ON OUR OWN TERMS

ON OUR OWN TERMS

Race, Class, and Gender in the Lives of African American Women

Leith Mullings

Routledge
New York & London

Published in 1997 by

Routledge
29 West 35 Street
New York, NY 10001

Published in Great Britain by

Routledge
11 New Fetter Lane
London EC4P 4EE

"Notes on Women, Work, and Society" from *Genes and Gender,* vol. 3, E. Tobach and B. Rossoff, eds. (New York: Gordian Press, 1980). Reprinted in *Freedomways* (1980, 20: 15–24) and *Anthropology for the '90s,* J. Cole, ed. (New York: Free Press, 1988).

"Uneven Development: Class, Race, and Gender Before 1900" from *Women's Work: Development and the Division of Labor by Gender,* E. Leacock and H. Safa, eds. (MA: Bergen and Garvey, 1986).

"Minority Women, Work, and Health" from *Double Exposure,* W. Chavkin, ed. (New York: Monthly Review Press, 1984).

"Anthropological Perspectives on the African American Family" from *The Black Family: Mental Health Perspectives,* M. Fullilove, ed. (San Francisco: Department of Psychiatry, UCSF School of Medicine, 1986) and the *Journal of Social Psychiatry* (1986, 6(1): 11–16).

"Households Headed by Women: The Politics of Race, Class, and Gender" from *Conceiving the New World Order: The Global Politics of Reproduction,* Ginsburg and Rapp, eds. (Berkeley: University of California Press, 1995).

"Symbols, Ideology, and Women of Color" from *Women of Color in U.S. Society,* Maxine Baca Zinn and Bonnie Dill, eds. (Philadelphia: Temple University Press, 1994).

"Gender and the Application of Anthropological Knowledge to Public Policy in the United States" from *Gender and Anthropology: Critical Reviews for Reading and Teaching,* Sandra Morgan, ed. (Washington, DC: American Anthropological Association, 1989).

"Race, Inequality, and Transformation: Building on the Work of Eleanor Leacock" from *Identity* (1994, 1(1): 123–29).

"Reclaiming Culture: The Dialectics of Identity" from *Race and Reason* (1994, 1(1)).

Library of Congress Cataloging-in-Publication Data

Mullings, Leith.
    On our own terms : race, class, and gender in the lives of African
    American women / Leith Mullings.
        p.   cm.
    Includes bibliographical references and index.
    ISBN 0-415-91285-7 (hbk.). — ISBN 0-415-91286-5 (pbk.)
    1. Afro-American women—Social conditions.   I. Title.
E185.86.M945   1996
305.48'896073—dc20   96-28853
                                                      CIP

To:

the memory of my mother, Lillieth Mullings,
my sisters everywhere and especially Sandra, Pauline, and Pansy Mullings,
and my children, Alia and Michael Tyner

Contents

Acknowledgments

Over the years in which these essays were written, innumerable colleagues, friends, comrades, and family members have given me help and support. In addition to those already mentioned in the text, I would like to thank Angela Gilliam for proposing the idea for the preface and for her insightful suggestions. Thanks also to June Foley for introducing me to the art of the memoir. Despite her very busy schedule, Barbara Ransby found time to give me invaluable comments on the "Introduction" and "Mapping Gender." Many thanks to Camella Bazemore, Michelle Hays, Jeanne McGettigan, Patricia Tovar, and Alia Tyner for their help in preparing the manuscript.

Though this book centers on the experiences of women, I would like to acknowledge the many African American men, including my father, brother, and children's father who have been very important in my life. These men, in their own ways, symbolize the perseverance, strength, and courage that characterizes many African American men.

In particular, I would like to thank Manning Marable, whose courageous writing has been an inspiration to me. It was he who first suggested that I put this volume together and I am especially grateful for the many hours we spent discussing and debating ideas, particularly those in the introduction and chapter 7. It would have been difficult to complete this project without his consistent encouragement and principled intellectual sustenance. *Asante sana.*

Preface

This collection of articles represents an attempt, within the context of the academy and the academic endeavor, to illuminate the experiences of African American women and to theorize from the materiality of their lives to broader issues of political economy, family, representation, and transformation. The essays are informed both by my own experience as a participant observer and by my research into the lives of others. In this sense they reflect my theoretical, political, and personal journey as a woman of African descent in America. I have organized the essays around three themes that form the contours of my own experience and those of others: work, family, and resistance. My purpose in this preface is not to present an account of my own history but to describe selective experiences—particularly those bearing on the interface between the academy and daily life—that provide the context for these essays.

Like many African Americans, much of my life has been concerned with analyzing and challenging structures of inequality, which were initially expressed most graphically in the construction of race. Race mediated every move for most of us growing up in the 1950s and 1960s; it was only in the company of other people of African descent that race could cease to exist. Not surprisingly, the search for the "cure" for inequality has dominated my intellectual life. Engagement in a project of liberation can be a powerful stimulant; it may facilitate the development of oppositional paradigms unrestrained by the necessity to defend the status quo. However, I cannot help but think that one of the ranking crimes of racism is the tremendous squander of human potential: the intellectual time and energy spent theorizing this construct that must, in the course of human history, be seen as one of the more bizarre approaches to human organization. This is a waste of human creativity that could otherwise be employed navigating cultures, finding the cure for cancer, discovering unlimited energy or food sources for the peoples of the world, or creating art forms to make the spirit soar.

The African American intellectual tradition differs from "mainstream" Euro-American scholarship in key ways. First, it is corrective. Mainstream scholarship establishes the parameters that frame the discourse about African Americans. African American scholars are often compelled to expend our creative energies answering stupid questions posed by others; striving, often with no more success than Sisyphus, to push the boundaries of paradigms steeped in racism, sexism, ethnocentrism, and cold contempt.

Imprisoned in the preoccupation of responding, we often rebel and refuse to answer. But, as the existentialists say, there is no exit. We must challenge until we are able to transform the power relations that hold the discourse in place, and we must battle on grounds not of our own choosing—the terrain of unmarked white ethnicity. To refuse to engage the ideological offensive would be to abandon large numbers of people to the machinations of racist policy, unleavened by intellectual opposition.

In correcting the dominant paradigms, African American scholars are concerned with accurate description, with reclaiming our history. In doing so, we seek to unravel what is perhaps the most complex riddle of culture: the manner in which people create their own history out of circumstances given and transmitted from the past. It is essential, as John Gwaltney said, to "set the record straight," but how to do so is not always evident. To focus only on the strengths, accomplishments, and victories does not give sufficient attention to the system of domination. Yet to emphasize too heavily the structure of oppression underplays the creative energy and history of a people.

Growing up in the fifties, I never thought much about the issue of gender; race was too overwhelming. In a school of mostly working-class Euro-Americans, my annual private torture was to sit through the official account of how Abraham Lincoln "freed the slaves," preceded by an "apology" to me. To the teacher and most of my classmates, the slaves were clearly pitiful things without history, volition, or agency. Those few of us of African descent squirmed with discomfort and embarrassment, knowing something was wrong, but bereft of the knowledge that could empower us. It was not until later that I realized that describing them as "enslaved" (by someone) rather than "slaves" (an inherent state of being) shifts the burden of culpability and transgression.

What puzzled me was the discrepancy between the way people of African descent were represented and what I knew from my own experience to be true.

Although our parents strictly limited the time we spent in front of the television, it was a primary form of family entertainment for people whose options for leisure were limited. Television and film alike reflected and perpetuated the stereotypical representations of African American women as matriarchs, mammies, and whores. The virulence of the McCarthy hearings seemed mirrored in the bitchiness of *Amos and Andy*'s Sapphire, who made the life of her henpecked husband, Kingfish, miserable; for a change of pace there was the prototypical mammy, Hattie McDaniel, bemoaning the bygone days of *Gone with the Wind*, or the image of the beautiful, tragic mulatta (ironically played by a series of Euro-American actresses, from Susan Kohner to Ava Gardner) tainted by a drop of African blood. Needless to say, almost any characterization of African American womanhood compared unfavorably with the social construction of femininity for Euro-American women reflected in the reigning mothers of *Father Knows Best* or *Leave it to Beaver*.

But in my own life, my models were such women as Rosa Parks, my grandmother, and my mother, who conformed to neither set of representations confronting young women in the fifties and sixties. They built the foundation for a new gender identity out of the reality of their experience. My father's mother cleaned houses for white people six days a week, but on the seventh day she rested in her spacious apartment overlooking Lenox Avenue (now Malcolm X Boulevard) in Harlem and took me to Abyssinian Baptist Church to hear Adam Clayton Powell. Yet we were subject to the ideal imagery of mothers who wore pearls and remained at home with the children. As a young girl, it was a source of pride that my mother, who had been raised in the Jamaican middle class, remained at home for the early years of her five children, while my father worked at least two jobs to put food on the table. I was disappointed when she went to work as a nurse as soon as the triplets—the youngest of us—entered school.

My early life mirrored the struggles and efforts of millions of Americans of African descent. My father worked at several jobs simultaneously while attending college at night; we lived for a time in a public housing project on the Lower East Side and for a brief period received welfare. Throughout, my parents retained a faith in education as a liberating force, as did many African Americans. Because the City University of New York was at that time tuition-free, my father, mother, and all five children were eventually able to attend college. But it was always clear that it was not hard work (though we worked hard enough) but the luck of being in the right place at the right time that separated our fortunes from those of others who struggled as hard.

In the two years of college courses I was required to take before entering nursing school, I included one anthropology course. Though I should now be embarrassed to confess to this, I was intrigued by Hortense Powdermaker's descriptions of her fieldwork experiences of "dancing with the natives" and her reflections about how taken aback her white southern family would have been. Against the backdrop of daily television images of people of African descent being attacked by dogs and fire hoses as they struggled to desegregate lunch counters, schools and voting booths, the idea of entering another culture, albeit through the anthropologist's representation of the "other," was seductive.

I went on to nursing school with the expectation that by becoming a public health nurse, I could help to "fix" society. My class of approximately fifty nursing students included, for the first time in the school's history, two African American women. In the hospital where I worked, the nurses were predominantly white and the nurses' aides generally of African descent. These latter women supported their families by doing the dirtiest work in the hospital. Though they often came to work with swollen feet or were sometimes bent with back injuries, they sustained me throughout my training, waking me when I fell asleep on night shift and feeding me when I forgot to eat. When they attempted to unionize, the hospital administration was able to engineer a narrow defeat for the union by adding to their ranks nursing students, who worked also as nurses' aides, and ordering us to vote against the union. It was in this bastion of "culture-free" hard science that I came to the realization that illness and health had much more to do with society than biology. I went on to graduate school to study anthropology.

Though I came to love the possibilities of anthropology, the questions for which I sought answers were not even posed in the polite society of the academy. I entered graduate school at the University of Chicago during the height of the Vietnam War. Because men, including students, were being drafted, the anthropology department admitted more women than ever before. In a class of nearly thirty students, almost one third were women. In another departure, three were of African descent. The class was greeted by a faculty member who noted, "For this class, we have admitted the maimed, the infirm, and the female."

Though some departments of the University of Chicago were more willing than those of other elite schools to prepare African American scholars, they were rarely inclined to hire them. Consequently many of the African American students, whatever their discipline or topical interest, worked with Charles Long, an African American professor of religion.

It is perhaps difficult for many young students today to fully comprehend what it meant to have virtually no faculty of color, few courses that reflected our experiences, and—almost always—highly distorted accounts of the lives of people of color. African American and progressive students all over the country went out on strike, sat in, and took over buildings in attempts to compel universities to establish departments and courses that would return people of color, women, and working people to history. While seeking to transform the academy, we had to live within it; we rejected their models, but had to do so in their language. We knew that much of what passed as objective knowledge was at best inadequate and distorted and at worst racist, oppressive, and false. The student of color often labored to reformulate the paradigm without assistance from sympathetic faculty. In retrospect, this is not surprising when one considers that the critique entailed challenging not only the paradigms but also the institutions that support them. In the space where the student flounders, struggling to articulate and refine her instinctive knowledge about what is wrong with the social sciences, lack of support may force her out of the academy. Or the stresses of living within the contradictions may force her to dull, rather than develop, her critical and creative faculties, in order to produce "acceptable" work.

As graduate students, we decoded symbols while Chicago burned. In those days the University of Chicago was the vanguard of the symbolic approach to anthropological analysis. The department had assembled the grand old men of symbolic theory—Clifford Geertz, Victor Turner, and David Schneider. The lectures for our introductory class, taught by Clifford Geertz, later appeared in his influential book *The Interpretation of Cultures*, in which he elaborated his well known approach to ethnography as "the power of the scientific imagination to bring us into touch with the lives of strangers" (Geertz 1975:16).

But as African American graduate students, we were the strangers. Hyde Park, the neighborhood surrounding the University of Chicago, was in many ways a secluded enclave. The real Chicago, just beyond the university's gates, was the Chicago of the late sixties: the Chicago that burned after the assassination of Martin Luther King Jr.; the black communities just across the Midway that were occupied by the National Guard; downtown Chicago, where students were brutally beaten for protesting the war at the Democratic National Convention; the inner city, where the Black Panther leader, Fred Hampton, was assassinated by the police while he slept.

For some of us, the answer to profound alienation from the university was to limit our contact with the academy as much as possible and to hang out in the "community." The "communiversity" became a place where university students of African descent and residents of the black neighborhoods in Chicago met to teach and to learn a range of subjects, including African history, a people's history of the United States, and political economy. Many of us accepted at some level, the view that because African American men had been denied the prerogatives of masculine roles by Euro-Americans, men should be put forward as the leaders of our movements, and we women often took supportive roles. I taught first aid, dressed bullet wounds, attended Marxist study groups, and worked as a nurse in a community clinic while I wrote my master's thesis and studied for the qualifying examinations for the doctorate.

Fieldwork in Africa was a liberating experience. I spent the first six months in Tanzania, an exciting place in the early 1970s. The project, to develop an African form of socialism—*ujamaa*—drew people from all over the world. One could encounter African, African American, and Caribbean freedom fighters seeking asylum from their respective governments. I worked parttime as a teaching assistant at the University of Dar es Salaam, where a core of scholars created a politically and intellectually stimulating environment. The most exciting of these was Walter Rodney, author of the seminal volume *How Europe Underdeveloped Africa* (1972), who was later assassinated in 1980 at the age of 38.

It was a time of optimism. Wars for liberation were being fought at that moment, and we felt that the forces of history were on the side of decolonization and national liberation. Most important to me was the opportunity to spend time with cadres from the liberation movements of southern Africa, particularly the African National Congress of South Africa. This experience, which provided a context for reflection on the United States, had a major effect on how I understood history and what I hoped for in the future.

In Ghana, I explored the historical, social and cultural setting of religion, healing and medicine. This allowed me to pursue my concerns about medicine first encountered in nursing school, and later to challenge the hegemony of various aspects of biomedicine through my work in medical anthropology. Though my research concerned ideology and healing (Mullings 1984), I could not help but observe Ghanaian women's independence, despite the fact that they had definite prescribed roles that were different from those of men. My experience in Africa validated my textbook studies of historical materialism as a method of analysis as well as my intuitive feelings about the cultural construction of gender. The range of tasks mastered by women and the ways in which they handled pregnancy and childbirth presented me with a vivid contradiction to the view that the basis of gender relationships is biological.

My first article about gender (which was also my first published scholarly article), "Women and Work in Africa" (1976), reflected this rather naive, optimistic enthusiasm about the implications of my findings. Second-wave feminism, though not yet in full swing, had newly discovered, as had I, that in West Africa, despite the dearth of discussion about women's roles, women did most of the farming, consequently producing much of the food resources of the region's societies. I also discovered Engels's 1887 study *The Family, Private Property, and the State* as well as Eleanor Leacock's work on women and equality. In my article I tried to address questions about cross-cultural constructions of equality by distinguishing between *inequality,* as defined by one's relationship to the resources of society, and *asymmetry,* in which men and women might hold different roles but are not necessarily involved in hierarchical relationships of domination and subordination; further, I explored the conditions under which asymmetry would give rise to inequality. In "Notes on Women, Work, and Society" (chapter 1) I tried to demonstrate how both the cross-cultural literature and the history of African American women gave the lie to the notion that gender inequality can be attributed to biological difference.

As I began to challenge traditional assumptions about gender and work, I reflected on my own experience. Though my own career was certainly more privileged in terms of educational and occupational options than those of most of my sisters, much of my life, like theirs, had been defined by work outside the home. The experience of my grandmother and mother embodied the transition African American women made from domestic work to service work. Like many African American women, I had supported myself for my entire adult life. I had begun to work part time at the age of sixteen at low-level service and clerical jobs, then worked as a nurse's aide and as a nurse.

I began teaching full-time at Yale University directly upon my return from fieldwork in Africa. Though I had always wanted to teach in the public sector, I took my father's advice to start in the Ivy League in order to understand the full spectrum of higher education. When I was hired at Yale in 1972, the three other new faculty members in the anthropology department were all Euro-American women. As women, we shared some experiences. We laughed together over the query of a male faculty member as to whether they could continue their Friday "beer and peanuts" now that the "ladies" had arrived.

But my colleagues could not share my anguish over the police brutality in the black neighborhoods of New Haven, nor did they share aspects of my teaching experience that were perhaps the result of the particular nexus of race, class, and gender. For example, on the first day of every large undergraduate class, as soon as I walked into a classroom, before I opened my mouth to speak, before the students had any information about me except that I was an African American woman, four or five male students would simply stand up and walk out of the classroom.

Throughout this experience I reflected on the areas of unity, but also the points of difference that made my life in many ways remote from that of my Euro-American female colleagues. As I researched the lives of African American women, it seemed clear that it was not simply contemporary experiences but their distinct history of work, resulting in an implicit sense of self-reliance, that separated them from Euro-American women. I sketched out some of these differences in "Uneven Development: Women and Work in the United States Before 1900" (chapter 2).

I confronted issues of gender most directly when I married, had children, and, like millions of other women, had to deal with balancing work outside the home with domestic responsibilities that included small children. After commuting for one year between New Haven and New York, where I was living, I took a job at Columbia University in 1974.

At Columbia too there were the usual, and some unusual, consequences of being the only African American woman in the Graduate School of the Arts and Sciences. The more common situations included sexual harassment as well as serving as faculty advisor for a huge number of African American and women students who felt they had no one else with whom to work. Among the more unusual events was the appearance near my office of the painted word *nigger* and the mysterious fire in my office that consumed two years of painstakingly gathered lecture notes (we had no computers at that time) and barely missed my nearly completed dissertation.

As is true for most African Americans, the support of family and community is essential in negotiating the outside world. For example, I was able to complete my dissertation while working full-time because my three sisters, who were themselves in graduate or professional schools, spent several weekends typing successive drafts of my dissertation.

Being pregnant at Columbia, where at that time the anthropology department had not tenured a woman since Ruth Benedict in 1948, was a challenging experience. One male faculty member could not resist touching my abdomen at every opportunity because he liked to "feel life"; another would avert his eyes every time I entered a room and never mentioned my pregnancy, subsequent delivery, or children (in fairness, I believe he thought that the professional way to treat a pregnant colleague was as though she had an unmentionable chronic disease); another, noticing that I barely had the energy to do any reading other than what was necessary for teaching and publishing, would berate me if I had not read the Sunday *New York Times* and assured me that unless I could quote the *Times* to my colleagues, I would never amount to anything. When I moved to the City College of New York in 1981 after the birth of my second child, I was bemused by the contrast formed to these men by my colleague Eleanor Leacock, who, understanding my situation from her own experience, clipped articles she thought would be of interest to me as she read the paper.

It was essential that my children be born in the summer, preferably early summer. In 1976 Columbia did not have paid leave for pregnancy, and disability coverage could not be extended to pregnancy. My husband was a left activist who made very little money, and my salary from Columbia was the primary source of income for our household, which included two children from his former marriage. Furthermore, Columbia's medical plan did not provide coverage for childbirth. Therefore I could not afford to be without my $12,000 salary from Columbia.

Despite our best efforts at planning, my daughter, Alia, was not born until August sixteenth, two weeks before I had to go back to work. That semester, as I dragged myself around, the Equal Rights Amendment was being debated. Several major unions had come out against the ERA because they feared it would eliminate protective legislation for women. The mainstream women's organizations were furious at what they viewed as the sexism of the unions. Having worked at other jobs, I knew that, tired as I was, my job as a professor was physically easy compared to that of a factory, service, or clerical worker, the jobs at which most African American women were employed. As I discussed this with students, I realized once again that my own ambivalence toward the mainstream women's movement was rooted in issues of race and class.

The search for child care similarly brought home gender matters. Adequate child care was so expensive that even when I worked in the child care center one day a week in exchange for a rebate on the expenses, it still took a significant proportion of my salary. My son, Michael, was born in June 1981, and when I had not found child care by September, when I had to start work at a new job at City College, I pounded the sidewalk, with my son on my back, searching for child care. And as every mother/professor knows, as wonderful as the children are, they always get sick during the breaks when you think you are about to get writing done.

Consequently, it was while juggling work outside the home, small children, and household responsibilities, both in a marriage and later when I became a single parent, that several of the articles were written. The search for patterns, the discovery of common experience, was often exhilarating. My article "Minority Women Workers and Health" (chapter 3) was based on a talk I gave to a group of workers from Local 1199 Hospital and Health Care Employees Union. As we discussed the common social circumstances that condition the generally poorer health status of African American women, these hardworking women began to stand up and speak about their lives, often weeping with emotion as they realized that their experiences were neither unique nor the result of personal failings. This was one of the rich ethnographic moments of my scholarly career, in which I graphically understood the responsibility of the scholar to her community: We have the moral and theoretical responsibility to employ the time for reflection allowed by our relatively privileged status to address people's real problems.

This is just one example of an encounter that underscored the African American woman's constant struggle with, among other things, representation and the power to represent in an increasingly media-driven world. In a society in which ideal models continue to valorize dependency and hierarchical gender roles, the pain that fills the space between the idea and the reality will be felt in intimate relationships as well as in our daily encounters with the larger society.

Most rewarding were my political activities, particularly those concerned with women, through which theory could be tested in practice. Through involvement in local, international, and academic activities, I developed an understanding of class, race, and gender as sites of contestation. I also committed myself to try to develop a style of writing that embodies a recognition that knowledge should be accessible to all and that clarity, rather than obfuscation, is the measure of proficiency. I believe that scholars have the responsibility to "speak truth to power," but to do so in a manner that avoids sterile abstractions and the self-indulgent rhetoric that seems to be the hallmark of some contemporary scholarship.

Having lived in various parts of Harlem for twenty years, I was moved by the women I met every day in organizing the Harlem branch of Women for Racial and Economic Equality, in trade union work, teaching at the City University of New York, or through research projects (most recently a proposal for an "opportunity zone" in Harlem, written for the office of the Manhattan borough president, and research on gender roles in central Harlem sponsored by the Centers for Disease Control). These women moved me to try to analyze the constraints under which women operated and also to record the spirit of struggle with which they overcame tremendous obstacles and developed, in Angela Davis's words, "standards for a new womanhood." Some of the ideas developed in the articles then formed the basis for a forthcoming ethnographic study of women and activism in Central Harlem.

Conditions that I observed on a local level often reflected global processes, and through involvement in antiapartheid work and other kinds of international solidarity movements I met women from various areas of the world. I used these experiences to build upon the cross-cultural perspective of anthropology and to provide me with insight into the transnational structures of race, class, and gender.

Within the last two decades, women, including women of color, have gained a voice in the academy, albeit a muted one. However, while anthropology is more open than most disciplines, mainstream anthropology, even when claiming to critique hegemonic representation, is still largely dominated by white males. This period, nevertheless, was characterized by ideological confrontation; publications such as *Gender and Anthropology* (Bookman and Morgen, eds. 1989) marked an attempt to go beyond reclaiming and documenting women's roles and to demonstrate the manner in which social processes are distorted by excluding the analysis of gender. But as Lynn Bolles (1995) reminds us, though "the feminist project is influencing and reconfiguring" anthropology, it renders "Black feminist anthropologists invisible" (p. 2) by excluding them from "citation and other canon-setting patterns" (p. 10).

Yet African American women have written themselves into history. In the social sciences, since the appearance of Angela Davis's pioneering book *Women, Race, and Class* in 1981, there have been many creative and eloquent accounts of the lives of African American women. These build on previous work and represent an attempt to create a new tradition in the social sciences—to place African American women within history and to establish a theoretical critique. For example, in 1981 the Center for Research on Women of Color and Southern Women, based at Memphis State University, began to organize workshops on curricula and research in which those of us studying and teaching about women of color could learn from each other. For scholars like me, based in predominantly white institutions where few people did work on women of color, the center provided a welcome, supportive oasis. Furthermore, the center directly addressed ideological domination through concrete measures such as conferences, workshops, curriculum development, newsletters, and data bases.

The struggles over the core curriculum in higher education that have taken place during the last decade go well beyond the goals of the student movements of the 1960s and 1970s. As students, we struggled to establish departments and courses that would validate labor studies, women's studies, and ethnic studies as areas of inquiry, but contemporary contestation over the core curriculum goes to the heart of ideological hegemony by challenging the foundation of what is defined as knowledge.

These essays, written over a period of 15 years, reflect varying degrees of anger and hope. For this I do not apologize. As I write, much of what we have struggled for is under attack, but I am proud to be a part of a new generation of scholars continuing the tradition of reclaiming the experiences of African American women.

June, 1995
New York City

References

Bolles, A. Lynn. 1995. "Faceless and Voiceless: African American Anthropologists and the Citation Wars." Paper presented at the annual meeting of the American Anthropological Association. Washington, D.C.

Geertz, Clifford. 1973. *The Interpretation of Cultures.* New York: Basic Books, Inc.

Morgen, Sandra, ed. 1989. *Gender and Anthropology: Critical Reviews for Reading and Teaching.* Washington, D.C.: American Anthropological Association Press.

Mullings, Leith. 1976. "Women and Economic Change in Africa." In Nancy Hafkin and Edna Bay, eds. *Women in Africa: Studies in Social and Economic Change,* Stanford: Stanford University Press.

———. 1984. *Therapy, Ideology and Social Change: Mental Healing in Urban Ghana.* Berkeley: University of California Press.

Rodney, Walter. 1972. *How Europe Underdeveloped Africa.* Dar es Salaam: Tanzania Publishing House.

Introduction

A t its best, the intellectual tradition of African American women's studies is
the creation of theory from the practice of everyday life, arising from reflection on lived experience. Contributions to this tradition have come from
activists, political leaders, poets, writers, and grassroots organizers. Throughout
the nineteenth century, women such as Harriet Tubman, Sojourner Truth, Ida B.
Wells, and others reflected on their experiences and reconstructed "ways of
knowing" through creating an alternative body of knowledge about themselves
and their communities, providing both a catalyst and guide for acts of struggle
and advocacy.

African American Women's Studies in Society and the Academy

It is only since the late 1960s, however, that an African American women's feminist critique has emerged, fostering an explosion of extraordinary work by and
about African American women. The 1960s were an era characterized by social
movements. On the international front, women were active participants in the
liberation movements of Asia, the Caribbean, Latin America, and southern
Africa. In the United States, women played critical roles in the civil rights,
anti–Vietnam War, and second-wave feminist struggles. At the end of a long day
of work in 1955, a seamstress, domestic worker and long time NAACP activist in
Alabama named Rosa Parks refused to give up her seat on the bus to a white
man, sparking the Montgomery bus boycott of 1955–56. Women as well as men

were beaten, attacked by police dogs, doused with fire hoses, and left to languish in jail—or graves. As the conflict shifted to urban areas, women as well as men in the Black Panther Party carried arms in self-defense, and in 1970 Angela Davis, a young philosophy professor and member of the Communist Party, spent two years in jail for allegedly plotting the escape of George Jackson, a political prisoner who was later assassinated by prison guards.

The experiences of women within these movements became a touchstone for reflections on the deconstruction of gender and the need to assess, critique, and rethink the roles that African American women played in the civil rights and black power movements. While these struggles had to some extent been successful in transforming the meaning of race (Omi and Winant 1986), this was not the case for gender. Indeed, in some instances the commitment to traditional hierarchical gender roles was revitalized, as organizations often fused demands for group empowerment with male dominance (see chapter 7).

The social movements of the sixties and early 1970s had repercussions in the academy, creating the context for demands for greater access for people of color and the establishment of departments of ethnic, women's, and labor studies. Within the larger theoretical challenge to traditional paradigms, they often took the lead in developing alternative approaches that laid the groundwork for rethinking the general curriculum. While these developments created some space for African American women's studies, often their specific histories were lost between women's studies and black studies, as captured in Hull, Scott, and Smith's provocative title *All the Women Are White, All the Blacks Are Men, But Some of Us Are Brave.*

By the mid-1980s, many of the community, civil rights, worker, and other mass movements that anchored activist work on and by African American women had been actively targeted for repression by the state or had declined due to their own internal contradictions. The consequences of the conservative retrenchment of the Reagan era and the destruction of mass movements were evident in the increasing disparities in wealth seen in the United States. By the beginning of the 1990s, a resurgent racism and antifeminist backlash was expressed in political and ideological offensives against people of color, women, and particularly women of color. At the same time, certain currents of popular urban culture, and media events such as Anita Hill's testimony during the Clarence Thomas confirmation hearings, highlighted gender tensions in the African American community.

Within the academy, the retreat from affirmative action in student activism and faculty recruitment, the expulsion of radical faculty, and the elimination of many ethnic studies departments and minority programs contributed to the decline of activist social theory in this arena. Simultaneously, the rise of postmodern and poststructural theoretical paradigms, while problematizing the traditional canon, tended to neutralize challenges to the structure of power.[1] Within these historical currents, the work on African American women—at its best nurtured in the materiality of experience but also influenced by the mediating currents of theory in the academy—seeks to retrieve and transform history.

Writing African American Women into History

Because the realities of African American women's existence was not part of the historical record, it was first necessary to recover and describe the substance of our experiences. While much of the early writing on the lives of African American women appeared in works of literature and literary criticism,[2] as well as in personal and biographical statements such as Michelle Wallace's controversial *Black Macho and the Myth of the Superwoman* [1979] (1990), there were several interdisciplinary collections that projected the voices of women of color and argued that they had a distinct experience. Among them were Toni Cade Bambara, *The Black Woman* (1970); Sharon Harley and Rosalyn Terborg-Penn, *The Afro-American Woman: Struggles and Images* (1978); Gloria Anzaldúa and Cherrie Moraga, *This Bridge Called My Back: Writings by Radical Women of Color* (1981); La Frances Rodgers-Rose, *The Black Woman* (1980); and Barbara Smith, *Home Girls: A Black Feminist Anthology* (1983). *All the Women Are White, All the Blacks Are Men, But Some of Us Are Brave* (Hull, Scott, and Smith 1980) contained an interdisciplinary set of papers from a 1979 conference directed toward developing "a radical black women's studies." This volume also included "A Black Feminist Statement," first published by the Combahee River Collective in 1977, which explored black feminism and affirmed a commitment to combat the "simultaneous" oppression of race, sex, class, and gender.

Various theoretical perspectives within African American feminist thought share a commitment to grounding in the real experiences of African American women, taking seriously the centrality of race and racism in their lives. By examining African American women's roles in the workplace, family and communities (see chapter 8), and underscoring the manner in which the experiences of African American women differed from that of Euro-American women, this body of work demonstrates the weakness of an abstract, essentialist view of gender that does not acknowledge the distinct experiences of women of color.

But people also theorize from different locations, strata, and experiences. While most African American feminists analyze the interaction of race and gender, their work reflects varying degrees of critique of other kinds of oppression; scholars frequently disagree about the sites and causes for the dynamics of oppression. Hence within African American feminist thought there is a series of discourses and critiques examining gender—specifically, its contradictions and inequalities—as it relates to the African American experience. The project includes overlapping, sometimes contradictory voices and competing ideological perspectives that reflect the different economic, social and political tendencies and experiences of African American women.

Alternative visions begin to appear in the early 1980s, with the publication of a number of books that marked the maturation of the social science perspective but also prefigured distinct theoretical approaches, paradigmatic standpoints, and political perspectives, which themselves reflect historical currents in the African American community (see chapter 7). What follows is by no means an exhaustive review of the now sizable literature in African American women's studies, but rather a discussion of examples of representative trends.

Paula Giddings's 1984 volume *When and Where I Enter: The Impact of Black Women on Race and Sex in America* is illustrative of one current. Largely descriptive rather than analytic, it is a "narrative history of Black women" (p. 6) and, like the more scholarly works of many African American women historians, makes a major contribution to revising our history. While describing the impact of race and sex on the lives of African American women, her analysis does not focus significantly on class, nor does it provide a fundamental critique of society. Rather, she advocates an extension of rights, concluding that "we must be as vigilant about sex discrimination as racial discrimination" (pp. 350–51).

In the second body of work there is much more emphasis on cultural continuity, often selecting women in the African diaspora as the unit of analysis. But even within this category there are different approaches to the essence of underlying unity. For example, Filomena Steady's introduction to *The Black Woman Cross-Culturally* (1981) claims that an "African brand of feminism" influences women of African descent in the United States, Africa, the Caribbean, and South America but also suggests that these women are united by "economic exploitation and marginality." Similarly, the editors of *Women in Africa and the African Diaspora* (Terborg-Penn, Harley, and Rushing 1987), in compiling papers from a 1983 conference, seek to analyze "how women of African descent view themselves and provide their own cultural parameters" (p. xii) but place less emphasis on the structural relations of oppression.

The third body of work to emerge in the 1980s is critical of capitalism both as a socioeconomic system and as a cultural one. In this sense, it contrasts with the liberal approach, which is not judgmental about the underlying socioeconomic structure but rather advocates an extension of privileges to blacks and women. It also differs from the nationalist approach, which, while often censorious in its emphasis on cultural continuity, does not always address economic and political structures. These critiques of capitalism on the other hand, take the analysis of race, class, and gender as a central problematic. Here too there are different approaches. For example, two important works published in 1981 by bell hooks and Angela Davis lead in strikingly different directions. While hooks's work fosters an incisive critique of cultural forms, Davis's theoretical anchor is a political project that confronts and challenges capitalism.

bell hooks's *Ain't I a Woman* (1981) shares some of the autobiographical character of Michelle Wallace's 1978 book, as well as the narrative style of Giddings's work. Like Giddings, her major thesis is that "sexism looms as large as racism as an oppressive force in the lives of African American women" (hooks 1981, 15). While hooks's *Ain't I a Woman* mentions issues of class, particularly in the final chapter, psychological and cultural issues are at the center of her analysis. These themes are developed even further in her subsequent work.

With the growing postmodern emphasis on cultural critique (and, in hooks's case, cultural resistance, though here resistance is often distanced from an organized political project), there is an increasing focus on the politics of identity. Hence for hooks, "identity is evoked as a stage in a process wherein one constructs radical black subjectivity" (hooks 1990, 20); she is concerned with "assertions of identity that bring complexity and variety to the constructions of black subjectivity." hooks's writing has introduced feminist concepts to many African American women, and her work has a popular, if not academic, following. In an extremely harsh critique of hooks, Michelle Wallace (1995) describes hooks's later work as "self-indulgent and undigested drivel that careens madly from outrageous to self-pity, poetic and elliptical, to playful exhibitionism to dogmatic righteous sermonizing" and asserts that progressively her analysis has become more and more "self-centered, narcissistic, and even hostile to the idea of countervailing perspectives."

Published the same year as *Ain't I a Woman*, Angela Davis's *Women, Race, and Class* employs a consistent analysis of the interaction of race, class, and gender. In contrast to hooks, her analysis is anchored in a political project that explicitly critiques the structure of power. Hence she positions African American women not only within a structure of racial oppression and gender subordination but also in relation to a class hierarchy. This analysis suggests complex commonalities and differences among women and points to a political intervention that is directed at an underlying socioeconomic and political structure and which involves potential alliances and coalitions that go beyond race and gender. Davis's volume, along with work by other scholars published in the 1970s and early 1980s, was important in indicating the broad outlines of the race, class, and gender nexus at which the African American woman stood, but the theoretical underpinning was yet to be elaborated.

Race, Class, and Gender

In the 1990s, in addition to the expanding work in literature, literary criticism, and representation, there is an important current of scholarship analyzing race, class, and gender as interlocking systems that most severely affect African American women. This work emerges against the backdrop of a resurgence and elaboration of feminist essentialism among many Euro-American scholars.[3]

While black feminist scholars concerned with class, race and gender are unanimous in their condemnation of these new forms of essentialism they, too, have different perspectives and emphases that follow in the tradition of earlier works. For example, Patricia Hill Collins maintains the "simultaneity of race, class and gender oppression" (Collins 1991, 416). Yet her analysis, in its emphasis on cultural continuity and uniformity, is equally influenced by the cultural tradition of "African feminism," as discussed by Steady (1981) and others. For Baca Zinn and Dill (1994), on the other hand, who, in the "coalitional" tradition, assume "women of color" as a productive unit of analysis,[4] "labor relations are at the core of race and gender inequalities" (p. 5) and are the foundation for the analysis of the similarities and differences among women of color. Similarly for Brewer (1993, 17), "gender takes on meaning and is embedded institutionally in the context of the racial and class order—the productive and social reproductive relations of the economy."

It is important to make the point that race, class, and gender are not additive categories; rather, they are interlocking, interactive, and above all relational ones. Hence their relationship has been described as "multiplicative" (King 1988, 42), and in terms of "the articulation of multiple oppressions" (Brewer 1993, 13) and of "simultaneity" (Anderson and Collins 1995, ii). Having said this, however, it may not be enough to point to a matrix of interaction. We must ask what are the implications for practice of descriptors such as *interactive, multiplicative,* and *simultaneous.*

Themes

Though I am aware that the phrase "race, class, and gender" has become something of a mantra, the essays in this volume argue that for the majority of African American women, race, class, and gender are the analytic constructs that have the greatest explanatory power in interpreting and predicting their conditions of existence.

As axes of stratification, they are fluid systems that intersect in different ways for different populations at different historical periods. However, I suggest that in the United States today, and in other stratified societies, class fundamentally prefigures the meaning and experience of both race and gender. To assert this is not to simplistically privilege or give primacy to class—that is, the productive relations and distribution of resources and power: class relationships *prefigure*, not dictate, a range of possibilities. This is not to suggest that either race or gender is reducible to class, nor is it to imply that other differences such as sexuality and age are irrelevant. Rather, this approach advocates analysis of how the totality of markers of difference emerge and function in any given historical period.

Though a group's relationship to resources and power is always critical, its manifestations vary historically. At a given historical moment, class may be primarily manifested as gender or race. For example, in the United States, the class relationships of slavery conditioned what race was to mean for the next three hundred years. Hence race is the lens through which we perceive and understand relationships of power and domination, coding reality through a glass darkly, as it were. But it is the deep structure of class—the distribution of resources and power—that gives race its meaning. As Marable points out, "In a racist society color symbolizes the inequality of power relations, the ownership of property and resources, between various groups and classes" (Marable 1995, 125). The experience of gender is conditioned by the intersecting systems of class and race.

At the same time, the essays in this volume suggest that class and culture are not dichotomous frames of reference, describing the role of culture as hegemonic discourse, on the one hand, and as community and protest, on the other. Throughout the essays, I suggest that mutually supportive paradigms of culture and biology underlie much of the hegemonic discourse rationalizing inequality and defending white privilege (see chapters 8 and 9 of this book). Their contemporary manifestations in the recent books *The Bell Curve* (Herrnstein and Murray 1994) and *The End of Racism* (D'Souza 1995) assert that genetics in the form of IQ (Herrnstein and Murray) and culture in the form of a "civilization gap" (D'Souza) rather than white privilege are responsible for racial stratification.

But culture is also central to the development of community, struggle, and protest. Hence this book discusses the manner in which African American women and men have created culture, the construction of alternative (sometimes oppositional) identities and institutions, and the struggle of African American women to reject the view that a woman is primarily defined by the love of a man and to seek meaningfulness in a range of human activities.

When we position African American women within a framework of class, race, and gender, the study of their experiences demystifies general social processes and has been central to rethinking several key questions that elucidate our understanding of gender—the relationship between men and women. For example, examination of African American women's experience has contributed to deconstructing the separate-spheres theory (see chapter 2), according to which historical and cross-cultural subordination of women is associated with universal restriction to the private or domestic sphere and exclusion from the public sphere. For many Euro-American women of the 1970s, the slogan "the personal is political" represented a critique of the private/public distinction and an attempt to make what had been considered private—particularly domestic issues—integral to the national political agenda (Morgen and Bookman 1988). The work on African American women demonstrated not only their participation in the public sphere as slaves and workers (see chapters 1 and 2), but also the manner in which the political and economic relations of the larger society structure reproduction and the domestic arena (see chapters 3 and 4). Combined with the study of women in other countries and working-class women in the United States, this work helped to clarify the historical particularity and ideological construction of "public" and "private" spheres and their interpenetration in the lives of all women (and, for that matter, men). These insights have implications for several theoretical questions.

Analysis of African and African American women's participation in production (chapters 1 and 2), for example, was important in deepening our understanding of the still unresolved issue of women's status in relation to their participation in production, first raised by Frederick Engels in *The Origin of the Family, Private Property, and the State* and later studied by Leacock (1981) and Sacks (1979). In investigating the extent to which participation in production gave African American women and women in other countries more equality in other spheres, the complexities of the double and triple day (see chapter 3), the need to consider women's roles in reproduction, the redefinition of male and female roles, and the emergence of influential women's organizations (cf. Leahy 1986, 127) became evident. Though scholarly interest in the workplace has declined, this continues to be an important area of study as women all over the world increase their participation in the labor force.

In the domain of family and community, by demonstrating the varied forms domestic groups can take and the diverse roles women have played within them, the exploration of the African American experience has contributed to deconstructing the Eurocentric, masculinist notion of the patriarchal family as "natural." On the other hand, observation of African American women, for whom building a family may be inherently an act of resistance, has refined and nuanced our analysis of the significance of kin, family, and community (chapters 4 and 5).

The separate-spheres theory has also shaped the work on women and resistance. The emphasis on workplace (public) activism and the neglect of community and domestic activism has often led to the invisibility of women's involvement in struggle (Susser 1988; Bookman and Morgen 1988). For African American women, transformative strategies directed toward the household have frequently necessitated involvement in public policy (chapters 5 and 6). For example, efforts to educate or protect children might require desegregating public schools or protesting police brutality, transcending the boundary between the domestic and public spheres. The study of activism among African American women as they challenge definitions of race, class, and gender has expanded our understanding of the meaning of struggle embedded in community (chapter 7).

These essays affirm the importance of positioning African American women not only in relationship to other women of color and to Euro-American women in the United States but also solidly within a global context. One direction this might take involves drawing out the common themes in "cultures of resistance" among African American women and their sisters in the diaspora and throughout the third world. There is a basis for this work in the early work of Steady (1981), Terborg-Penn, Harley and Rushing (1987), and Mohanty (1991). However, race is fluid, cultures are continually reimagined, and national boundaries are moving targets. For this reason, such an analysis must go even beyond the boundaries of Mohanty's "imagined communities of women with divergent histories and social locations woven together by the political threads of opposition to forms of domination that are not only pervasive, but also systemic" (Mohanty 1991, 4) in order to concretely understand how the global order structures, even while constantly transforming, the meaning of gender and race,[5] as well as the manner in which constructions of race and gender are challenged, contested, and re-created.

The essays included in this volume were written over a period of 15 years. They reflect the time and context in which they were written and our collective efforts to define ourselves and our community from a set of shared and individual experiences. My ideas have evolved over time, but I have included earlier essays that illustrate steps in this evolution, as well as the struggle to find my own voice. As in any collection of essays, there is some repetition of ideas. Several central themes, discussed above, run through the essays and are developed and restated in different ways. Several articles have been slightly revised for style and clarity and to avoid repetition.

Finally, the essays embody my interest in the link between a theoretical project and collective struggles that seek to transform structures of power. The question of race, class, and gender is not merely academic, so to speak. It is important precisely because our understanding of the source of our oppression informs what we do about it. In the aftermath of the cold war and the fall of socialist governments in Eastern Europe, it has become unfashionable to attribute inequalities to the workings of capitalism. Some argue that class and social movements are categories that no longer matter. Those of us who employ a class analysis are often accused of a variety of intellectual heresies: "totalizing," "universalizing," "reductionist," and, perhaps more dismissive, simply "old-fashioned." If such critics were to look out their tower windows, they would realize that the contradictions of capitalism—a socioeconomic system built on harnessing the labor of others and constructing inequality from difference—are more profound than ever before and continue to impoverish the lives of millions of people. Any liberation project, including feminism, must take account of this. Because the basic problem in the United States is still the inequitable distribution of resources, which is expressed primarily in relationships of class and race and secondarily through gender, I remain an unabashed advocate of privileging class, race, and gender in explaining oppression and seeking to transform history.

Notes

1. For a discussion of this, see *Monthly Review* 47, no. 3 (1995), a special issue devoted to the postmodern agenda, especially chapter by Wood.

2. See, for example, works by Alice Walker, Lorraine Hansberry, Sonia Sanchez, Toni Cade Bambara, Barbara Smith, Barbara Christian, Helen Carby, Toni Morrison, Ntozake Shange, and Nellie McKay, among others.

3. See di Leonardo 1993, Morgen and Bookman 1988, and Stabile 1995 for a critical account of this trend.

4. Seminars and workshops sponsored by the Center for Research on Women (CROW) at Memphis State University were very influential in developing this body of literature.

5. The new work on race, particularly on the social construction of whiteness (see Roediger 1992; Frankenberg 1993), is important here.

References

Andersen, Margaret L., and Patricia Hill Collins, eds. 1995. "Preface." *Race, Class and Gender: An Anthology.* 2nd ed. Belmont: Wadsworth Publishing.

Anzaldua, Gloria, and Cherrie Moraga, eds. 1981. *This Bridge Called My Back: Writings by Radical Women of Color.* New York: Kitchen Table: Women of Color Press.

Baca Zinn, Maxine, and Bonnie Thornton Dill. 1994. *Women of Color in U.S. Society.* Philadelphia: Temple University Press.

Bambara, Toni Cade, ed. 1970. *The Black Woman.* New York: New American Library.

Bookman, Ann, and Sandra Morgen, eds. 1988. *Women and the Politics of Empowerment.* Philadelphia: Temple University Press.

Brewer, Rose M. 1993. "Theorizing Race, Class, and Gender: The New Scholarship of Black Feminist Intellectuals and Black Women's Labor." In Stanlie M. James and Abena P. A. Busia, eds., *Theorizing Black Feminisms: The Visionary Pragmatism of Black Women.* London: Routledge.

Collins, Patricia Hill. 1991. *Black Feminist Thought: Knowledge, Consciousness, and the Politics of Empowerment.* New York: Routledge.

Davis, Angela. 1981. *Women, Race, and Class.* New York: Random House.

di Leonardo, Micaela. 1991. "Introduction: Gender, Culture and Political Economy." In Micaela di Leonardo, ed., *Gender at the Crossroads of Knowledge: Feminist Anthropology in the Postmodern Era.* Los Angeles: University of California Press.

D'Souza, Dinesh. 1995. *The End of Racism.* New York: Free Press.

Engels, Frederick. 1942 [1884]. *The Origin of the Family, Private Property, and the State.* New York: International Publishers.

Frankenberg, Ruth. 1993. *White Women, Race Matters: The Social Construction of Whiteness.* Minneapolis: University of Minnesota Press.

Giddings, Paula. 1984. *When and Where I Enter: The Impact of Black Women on Race and Sex in America.* Toronto: Bantam Books.

Harley, Sharon, and Rosalyn Terborg-Penn, eds. 1978. *The Afro-American Woman: Struggles and Images.* Port Washington, NY: Kennikat Press.

Herrnstein, Richard, and Charles Murray. 1994. *The Bell Curve: Intelligence and Class Structure in American Life.* New York: Free Press.

hooks, bell. 1981. *Ain't I a Woman: Black Women and Feminism.* Boston: South End Press.

———. 1990. *Yearning: Race, Gender, and Cultural Politics.* Boston: South End Press.

Hull, Gloria T., Patricia Bell-Scott, and Barbara Smith, eds. 1982. *All the Women Are White, All the Blacks are Men, But Some of Us Are Brave: Black Women's Studies.* Old Westbury, NY: Feminist Press.

King, Deborah. 1988. "Multiple Jeopardy, Multiple Consciousness: The Context of A Black Feminist Ideology." *Signs: Journal of Women, Society and Culture* 14(11): 42–72.

Leacock, Eleanor. 1981. *Myths of Male Dominance: Collected Articles on Women Cross-Culturally.* New York and London: Monthly Review Press.

Leahy, Margaret. 1986. *Development Strategies and the Status of Women: A Comparative Study of the United States, Mexico, the Soviet Union and Cuba.* Boulder, CO: Lynne Rienner Publishers.

Marable, Manning. 1995. *Beyond Black and White: Transforming African American Politics.* London: Verso.

Mohanty, Chandra Talpade, Ann Russo, and Lourdes Torres, eds. 1991. *Third World Women and the Politics of Feminism.* Bloomington: Indiana University Press.

Morgen, Sandra, and Ann Bookman. 1988. "Rethinking Women and Politics: An Introductory Essay." In Ann Bookman and Sandra Morgen, eds., *Women and the Politics of Empowerment.* Philadelphia: Temple University Press.

Omi, Michael, and Howard Winant. 1986. *Racial Formation in the United States: From the 1960s to the 1980s.* New York: Routledge.

Rodgers-Rose, La Frances, ed. 1980. *The Black Woman.* Beverly Hills: Sage Publications.

Roediger, David. 1991. *The Wages of Whiteness: Race and the Making of the American Working Class.* London: Verso.

Sacks, Karen. 1979. *Sisters and Wives: The Past and Future of Sexual Equality.* Westport, CT: Greenwood Press.

Smith, Barbara, ed. 1983. *Home Girls: A Black Feminist Anthology.* New York: Kitchen Table: Women of Color Press.

Stabile, Carol. 1995. "Postmodernism, Feminism and Marx: Notes from the Abyss." *Monthly Review* 47(3): 89–107.

Steady, Filomina Chioma, ed. 1981. *The Black Woman Cross-Culturally.* Cambridge, MA: Schenkman.

Susser, Ida. 1988. "Working-Class Women, Social Protest, and Changing Ideologies." In Ann Bookman and Sandra Morgen, eds., *Women and the Politics of Empowerment.* Philadelphia: Temple University Press.

Terborg-Penn, Rosalyn, Sharon Harley and Andrea Benton Rushing, eds. 1987. *Women in Africa and the African Diaspora.* Washington, D.C.: Howard University Press.

Wallace, Michelle. 1990 [1978]. *Black Macho and the Myth of the Superwoman.* London: Verso.

———. 1995. "For Whom the Bell Tolls." *Voice Literary Supplement* (November): 19.

Wood, Ellen Meiksins. 1995. "What is the 'Postmodern' Agenda? An Introduction." *Monthly Review* 47(3): 1–12.

PART 1

WOMEN, WORK, AND COMMUNITY

Introduction

Analyzing the record of African American women's labor is crucial to understanding their history in the United States. Many women are involved in several dimensions of labor simultaneously: wage work in the formal sector; informal-sector production; reproductive labor in the household, as well as the social reproductive labor involved in caring for the elderly and the sick; and transformative work directed toward changing conditions in the community and larger society.

Documenting the roles of African American women in production has been central to demystifying social processes that affect all women. Their history of work—in Africa (Mullings 1976), during slavery, and after emancipation, highlighted the social and historical basis of the division of labor by gender and demonstrated that hegemonic notions about gender and work were often displaced. These discoveries helped to undermine arguments supporting the biological rationale for gender divisions. Their role as workers was pivotal to their relatively independent role in the family and participation in strategies of resistance. Many of the major studies of African American women and work were carried out the 1970s and 1980s. The decline of interest in this area reflects not only the changing currents of the academy but also real transformations in labor force participation.

African American women progressed from domestic work to service, clerical, and industrial work, and today they generally do the same work as Euro-American women. However, there are some notable differences. For example, only one fifth (20.5 percent) of employed African American women hold man-

15

agerial and professional jobs compared to almost one third (29.3 percent) of white[1] women. Twenty-eight percent of African American women are service workers, as compared to 16.7 percent of white women. African American women hold jobs as operatives, fabricators, and laborers at almost twice the rate of white women (11.5 percent as compared to 7 percent) (see Table 1).[2]

Table 1

	Occupational Distribution By Race	
Occupation in 1993	African American	White
Managerial and professional specialty	20.5	29.3
Technical, sales, and administrative support	37.8	43.9
Service	27.5	16.7
Farming, forestry, and fishing	0.3	1.0
Precision production, craft, and repair	2.5	2.0
Operators, fabricators, and laborers	11.5	7.0

Source: Bennett, Claudette E. 1995. "The Black Population in the United States: March 1994 and 1993." U.S. Bureau of the Census, *Current Population Reports*, P20–480. Washington, D.C.: U.S. Government Printing Office, p. 83.

Though African American women have historically had higher rates of labor force participation than Euro-American women, the 1993 rates of African American (57.4 percent) and white women (58 percent) are roughly equal. However, African American women are more likely to be unemployed; their unemployment rate is 12 percent, as compared to 5.7 percent for white women. However, unemployment rates, which include only those who report themselves as looking for work, are not a sufficient measure of real unemployment. These figures do not measure the number of people who are not in the labor force, which would include (among others) discouraged workers, those working in the informal sector, and those existing on transfer payments, help from relatives, and such.

Table 2

Labor Force Status in 1993	African American Women	White Women
Percent in civilian labor force	57.4	58.0
Percent unemployed	12.0	5.7

Source: Bennett, Claudette E. 1995. "The Black Population in the United States: March 1994 and 1993." U.S. Bureau of the Census, *Current Population Reports,* P20–480. Washington, D.C.: U.S. Government Printing Office, p. 83.

In 1993, there were more African American women (7.0 million) than men (6.9 million) in the civilian labor force (Bennett 1995, 17). The economic conditions of African Americans reflect transformations in the political economy of the United States over the period from slavery through industrialization to deindustrialization. These, in turn, are shaped by an international political economy now characterized by low-wage service jobs and "jobless growth."

The chapters in this section focus on work, or, more broadly, the division of labor in production, taken in the context of work, family, and resistance.

"Notes on Women, Work, and Society" was written in 1979 and presented to a conference commemorating the International Year of the Child, sponsored by the Genes and Gender Collective, organized by Ethel Tobach, a biologist, and Eleanor Leacock, an anthropologist. In the late 1970s, newly armed with cross-cultural and historical "discoveries" that undermined biological reductionism and genetic determinism, we were perhaps more optimistic about the persuasive power of these findings. Unfortunately, notions of biological and genetic determinism are still current, though they now appear in different (and occasionally more sophisticated) forms. Furthermore, this essay (as well as others in this volume) was written at a time when trade union and black liberation movements were more active than in the 1990s. A level of militancy and hopefulness about possibilities for change informed the movements and is reflected in my writing.

Participation in conferences such as this allowed feminist scholars to exchange ideas about topics that would become central to the feminist corpus: the evolution of the gendered division of labor and the relationships among class, race, gender, and work in a racialized, gendered political economy. But in many feminist gatherings, "woman" was a generic category defined primarily by the conditions of privileged Euro-Americans. Issues of race and class were frequently viewed as divisive and we had to insist, often in terms that today might seem strident, in telling the stories of African American women. Nonetheless, perhaps most important was the empowering potential of placing the experiences of African American women in a cross-cultural and historical context, through which our experiences became part of the stream of international and historical processes rather than marginal or aberrant.

"Uneven Development: Class, Race, and Gender Before 1900" attempts to address these issues by exploring the manner in which race and class have conditioned the experiences of women historically and by highlighting the contribution of African American and working-class women's labor to the development of the United States as a world power. The original essay was written for presentation at a conference on Women and Development, sponsored by the Wenner-Gren Foundation for Anthropological Research, held in Austria in the summer of 1979. At this conference, as has often happened since, I was struck by the differences rather than the similarities in women's experiences and bemused by the indictment of "men" by some Euro-American feminists, whose lives were much more privileged than those of the men of my race. This essay, which prefigures some of the arguments about class and race presented much more forcibly by Angela Davis in *Women, Race, and Class* (1981), explored some of those differences historically. This article was one of a number of studies appearing in the early 1980s asserting that class and race modify the experience of gender and exploring the ways in which they mediate the productive and reproductive spheres. There is now a significant body of work on African American women and slavery (see, for example, White 1985, Jones 1985, and Fox-Genovese 1988), as well as advanced analyses of the interpenetration of public and private spheres.

While chapter 2 explores the "double day," examining work and household responsibilities, chapter 3, "Minority Women, Work, and Health," introduces the concept of the "triple day," broaching the subject I later refer to as transformative work. This article, which was based on a presentation to several unions in the early 1980s, considers the cost of the triple day to the health status of women of color. The central argument—that the interrelated arenas of work, household, and community must be analyzed in order to understand health—became the basis of the ethnographic component of a successful proposal to the Centers for Disease Control to study social conditions and health among women of Central Harlem through integrating community collaboration into the research process. The results of this and other research in Harlem are forthcoming in a volume coauthored with Alaka Wali.

In writing this article I was concerned with deconstructing current explanations attributing health disparities between African Americans and Euro-Americans to biological or cultural inferiority. This critique is elaborated in a more recent article (Mullings 1989) in which I also suggest that should policies initiated in the Reagan era continue, these inequalities in health status will persist. Currently, with the virtual dismantling of the Occupational Safety and Health Administration, the decline of unions, the rise of unemployment, and continuing inadequate access to health care, it is not surprising that such disparities remain and in some cases have intensified.

Notes

1. Black women are compared to all white women, including Hispanic whites.

2. These occupational categories can be somewhat misleading in that they obscure significant differences within categories and concentrations of African Americans in particular jobs. For example, within the "managerial and professional specialty," while roughly the same percentage of African American and white women are found in professional occupations, white women are three times more likely to hold executive and managerial jobs.

References

Bennett, Claudette E. 1995. "The Black Population in the United States: March 1994 and 1993." U.S. Bureau of the Census, *Current Population Reports,* P20–480. Washington, D.C.: U.S. Government Printing Office.

Davis, Angela. 1981. *Women, Race, and Class.* New York: Random House.

Fox-Genovese, Elizabeth. 1988. *Within the Plantation Household: Black and White Women of the Old South.* Chapel Hill: University of North Carolina Press.

Jones, Jacqueline. 1985. *Labor of Love, Labor of Sorrow: Black Women, Work, and the Family from Slavery to the Present.* New York: Basic Books.

Mullings, Leith. 1976. "Women and Economic Change in Africa." In N. Hafkin and E. Bay, eds., *Women in Africa: Studies in Social and Economic Change.* Stanford: Stanford University Press.

———. 1989. "Inequality and Afro-American Health Status: Policies and Prospects." In Winston Van Horne, ed., *Race: 20th Century Dilemmas—21st Century Prognoses.* Milwaukee: University of Wisconsin Institute on Race and Ethnicity.

White, Deborah Gray. 1985. *Ar'n't I a Woman: Female Slaves in the Plantation South.* New York: W. W. Norton.

1

Notes on Women, Work, and Society

We are called to struggle against those practices that result in differential treatment of children according to gender, race, and socioeconomic status, and to promote those practices that enable children to enrich their own lives and our society. One of the most pernicious theories that has, for centuries, consistently promoted and rationalized the differential access of human beings to the resources of society is that of genetic determinism. In its various forms, this view serves to justify the ranking of people on the basis of class, race, ethnicity, and gender. It suggests that such distinctions have biological implications, determining potential, ability, and, ultimately, life chances. This concept serves to rationalize the sentiment that categories of people, defined by class, race, and gender, are relegated to certain tasks and socioeconomic levels because their biological programming limits them to such statuses.

That there are anatomical differences between males and females is undisputed. What remains very much at issue is the meaning of these differences. In general, genetic determinists have argued that biological differences have "natural" consequences, that the division of labor—usually some variant of the home/work, private/public dichotomy—and, indeed, the inequalities between men and women have a genetic origin and therefore will persist in some form regardless of the structural arrangements of society. Much of the cross-cultural and historical data calls such a view into question. In this chapter I will review some of the evidence suggesting that the division of labor by gender and the ideology of sex roles are ultimately determined not by biological constraints but by the structural arrangements of a given society.

Upon examination of the cross-cultural evidence, anthropologists of very different perspectives find that in general, the ways in which labor is divided between men and women are so diverse that it is difficult to correlate the division of tasks with the biological or physical attributes of either gender (Hammond and Jablow 1976; Lévi-Strauss 1971; Liebowitz 1978). We find that assignments vary from one culture to another. Such tasks as agriculture, animal herding, marketing, or the transporting of heavy loads are performed by women in some cultures and by men in others. Whatever the nature of the division of labor, however, the rationale for it is usually biological. For example, the Arapesh say that women have stronger heads than men and that is why it is women who transport heavy loads on their heads. The Kota of India claim that women have stronger heads but weaker arms; women carry all loads on their heads while men carry the loads in their arms (Hammond and Jablow 1976). Even within the same geographic area, neighboring societies may make different assignments of gender-related roles: Navajo women in the southwest United States do the weaving, but among the neighboring Pueblo, weaving is undertaken by the men (Hammond and Jablow 1976).

It is not necessary to look to other societies to find that assignment of sex-segregated tasks is more related to the exigencies of historical development than to biological differences. Blau (1978) notes that in the United States the gender composition of occupations is subject to regional variation. For example, in the Midwest cornhuskers are traditionally women, while trimmers are always men; in the Far West, cornhuskers are men and trimmers are women. An occupation that is predominantly female in one industry may be predominantly male in another; thus, in electrical machinery equipment and supplies, the 1960 census reported that 67 percent of the assemblers were women, while in motor vehicles and motor vehicle equipment only 16 percent of the assemblers were women.

The correlation between anatomical differences and gender-related tasks, then, is far from clear. Historically, the major exception seems to be hunting, which was long thought to be almost universally assigned to men, leading investigators to conclude that the biological fact of women's reproductive capacities constrained their ability to hunt, determining this initial division of labor. Sociobiologists have taken this further, suggesting that because the early division of labor revolved around the anatomical differences between males and females, it was likely to persist in all types of societies:

> In hunter-gatherer societies men hunt and women stay home. This strong bias persists in most agricultural and industrial societies, and on that ground alone appears to have a genetic origin. . . . My own guess is that the genetic bias is intense enough to cause a substantial division of labor even in the most free

and most egalitarian of future societies . . . even with identical education and equal access to all professions, men are likely to continue to play a disproportionate role in political life, business and science. (Wilson 1975, 48)

Recent evidence calls many of these assumptions into question. In a provocative account of the evolution of the family and women's roles, Lila Liebowitz argues persuasively that the early division of labor was molded by socioeconomic considerations, not by biological imperatives in and of themselves (Liebowitz 1978). Greatly simplified, her argument runs as follows: the division of labor by gender whereby men hunt and women gather and care for the children is not a "natural" outcome of anatomical differences, but rather was the result of specific socioecological transformations. Though it is generally assumed that women were excluded from all types of hunting,[1] Liebowitz suggests that a gendered division of labor was associated with the emergence of a form of hunting that involved pursuing and killing large animals with the use of projectile weapons, as compared to earlier types of hunting, such as drives, individual hunting of small game, or surround hunting. It was in the specific conditions under which meat became a regular part of the diet and resources were scarce, thus making dispersal into small groups a necessity, that projectile hunting was associated with a sexual division of labor. As the ability to remain inconspicuous and to surprise the animal was key in this type of hunting, small groups became more efficient, unlike surround or drive hunting, where large groups were required.

It was with the development of these socioecological circumstances, characterized by small groups and projectile hunting, that a woman with children found herself encumbered as a hunter. Infants must nurse often, and young children need constant care. In a small social unit having few nursing mothers and in which a nursing mother could not easily count on another nursing mother for care of her children, the assignment of men to hunt and women to gather and care for children becomes predictable, practical, and adaptive. Moreover, since men cannot nurse children, the loss of a woman in the relatively dangerous occupation of hunting would have been more serious than the loss of a man. Since effective hunting requires a certain skill acquired through training, differential training and socialization of the sexes established, reinforced, and perpetuated this division of labor.

If Liebowitz's assertions are valid, it seems that while anatomical differences determined which gender cared for children, the necessity for a gendered division of labor arose not from biological or genetic imperatives but only as a result of a particular configuration of ecological, economic, and historical transformations. Thus, division of labor by gender may not be "natural" and therefore enduring, but social and subject to change as social arrangements change.

Numerous studies have pointed to the impact of such factors as private property, the evolution of the state, and warfare on the status of women, often transforming the division of labor into relationships of domination and subjugation (for example, see Harris 1977; Leacock 1978; Mullings 1976; Rapp 1978).

Although the evidence is not yet all in and reconstruction of earlier epochs must be undertaken with caution, a glance at the history of women's roles in the United States suggests a similar conclusion: It is not biology but society that ultimately determines the division of labor. The division of labor by gender has not been fixed but rather has varied according to historical circumstances, and it has been very different for different classes. While in the seventeenth and eighteenth centuries European women were routinely employed as mowers, reapers, and haymakers (Blau 1978), in Colonial America among the nonslave population agricultural tasks were primarily the domain of men, with women being employed in the household industries and producing most of the colonies' manufactured goods. As labor shortages increased with the invasion of the West, the division of labor was modified to fit the needs of the society. Indeed, the transformation occurred during the journey itself. At the beginning of the westward journey, gender tasks were rigidly segregated; by midjourney, due to the vicissitudes of the trail, most women worked at male tasks (Bernard 1976). Increasing labor shortages in the evolving frontier society found women in a variety of nontraditional occupations, such as tavern keepers, traders, printers, and publishers, as well as the more traditional domestic ones (Blau 1978). Despite the separation between the home and the workplace fostered by industrialization, women played a crucial role in the development of the factory system. With the introduction of the power loom in 1814 and the creation of the textile industry, women—working-class women—constituted the bulk of this industrial work force. At various points during the nineteenth and twentieth centuries, labor shortages, fluctuations in demand, and technical innovations resulted in a shift toward greater numbers of female employees in such industries as shoe manufacturing, teaching, cigarmaking, and clerical work. It appears that the question of whether or not women were in the home, of what they did or did not do, has been related more to class than to gender, determined by society rather than biology.

The discrepancy between the roles of women of different classes has perhaps been greater than that between men and women of the same class. With the advent of industrialization, while femininity was described in terms of nonparticipation in the labor force and upper-class women were allegedly fainting in parlors, immigrant working-class women were laboring twelve hours a day in factories and African American women were toiling for sixteen hours or more in the fields. While womanliness was projected as intertwined with homemaking, and although single women constituted the majority of working women, the working wife seems to have been more prevalent than is generally assumed. An annual report of the Massachusetts Bureau of Statistics, cited in the April 1875 issue of *Scientific American,* concluded on the basis of visits with 397 families that in the majority of cases working men did not support their families by their own earnings alone but depended on their wives and children for one fourth to one third of the family earnings.

Perhaps the most dramatic, and heroic, example of the discrepancy between the ideology that divisions of labor are biologically rooted and the actual divisions that the socioeconomic system and the class position determine is that of African American women. Under conditions of chattel slavery, where the goal was the greatest exploitation of labor, the "flowers of southern womanhood" languished in plantation parlors while African American women often did the same work as men—under conditions to which no human being, male or female, should be subjected (Lerner 1972). The contradiction between the ideology of "women's place" as determined by their biology and the roles of African American women is movingly described in Sojourner Truth's address to the Akron Convention for Women's Suffrage:

> That man over there says that women need to be helped into carriages, and lifted over ditches, and to have the best place everywhere. Nobody ever helps me into carriages, or over mud-puddles or gives me any best place, and ain't I a woman? Look at me! Look at my arm. I have ploughed, and planted, and gathered into barns, and no man could head me! And ain't I a woman? I could work as much and eat as much as a man—when I could get it—and bear the lash as well! And ain't I a woman? I have borne thirteen children, and seen them most all sold off to slavery, and when I cried out with my mother's grief, none but Jesus heard me! And ain't I a woman? (Cited in Rossi 1973, 428)

The effects of racism against African American men and women in the areas of employment and wages since emancipation have compelled African American women to work to help support themselves and their families, and their rate of labor force participation has always exceeded that of Euro-American women.[2] Despite the desire of married African American women to withdraw from the labor force after slavery, large numbers of rural women were forced to labor alongside men as field hands (relatively few worked as servants or washerwomen—occupations that were more common among urban African Americans) (Gutman 1976).

While their long history of labor force participation may have produced more egalitarian arrangements within the household, African American women remain the most exploited in the public arena, receiving the lowest returns for the sale of their labor. The Census Department calculated that in 1973 the median annual income of minority women was 49.6 percent that of white men (as compared to 56.3 percent for Euro-American women).[3] This is primarily a result of the disproportionate confinement of African American and other minority women to the lowest-paying sectors of the labor force.[4] The example of African American and other working-class women dramatically demonstrates the discrepancy between their roles as determined by the division of labor and the ideology that "a woman's place is in the home."

The relationship between the ideology of the division of labor—how differential roles of men and women are rationalized and explained—and actual social conditions deserves much more elaborate treatment than I am able to undertake here. However, I would like to speculate on how the dominant ideology bears on the position of African American and other working-class women. Throughout most of the history of the United States normative notions of what a woman ought to be have reflected what upper-class women were able to be. Upper-class women, unlike all other women in the society, have no need to work and can therefore present themselves as ideal wives, mothers, and representatives of "high culture" (Rapp 1978, 299). These women, who "become symbols of domesticity and of public service," influence our views of what feminine behavior should be. The ideology of the division of labor, then, is often far removed from the reality of the experience of minority and other working women, yet it remains the cultural ideal, often buttressed by the canons of religion and rationalized as "natural" by biologically and genetically based explanations of science.

To bridge the gap between the ideology of gender roles and the real division of labor, between the biological sex of these women and their status as slaves and workers, requires a new ideological twist. In contemporary society, this takes the familiar form of blaming the victim: sex role ideology is used by apologists for the social system to castigate women workers and thus rationalize and deepen their oppression. The cynical theoretical circularity of the argument is most evident in the case of African American women. African women, along with men, were captured, torn from their families, and forced into slave labor without regard for the constraints and privileges of gender differentiation. (The ideological rationale at that time was to limit the definition of what was human—another example of genetic determinism.) After emancipation, African American women were coerced, by necessity and otherwise, into the labor force. Gutman (1976) reports numerous local situations in which planters complained about the lack of cheap field labor because women did not want to work and wished to be supported by their husbands. One Louisiana planter instructed that rent be charged to any nonworking wives of ex-slaves.

Today, the effects of racism—wage and employment discrimination, the high rate of death and disability of African American men as a result of lack of access to health care, disproportionate death from war, unemployment, and more-dangerous work conditions, as well as many other poverty-related stressors—continue to press African American women into the work force. In general, they do not have the option of choosing whether or not they wish to work. These women, who must work to ensure the survival of their families, are then attacked as "matriarchal" (Moynihan 1965).

Just as the ideology of racism bridges the gap between the folk belief of an open society with equal opportunity and the superexploitation of African American labor, the ideology of the "castrating" African American woman obscures the role of the socioeconomic system and, further, bridges the contradiction between sex role ideology and the reality of what women do. To the extent that the ideas of the ruling class become the ruling ideas of society, in the same way that the ideology of racism has divided the working class, sex role ideology penetrates the home and the workplace. Because the wage paid by the employer to an African American man will not support the family and therefore the woman must work, tensions and strains arise in the home as a result of the inability of both spouses to "live up to" the sex roles defined as models by the ruling class. In the workplace, ideologies of racism similarly divide those who should be united.

It seems clear that the division of labor by gender, though rationalized in terms of biological, genetic, and personality differences, is ultimately determined by social conditions. There is much disagreement among social scientists about which configuration of social processes is most relevant to explicating the status of women, and I will not recount the debate here. (See Amsden 1978 for a discussion of the various economic explanations; these models also have their counterparts in the sociology literature.) While production is not the only arena in which the inequality of women is expressed, the establishment and perpetuation of the division of labor seem to be rooted in the productive processes as well as in the relationship of the household to the resources of society. With this in mind, I will briefly indicate some of the functions served by inequality of contemporary American women in the workplace. (See Rapp 1978 for a discussion of inequality in the household.)

In a social system based on the accumulation of profit through the exploitation of labor, the division of labor by gender functions to strengthen those arrangements and to increase profits. Clearly, gender-segregated occupations tend to result in women's receiving less pay for the same work than men, hence maximizing profits. One well-documented example of this practice was the case of American Telephone and Telegraph Company (AT&T), whose discriminatory practices were investigated and described in a 1972 report of the Equal Employment Opportunity Commission (EEOC 1972). The EEOC report estimated that wage discrimination against women, through which AT&T was able to hold wages down and increase profits, amounted to $422 million a year in a total of thirty metropolitan areas (Perlo 1975). The widespread nature of such discriminatory practices is indicated in the male/female wage differential; women earn approximately 60 percent of what men earn (Amsden 1978).

With the growth of an organized labor movement and labor militancy, which may block companies' efforts to put short-term profit-maximizing strategies into effect, the existence of components of the labor force that are subject to discriminatory practices may serve other functions. Because marginally employed and underemployed people have fewer options and a higher rate of unemployment, they constitute a "reserve army" of unemployed who can be utilized to inhibit the wages-and-benefit demands of fully employed workers. The AT&T case illustrates the way in which this process operates. The EEOC report cites AT&T vice president Walter Straley's explanation of why, after years of discrimination, AT&T finally began to hire more minority women: "What a telephone company needs to know about its labor market (is) who is available for work paying as little as $4,000 to $5,000 a year. . . . It is therefore just a plain fact in today's world, telephone company wages are more in line with Black expectations—and the tighter the labor market the more this is true . . ." (cited in Perlo 1975, 136). Since a large majority of AT&T's employees were white, we can surmise that the company's ability to hire African American workers, particularly African American women, at lower wages because of their lack of options resulting from discrimination, contributed to AT&T's ability to hold down salary and benefit levels of Euro-American women workers to that at which they could hire African American women. Where males and females work at the same job, or where male workers can be replaced by female workers, this process can also be applied to male workers.

The threat of replacement buttressed by ideological justifications (e.g., men are superior to women, women's place is in the home, women are taking jobs from men) can inhibit the formation of unified working-class organizations that could, presumably, struggle more effectively for greater control of the workplace and better conditions for everyone. To make a case for the way in which the gender inequality functions to increase profits does not require a conspiracy theory; although conspiracy among corporate managers undoubtedly occurs, overt collusion is not a precondition to the perception of their (common) interests and the pursuit of (similar) actions to advance those interests.

Workers may also recognize and act on common interests. The extent to which differences between men and women, among ethnic groups, and among populations divide them partly depends on whether they organize to challenge such segmentation. It is to be hoped the ability of corporations such as AT&T to perpetuate conflict based on difference will decrease as women are organized into trade unions and women's groups concerned with advancing their interests in the context of the class struggle and the struggle against racism. African American women have frequently assumed leadership in such organizing (Foner 1974; Lerner 1972; Rossi 1973), but the success of these efforts will depend on the extent to which working people are able to unite behind their own interests, across gender lines and race boundaries. The importance of unity was recognized as early as 1869 by the Colored National Labor Union, when it convened in response to the exclusion of African Americans from Euro-American unions. Upholding the rights of women in industry and unions, the union's Committee on Women's Labor recommended "profiting by the mistakes heretofore made by our white fellow citizens in admitting women . . . that women be cordially included in the invitation to further and organize cooperative societies" (Foner 1974, 138). While "mistakes" of exclusion have by no means been fully corrected, workers and trade unions increasingly recognize the need for unity. Particularly interesting are the scattered incidents where workers have been able to use protective legislative measures designed for women in such a way as to extend them to increase benefits and protection for male workers as well.[5]

In summary, then, it is undisputed that there are anatomical differences between men and women. However, what these differences come to mean, and the significance they assume in a given society, appears to be determined not by the nature of the differences themselves but by the way in which the society is organized. In a society where profit is the driving force, anatomical differences between males and females, like culture history differences between ethnic groups and phenotypic differences between populations, are utilized to support inequality and maximize profits. Where such differences converge, as in the case of African American women, oppression will be particularly intense (Mullings 1978).

Policy implications, then, must relate to changing the basic structure of the socioeconomic system. While all forms of gender asymmetry will not disappear once the society ceases to be organized around profit, this seems to be the first step in creating the foundation for change. Explanations that do not account for the role of the social system in determining the division of labor, whether they attribute sexual inequality to the anatomy of women or to the congenital dispositions of men, ultimately function to assist in reproducing the socioeconomic system that so defines the division of labor and divides the people who are oppressed by it. If gender inequality is socially, not naturally, determined, the first step in eradicating inequality is addressing the system that profits from it—putting people before profits. Because the destinies of working people, men and women, are inextricably linked economically, politically, and socially, this requires the unity of working people and oppressed minorities, men and women, to create a better world for all our children.

Notes

I would like to thank Jean Carey Bond and Eleanor Leacock for reading and commenting on this paper.

1. I would like to thank Eleanor Leacock for pointing out that the "exclusion" of women from hunting large game among gathering-hunting populations is a popular, but undocumented, stereotype. She notes that although cross-culturally men do most of the hunting, data on the Inuit and Native Americans of the Canadian subarctic and some Australian groups indicate that women hunt large game when they need or want to.

2. In 1890 the labor force participation rate for white women was 16.3 percent compared to 39.7 percent for nonwhite women; however, the labor force participation rate for married white women was 2.5 percent, compared to 22.5 percent for married nonwhite women (Goldin 1977). In 1948, 31 percent of all Euro-American women and 45 percent of all nonwhite women were in the labor force (Blau 1978); by 1973, three out of five African American women worked for wages or salary, as compared to approximately half of Euro-American women (Perlo 1975). While the differential between African American and Euro-American women has been narrowing in recent years, the difference in the overall impact of the work experience can be understood more accurately if we examine, in addition to marital status, the proportion of women working in specific age groups. In the 25–34 age group—the principal childbearing years—there is a sharp decline in the participation in the labor market of Euro-American women, but an increase in African American women's participation; these are the years when the presence of children makes working more difficult but for some more necessary. It is in this age range that the excess of African American women over Euro-American women reaches its peak, with 61.1 percent of African American women working, as compared with 48.6 percent of Euro-American women (Perlo 1975).

3. There has been some confusion about the differential income of African American women that has resulted from comparison of aggregate annual incomes of Euro-American and African American women. Often these statistics, used to suggest that African American women's wages are higher than those of Euro-American women, do not take into consideration the fact that a greater number of Euro-American women are able to afford to work part time and to find suitable part-time work.

4. The U.S. Women's Bureau, in a survey of four states, reported that prior to 1929 the African American working woman averaged $300 annually, or $6 per week. In 1955, six out of ten African American women worked in domestic and service jobs, with only 20 percent in industrial, sales, and office jobs, in which 59 percent of the Euro-American women then working were employed (Foner 1974). In the last fifteen years the occupational distribution of African American women workers has dramatically changed, with a move away from domestic work and a shift into clerical, professional, and factory work (Reiter 1977). However, although there have been gains related to social status, these have not necessarily registered as equivalent economic gains. In 1959, the median earn-

ings of male clerical workers were $4,785; ten years later, the median annual earnings of female clerical workers were $4,232, and of African American female clerical workers $4,152 (Perlo 1975).

5. The issue of protective legislation is a very complex one. While it is true that protective legislation has been used in some cases to discriminate against women workers, it is also true that some of the measures ensure at least minimal protection against the hazards of the workplace and thus offer some protection to women workers. Where women's movements have been dominated by intellectuals, professionals, and housewives, the hazards faced by working-class women, particularly those in industry, have been neither understood nor considered. Where protective legislation is not clearly discriminatory, rather than seek to eliminate those few protective measures against the hazards of the workplace that are in existence, a more useful approach might be to fight to extend those protective measures to all workers.

References

Amsden, A. 1978. *An Overview of the Economics of Women and Work.* New York: Center for Social Sciences, Columbia University.

Bernard, J. 1976. "Historical and Structural Barriers to Occupational Desegregation." In M. Blaxall and B. Reagan, eds., *Women and the Workplace.* Chicago: University of Chicago Press.

Blau, F. 1978. "The Data on Women Workers, Past, Present, and Future." In A. Stromberg and S. Harkess, eds., *Women Working.* Palo Alto, CA: Mayfield.

Foner, Philip. 1974. *Organized Labor and the Black Worker, 1619–1973.* New York: International Publishers.

Gutman, Herbert. 1976. *The Black Family in Slavery and Freedom, 1750–1925.* New York: Pantheon.

Goldin, Claudia. 1977. "Female Labor Force Participation: The Origin of Black and White Differences, 1870 and 1880." *Journal of Economic History* 37: 87.

Hammond, D., and A. Jablow. 1976. *Women in Cultures of the World.* Menlo Park, CA: Cummings.

Harris, Marvin. 1977. *Cannibals and Kings.* New York: Random House.

Leacock, E. 1978. "Women's Status in Egalitarian Society: Implications for Social Evolution." *Current Anthropology* 19(2): 247–55.

Lerner, Gerda. 1972. *Black Women in White America.* New York: Pantheon.

Lévi-Strauss, Claude. 1971. "The Family." In A. Skolnick and J. Skolnick, eds., *Family in Transition.* Boston: Little, Brown.

Liebowitz, L. 1978. *Females, Males, Families: A Biosocial Approach.* Belmont, CA: Duxbury Press.

Moynihan, D. P. 1965. "Employment, Income, and the Ordeal of the Negro Family." *Daedalus* 94: 745–70.

Mullings, L. 1976. "Women and Economic Change in Africa." In N. Hafkin and E. Bay, eds., *Women in Africa.* Stanford: Stanford University Press.

―――. 1978. "Ethnicity and Stratification in the United States." *Annals of the New York Academy of Sciences* 318: 10–22.

Perlo, V. 1975. *Economics of Racism.* New York: International Publishers.

Rapp, R. 1978. "Family and Class in Contemporary America." *Science and Society* 42: 278–300.

Reiter, Rayna Rapp. 1977. "The Search for Origins: Unraveling the Threads of Gender Hierarchy." *Critique of Anthropology* 9–10: 5–24.

Rossi, A., ed. 1973. *The Feminist Papers.* New York: Bantam.

U.S. EEOC (United States Equal Employment Opportunity Commission). 1972. "'A Unique Competence': A Study of Employment Opportunity in the Bell System." *Congressional Record,* February 17: E1260–E1261.

Wilson, E. 1975. "Human Decency Is Animal." *New York Times Magazine,* October 12: 38–50.

2

Uneven Development

Class, Race, and Gender in the
United States Before 1900

It is by now well established that the modern world is characterized by uneven development—the development of Europe and the United States through the underdevelopment of Africa, Latin America, and Asia. Just as popular explanations of this disparity have ignored the exploitation of the underdeveloped world, so too have they frequently overlooked uneven development within the developed world, stemming from unequal exploitation and incorporation of labor. In the United States, stratification based on race and ethnicity, as well as class and gender, was both a prerequisite for and an effect of modern capitalist development.

During the nineteenth century, the United States entered a period of rapid economic development, becoming the most advanced capitalist country in the world. This set the stage for imperialistic enterprises such as the invasion of the Philippines and the Spanish-American War at the turn of the century and economic and military interventions in Africa, Asia, and Latin America later in the twentieth century. The wealth that enabled the buildup of military power was generated in part by the massive amount of free labor provided by enslaved Africans and African Americans and indentured Euro-Americans, as well as the cheap labor provided by free immigrant Euro-Americans.

As the status of women all over the world was affected by the manner in which development took place, it is also true women's labor was an integral aspect of economic development in the United States. Since the structure of labor varied by race and class as well as by gender, the experiences of women of distinct races and classes were fundamentally different.

The manner in which class and race have affected the lives of women has not been sufficiently recognized and analyzed by feminist scholars. Radical feminists, in particular, have tended to ignore these variables, suggesting that attention to them is divisive. Patriarchy stemming from the gender-ordered division of labor is held to be the major form of oppression, equally shared by all women. In industrial societies, the private/public dichotomy is seen as a basic mechanism for maintaining patriarchy. Heidi Hartmann summarizes this view, which is fairly common among scholars of women's history in the United States: "In our society the sexual division of labor is hierarchical, with men on top and women on the bottom. . . . It is my contention that the roots of women's present status lie in this sex-ordered division of labor" (1976, 137). Recently scholars concerned with class and race have suggested that the radical feminist perspective derives primarily from the experiences of upper- and middle-class Euro-American women and that the bases of gender oppression are a great deal more complex (Dill 1983, Davis 1981).

This chapter follows this line of reasoning by examining the ways in which class and race conditioned the experiences of women in the private and public spheres during the period of industrialization in the United States. I will first discuss the period prior to industrialization—loosely called the colonial epoch—since it creates the foundation for the developments we will find in the nineteenth century.[1] This is not meant to be a historical account, but rather one that will highlight certain ethnographic issues. Because African American women have been omitted so often from women's histories, I give special attention to their lives before and after slavery.

The Colonial Period

Women came both freely and in bondage to a world that was built on the land of the Native Americans, yet called "new." Patterns of labor exploitation that were to characterize the United States were established during the founding of the colony, imparting to women of different classes and ethnic groups, as well as their men, qualitatively different experiences.

The early colonial economy was characterized by small-scale agriculture and business. Economic conditions, along with the shortage of women, produced a marked flexibility in both public and household spheres for free Euro-American women, despite ideologies of gender differentiation. Women participated in economically productive work in the fields as well as in the house, and work was considered a duty for both married and single women. After the initial stages of settlement, work in the fields after the first crop was harvested became more infrequent for free Euro-American women, with custom decreeing that "only those wenches that are not fit to be so employed were put to the ground" (cited in Ryan 1983, 27). As we shall discuss, "unfit wenches" included enslaved African women.

While it was true that ownership of land accrued predominantly to male heads of households, in some locations—particularly in states that had been settled earliest—land could be owned by women. For example, in Virginia in 1634, opposition to women's legal entitlement to land ownership was overcome (Spruill 1938, 11). Villages in Massachusetts, Pennsylvania, and Maryland traditionally allocated land to women (Ryan 1983, 23). Women could inherit land from husbands and fathers, and widows often used such resources to work as independent traders and entrepreneurs. The elasticity in definition of women's roles allowed an important minority of women, particularly those in or near towns, to be employed outside the home in male-dominated commercial activities (Blau 1978, 30; Foner 1980, 8–9; Degler 1980, 365).

Within the household, free Euro-American women were granted some protection by law, custom, and theology. The family was considered to be a cornerstone of society, and colonial courts intervened if men dealt brutally with wives, daughters, or female servants (Ryan 1983, 37–38). Family handbooks of the seventeenth century advised husbands, in their behavior toward wives, "seldom to reprove: and never to smite her" (Spruill 1938, 163). In New England, some aspects of Puritan theology "worked to mitigate the domestic despotism of patriarchy," with wives admonished not to idolize their husbands (Ryan 1983, 38).

As colonial land grants were exhausted and private enterprise expanded, the distribution of wealth grew more uneven. This brought with it not only the widening chasm between male and female activities; as the planter and merchant elite was strengthened, the lives of women of different classes became more divergent. For free women of all classes, the developing separation of market and household spheres increased the centrality of household in their lives. However, upper-class women could delegate most of the actual household work to servants and spend much of the day in leisure activities. Nancy Shippen Livingstone, the daughter of a prosperous Philadelphia merchant and the wife of a New York aristocrat, described her routine as follows:

> This morning I gave orders to the servants as usual for the business of the day, then took a little work in my hands and sat down before the fire to think how I should dispose of myself in the evening. The morning generally devoted to

working and reading, and I concluded to go to the concert. Then I considered what I would dress in, and having determined this important part, I felt light and easy. (Cited in Ryan 1983, 93)

This lifestyle perhaps reached its extreme in the planter class, about which French traveller Marquis de Chastellux commented that the "natural indolence" of Virginia women was augmented by the luxury of being served by a large number of slaves (Spruill 1938, 76). The extent of available help is evident in the case of Elizabeth Pinckney, who, living alone after the marriage of her children, was said to keep a rather modest establishment. She described her domestic help as follows:

> I shall keep young Ebba to do the drudgery part, fetch wood and water, and scour, and learn as much as she is capable of Cooking and Washing. Mary-Ann cooks, makes my bed and makes my punch. Daphne works and makes the bread, old Ebba boils the cow's victuals, raises and fattens the poultry, Moses is employed from breakfast until 12 o'clock without doors, after that in the house. Pegg washes and milks. (Cited in Spruill 1938, 77)

George Washington wrote of the necessity of hiring a servant to "relieve Mrs. Washington from the drudgery of ordering, and seeing the table properly covered, and things economically used" (Spruill 1938, 77).

Indenture

The "drudgery" was generally performed by the unfree. In the early seventeenth century, domestics on plantations were frequently indentured servants. One of every three passengers disembarking from the Atlantic crossing in seventeenth-century Virginia was a woman, the majority of whom were indentured servants (Ryan 1983, 22). Indentured servants were bound to work for a limited period. Their death rates were high, though most of those who lived could look forward to freedom in the early colonial period and perhaps a subsidy of tools and land when their indenture was completed. The nature of work for female indentured servants was usually determined by the status of the family for which they worked: The servant of a small planter might do some fieldwork, while that of a wealthy planter would most often be a domestic servant.

Although female servants were undoubtedly vulnerable to sexual exploitation, the extent to which this occurred appears to have been limited by moral norms and legal protection (Carr and Walsh 1979, 30); female servants could and did

sue masters for support of children (Ryan 1983, 42). In general, indentured servants possessed some rights to life and contract and could bring suit to enforce
contract rights (Foner 1980, 5). After the term of indenture ended, a female servant could, and often did, become a planter's wife. Particularly where there was a
shortage of women, indentured servants experienced some liberty in making
their choices (Kennedy 1979; Carr and Walsh 1979; Lerner 1979).

Slavery

Indentured servants did not meet the growing labor needs of the colony, and
captured Africans were transported to the colonies against their will. In 1619 the
first group of twenty Africans was brought to Jamestown, Virginia. Though they
began as indentured servants, court decisions and special laws enacted between
1660 and 1682 transformed African servants into slaves. By the end of the seventeenth century, domestics on plantations were predominantly enslaved Africans;
with the expansion of tobacco, rice, and indigo plantations after 1700, the number of slaves rapidly increased.

The planters' concern for fullest exploitation and highest profits muted gender
differentiation among enslaved Africans in the public sphere. As Angela Davis
has put it, "the starting point for any exploration of black women's lives under
slavery would be an appraisal of their role as workers" (1981, 5). The majority of
slaves in the Deep South were agricultural workers, with women frequently doing
the same work as men. Owens notes: "A standard claim was that 'women can do
plowing very well and full well with the hoes and equal to men at picking'" (1976,
39). Julia Brown remembered: "I worked hard as always. You can't imagine what
a hard time I had. I split rails like a man. I used a huge glut and a iron wedge
drove into the wood with a maul, and this would split the wood" (cited in
Yetman 1970, 47).

The workday of the enslaved woman was very different from that of the Euro-
American plantation mistress:

> I never knowed what it was to rest. I just work all de time from morning till late
> at night. I had to do everythin' dey was to do on de outside. Work in de field,
> chop wood, hoe corn, till sometime I feels like my back surely break. . . . In de
> summer we had to work outdoors, in de winter in de house. I had to card and
> spin till ten o'clock. Never get much rest, had to get up at four de next mornin'
> and start again. Didn't get much to eat neither, just a li'l corn bread and 'lasses.
> Lordy, you cain't know what a time I had. All cold and hungry. I ain't tellin' no
> lies. It de gospel truth. It sure is. (Sarah Gudger, cited in Yetman 1970, 151)

Relationships in the households of enslaved people were, of course, constrained by the fact that the stability of slave families was at best uncertain: members could be sold, raped, or killed. Some indication of the prevalence of this disruption is evident in the post–Civil War marriage records. Analysis of data on marriage registrations of 2,880 African American couples by the Union Army in 1864–65 indicated that only 13.6 percent of the couples registered had been able to live together without disruption. Of those who had been separated from a previous spouse, over one third of the marriages were broken by the slave owner, presumably through sale, and approximately one half were disrupted by the death of a spouse. Similar conditions were reflected in a study of 450 slave marriages in Louisiana, where 35.7 percent were broken by the slave owner and 51.5 percent were ended by the death of a spouse (Degler 1980, 119).

For African and African American women, there were few protections in the reproductive sphere. In fact, as Davis (1981, 7) points out, rape became a weapon of terrorism used against enslaved people to facilitate the exploitation of labor. These mothers bore children but had no rights to them. A year after the importation of Africans was halted, a South Carolina court ruled that children could be sold away from their mothers because the "young of slaves . . . stand on the same footing as other animals" (cited in Davis 1980, 7). Delia Garlic recalled:

> Slavery days was hell. I growed up when de War come, and I was a mother before it closed. Babies was snatched from deir mother's breast and sold to speculators. Chillens was separated from sisters and brothers and never saw each other again. Course dey cry. You think they not cry when dey was sold like cattle? I could tell you about it all day, but even den you couldn't guess de awfulness of it. (Cited in Yetman 1970, 133)

Yet people take conditions that have been thrust upon them and out of them create a history and a future. Recently historians have documented the processes by which African Americans, using African forms where possible and creating new forms where necessary, put together families as best they could (see especially Gutman 1976). Some slave owners encouraged the formation of families. No doubt this was sometimes for humanitarian reasons, but clearly many sought to maintain labor discipline by exploiting the affective bonds between family members with direct and indirect threats and incentives. After the escape of one of his slaves, a slaveholder observed, "He would not go anywhere remote from his wife for whom he always indicated strong attachment" (cited in Owens 1976, 85). Noah Davis, a slave whose master allowed him to travel and deliver sermons to raise money for his freedom, said "How can I leave my wife and seven children, to go to Baltimore. . . . I thought my children would need my watchful care" (cited in Owens 1976, 198). The family was, as always, a place of refuge, a source of strength, and an inspiration for rebellion—but also a means of control.

Notwithstanding affective bonds, men and women resisted slavery. Women with children were perhaps inhibited from fleeing slavery, but some did, sometimes pregnant and sometimes with children. The late Lathan A. Windley's publication of the advertisements for runaway slaves from the 1730s to 1790 in Virginia, North Carolina, Maryland, South Carolina, and Georgia has been analyzed by Herbert Aptheker (1984).[2] Though there were a significantly higher number of male than female fugitives, the cases of some women were rather dramatic. For the five areas, 6,373 men, 1,258 women (including 26 who were described as pregnant), and 215 children under ten were sought as fugitives (Aptheker 1984, 10). Flight of women alone was somewhat unusual but did occur. For example, in 1785 in South Carolina, Charles H. Simmons of Charleston announced the flight of "THREE NEGRO WENCHES: JENNY, an elderly short wench; DIDO, her daughter about 35 years of age, middle stature; and TISSY, her granddaughter with a young child at her breast." An announcement that six adult slaves had fled a plantation in Savannah, Georgia, pointed out that two of these were women and that Sue, who was about thirty-five years old, quite short, and "is now and has been for a long time lame with the rheumatism, even to her finger ends (but nevertheless) . . . carried her three children with her, viz. Juno, a girl of about 10 years; Sarah, 7 years; and Dolly, 3 years old" (Aptheker 1984, 17).

Although slavery often drove blood relatives apart, shared oppression brought nonblood relatives together in extended family groups. (Generations later, the descendants of the slaves—faced with enclosure of land in the modern South and economic depression driving apart blood relatives—responded with fictive kin networks for collective survival.) Life in the slave quarters, a welcome retreat from the outside society, involved adoption of relatives, socialization of children, and care of the elderly. Although there is some disagreement about the division of labor by gender during slavery, most recent findings support Davis's contention that within the slave household the "salient theme is one of sexual equality" (1981, 17). Some measure of gender equality may be read into the marriage vows recited on one plantation. The groom pledged to perform the "duties of an affectionate and faithful husband" and the bride similarly pledged to be "an affectionate and faithful wife" (cited in Ryan 1983, 162) without assertions of obedience.

After work in the field and sometimes the factory, enslaved men and women both performed additional tasks for their own households. Men often hunted, fished, and farmed to help provide the family with food. Women often had domestic tasks to perform. Yet even here, the division of labor does not seem rigid; Owens notes that many young women were said to hunt with great success (1976, 196).

Women had the added burden of childbearing, frequently working up until childbirth and restarting soon afterward. Owens suggests that the general rule applying to enslaved women after childbirth was "make her do something, for as long as she hugs that sick house, she'll never get well" (cited in Owens 1976, 40). Carrying their newborns on their backs, enslaved women returned to work in the fields, nursing their babies when they could. Sometimes slaveholders permitted enslaved mothers to spend extra time caring for children, which would be made up by additional work performed by the children's father (Owens 1976, 200). The division of labor, to the extent that it existed, seemed geared toward facilitating the survival of the family. One of the ironies of slavery was that the disenfranchisement of both men and women meant that the enslaved family possessed no means by which one gender could control the other.

In this period women of different classes emerged with distinct experiences, options, and constraints. Their lives were at least as different from one another in these respects as they were from the lives of men of their own classes. For Euro-American women, class distinctions intensified and the public/private dichotomy became more salient. In the early phases, women of the planter class had access to resources primarily through their husbands and fathers but could command some independence through participation in manufacturing, agriculture, and some commercial enterprises. The extent to which they were subject to the limitations of gender role ideologies was modified by demographic and technological conditions. The limited political rights of female indentured servants, and later of poor Euro-American women, were shared with the men of their class. In the early period, the division of labor was probably less extreme, and availability of land allowed a certain flexibility in the mobility structure. In later periods, these women too were affected by the emerging gender role segregation.

The lives of enslaved women were very different. These women shared with men of their class a complete lack of property rights or even rights over their own bodies. They often did what was considered to be men's work. They shared the reproductive burdens of both the planter's wife and the indentured servant, but they were not entitled to protection of their sexuality or families, except that which they could muster themselves within the confines of the slave system. Here we find a major distinction between the lives of the free and the unfree. The division of labor by gender seems to have been greatest in the planter class. This was reflected in the household, and relationships seem to have been most patriarchal in the emerging merchant, planter, and artisan classes (see Farber 1973).

Given the realities of enslaved women's lives compared to the ideologies of gender-based role differentiation, it is not surprising that stereotypes emerged that continue to permeate the ideological landscape. Because African American women performed tasks usually reserved for males (that were thought to distinguish men from women) and possessed qualities considered taboo for women of this epoch, the feats accomplished by African American women were labeled unfeminine and contrasted to the model of Euro-American women (see chapter 6). Surely the images of the enslaved woman hewing wood and the shy, retiring plantation mistress, prone to fainting, have little in common.

Industrialization

In the first half of the nineteenth century, slavery, wage labor, and small-farm and artisanal labor competed for dominance. The victory of wage labor culminated in the Civil War, as industrial capitalism became the dominant mode of production. With industrialization and the rise of the so-called robber barons, who obtained the passage of government legislation authorizing them to seize natural resources and force out competitors, class differences intensified.

Distinctions between women of different classes, certainly clear during the previous epoch, became further entrenched and functioned to signify and strengthen class differences. By the mid-nineteenth century, the majority of Euro-American native-born women had husbands who were relatively comfortable farmers, shopkeepers, managers, clerks, and professionals, with only a small proportion being unskilled workers (Ryan 1983, 148). During this period, employment opportunities for middle- and upper-income women decreased as gender restrictions in businesses, trades, and professions became more stringent. Thus for most women, access to resources was largely a matter of the occupation of their husbands and fathers. However, in states such as Virginia, New York, and others, where married women were granted property rights, women seem to have had some independent access to financial resources.[3] There were also some avenues to independent income: for example, urban middle-class wives often increased their income by taking in boarders.

Domesticity: Elite and Middle-Stratum Women

The cults of domesticity and "true womanhood" that proliferated during this period reflected, on the ideological plane, the increased wealth that allowed some women freedom from work outside the home; the growing separation of home and workplace; and nascent consumerism. Asserting a separation between home and workplace, a contrast between male and female natures, and the idealization of motherhood (Harris 1978, 33), the cult of domesticity affirmed, for all classes, the home as the only sphere of the "true" woman. Although elite and middle-class women were discouraged from pursuing careers in business and the professions, their access to financial resources—or to the fruits of them—gave them privileges that neither men nor women of other classes possessed. They clearly experienced a separation between the public and private spheres, and their realm was the household. Within the household, however, much of the work was done by servants, leaving the women some leisure for pursuit of other interests.

Harriet Beecher Stowe, for example, who was by no means wealthy, plaintively expresses in a letter her boredom with the confines of domestic life but also indicates the extensive help she received from servants in her relatively modest household. In a letter to a Miss May written on June 21, 1838, she laments the change in her personality since becoming a wife and mother and describes her day:

> In the first place I waked about half after four and thought "Bless me, how light it is! I must get out of bed and rap to wake up Mina, for breakfast must be had at six o'clock this morning." . . . "Dear me broad daylight I must go down and see if Mina is getting breakfast." . . . Then back I come to the nursery, where, remembering that it is washing day and that there is a great deal of work to be done, I apply myself vigorously to sweeping, dusting, and the setting to rights so necessary where there are three little mischiefs always pulling down as fast as one can put up. Then there are Miss H—— and Miss E——, concerning whom Mary will furnish you with all suitable particulars, who are chattering, hallooing, or singing at the tops of their voices, as may suit their various states of mind, while the nurse is getting their breakfast ready. This meal being cleared away, Mr. Stowe dispatched to market with various memoranda of provisions, etc., and the baby being washed and dressed, I begin to think what next must be done. I start to cut out some little dresses. . . . By and by the nurse comes up from her sweeping. I commit the children to her, and finish cutting out the frocks. . . . But let this suffice, for of such details as these are all my days made up. Indeed, my dear, I am but a mere drudge with few ideas beyond babies and housekeeping. (Cited in Stowe 1889, 90–92)

While the work women performed in the home contributed to the growth of an industrial society, it was the working-class and enslaved men and women whose labor created the wealth that allowed the middle- and upper-class domestic lifestyles to exist. By the close of the eighteenth century, the first mechanical factories were taking entire families—including women—to work in conditions reminiscent of industrializing England.[4] Wages were determined by gender and age, with women and children making less than men (see Ryan 1983, 84).

Euro-American Women Workers

By 1850 women worked in nearly 175 industries in manufacturing, through their low wages creating the surplus value that helped to build the economy. The extent to which women worked outside the home was conditioned by class, ethnicity, and marital status. For many Euro-American working-class women, leaving the paid labor force upon marriage was an ideal to strive for, although it was not always attained. It was, however, attained more frequently by those Euro-American working women whose husbands were able to make a "family wage." The cult of domesticity, disseminated through the church, the educational system, and popular literature, sought to define femininity for all classes of women but also became the basis of the demand for the family wage that allowed women and children to stay at home.

For some, the ideal of the woman's sphere could become a reality. U.S. census figures for 1860 show that only about 15 percent of "adult women" were employed outside the home (Ryan 1983, 117). A study conducted by the Bureau of Labor in 1887 found that 75 percent of the female industrial labor force was under twenty-five and that 96 percent of them were single. As of 1890, the average tenure of women's work outside the home was only eleven years (Ryan 1983, 175–76).

These conditions, however, did not pertain equally to all strata of women. The Irish, for example, faced some of the worst socioeconomic conditions among Euro-American groups. In the Irish-dominated Sixth Ward of New York in 1855, 44 percent of women between the ages of fifteen and forty-nine were gainfully employed, primarily in domestic and personal service. While most women working outside the home in this area were young and single, most married women took in boarders in order to supplement their income (Groneman 1977, 85), a practice that was fairly widespread among urban working-class women (see Ryan 1983, 177).

Studies increasingly suggest that married women, depending on their socioeconomic circumstances, participated in the labor force more frequently than was originally believed. In Lowell, Massachusetts, for example, by 1860 one half of the households were female-headed (Degler 1980, 371). After the Civil War, as many as half of all Irish American women were without a spouse because of widowhood, desertion, or separation (Ryan 1983, 156). It is reasonable to assume that such women moved in and out of the labor force as necessary. Working-class Italian

American women, on the other hand, tended not to work outside the home to the same extent as other groups (Yans-McLaughlin 1977). In 1890 in New York City, fewer than one in twenty Italian American wives was employed outside the household; among Jewish wives, the figure was one in fifty (Ryan 1983, 177).

These women, too, were responsible for the domestic sphere, but this probably meant doing most of the work without servants. The extent to which participation in the labor force gave working-class women greater autonomy in the household is not clear, but the hypothesis that working gained them some autonomy is not unreasonable. Young single women contributed a major portion of their wages to their family of origin (Ryan 1983, 176), but their wages could also be used to gain power and privilege at home, to escape from social pressures, to leave home and decide how their wages were to be spent, and to have something comparable to a dowry when seeking a marriage partner (Kennedy 1979, 16–17). Most married women were not in the wage-labor force, but they worked at home, sewing or taking in boarders. In addition to the extra money made in this fashion, working-class wives usually had charge of the spending money for the household (Ryan 1983, 180–81), often the husband's entire paycheck (Degler 1980, 136). New research, unencumbered by the stereotype of the working-class male, is needed to clarify the extent to which working-class men wielded power in the household.

African American Women Workers, Slave and Free

While Euro-American working-class women toiled in the factories and elite women adorned parlors, several hundred thousand African American women, men, and children were undergoing massive disruption. Individuals were sold away and families separated as export agriculture shifted from the upper to the lower South between 1815 and 1860. These enslaved laborers planted and picked the cotton for the mills in which the free Euro-American labor force worked. By the mid-nineteenth century, seven out of eight slaves—men and women—were fieldworkers (Davis 1981, 5). Enslaved labor was also used for industry. In textile, hemp, tobacco, sugar refining, and rice milling factories, in the lumber and transportation industries, and in foundries, salt works, and mines, women did what was considered to be men's work (see Foner 1980, 99). The following observation of a Carolinian was probably typical and accurate: "In ditching particularly in canals . . . a woman can do nearly as much work as a man" (cited in Starobin 1970, 167).

For free African Americans,[5] who were not permitted to work as operatives in shops and factories, the Industrial Revolution did not change the type of work available to either men or women. In the South, free African American women worked as cooks, laundresses, and housekeepers. In the North, the work available to African Americans was not much different. According to the 1838 census of Philadelphia, among African Americans, eight out of every ten working men were unskilled workers, with 38 percent working as laborers, 11.5 percent as porters, 11.5 percent as waiters, 5 percent as seamen, 4 percent as carters, and 10 percent in miscellaneous laboring capacities (Hershberg 1972, 199). In 1847, less than .5 percent of the African American male work force was employed in factories (Hershberg 1972, 191). Of the women, more than eight out of ten were employed as domestic servants in day-work capacities. By 1880, one in every five adult African Americans in this area lived and worked in a white household as a domestic servant, demonstrating the pervasive employment discrimination at the same time that industrialization provided widening job opportunities for Euro-American men and women (Hershberg 1972, 191). Through 1859, there were no African American women employed in the cotton mills or other factories in the Philadelphia area (Foner 1980, 105). This situation was typical of the North, where African Americans were excluded from the burgeoning industrial sector.

After emancipation, African Americans in the South became sharecroppers and tenant farmers. Like Euro-American working women who had struggled for the family wage, African American women attempted to withdraw from the labor force and to demand for their men wages that would support a family. In 1865 an Alabama plantation owner complained to his daughter, "The women say they never mean to do any more outdoor work, that white men support their wives and that they mean that their husbands should support them." A plantation mistress had a similar complaint about one of her ex-slaves: "Pete is still in the notion of remaining but chooses to feed his wife out of his wages rather than get her fed for her services" (quoted in Gutman 1976, 167–68).

Inexpensive labor was important for getting out the cotton crop at the highest levels of profit. A Georgia planter predicted, "You will never see three million bales of cotton raised in the South again unless the labor system is improved. . . . One-third of the hands are *women* who *now* do not work at all" (quoted in Gutman 1976, 167). Boston capitalists worried about the effect on their profits of the withdrawal by southern African American women: "A very large proportion of the women have left the fields and stay at home in the cabins. This, in looking to the future, is a serious loss, one over which there is no control" (quoted in Gutman 1976, 168). There was some control, however, and in some cases immediate and direct measures were taken to force women back into the fields. For example, a Louisiana planter instructed that rent be charged to the nonworking wives of ex-slaves who were working on his plantation (Gutman 1976, 168). Given the prevailing ideology that a woman's place was in the home, it is ironic that John deForest, a Freedmen's Bureau officer in Greenville, South Carolina, concluded that families needing bureau aid had gone "astern simply because the men alone were laboring to support their families" and worried about the "evil of feminine loaferism" (quoted in Gutman 1976, 167).

Emancipation did not bring an end to job discrimination for African Americans in the North, either. In most cities, African Americans were confined by racism to lower-paying menial jobs, as a function of both wage differentials and job-category discrimination (see Mullings 1978). In the Boston of 1880, for example, which was considered to have unusually favorable opportunities for African Americans, 74 percent of all African Americans worked as waiters, servants, barbers, laborers, porters, laundresses, and seamstresses; the largest group were servants. As compared with Irish Americans, the lowest-ranking Euro-Americans, almost three times as many Irish Americans (19.8 percent) as African Americans (7.2 percent) were skilled workers. A similar situation was found in other cities (see, for example, Gutman 1976, 442–47).

In most U.S. cities, the constraints on the ability of African American men to earn a "family wage" forced African American married women into the labor market in greater proportions than Euro-American wives. By 1880, 50 percent of African American women were in the work force, as compared to 15 percent of Euro-American women (Degler 1980, 389). While the majority of working women of both races were unmarried, a significantly higher proportion of African American wives worked. Data from the 1890 census show labor force participation by white married women at a rate of 2.5 percent as compared to 22.5 percent among nonwhite married women. Separating out foreign-born women reveals a labor force participation rate of 3.0 percent among these wives (Goldin 1977, 88).[6] By 1900 there was a 26 percent employment rate among African American wives, as compared to 3.2 percent among Euro-American married women. Again, the comparison with immigrant wives sustains the contrast. In most American cities, the employment rate of African American married women was four to fifteen times higher than that of immigrant wives (Pleck 1972, 368).

Several factors may have had some bearing on the high labor force participation rate of married African American women. Scholars have suggested that slavery conditioned African American women to combine work and family (Goldin 1977) and that African American wives chose to go to work and keep their children in school rather than have their children go out to work, as was the case in Italian American families (Pleck 1972). It seems clear, however, that the major factor constraining the options of African American women was the pervasive discrimination against both men and women, eliminating the possibility of a family wage. Within the limitations set by the society, African American women made choices about how they fulfilled their responsibilities. For example, in most cities, African American married women chose to work as laundresses rather than as domestic servants in order to spend more time with their children (Gutman 1976, 167–69). Though there is some disagreement, most studies acknowledge that African American women have historically experienced greater independence in the household, manifested in more egalitarian decision making and the ability to terminate unsatisfactory relationships.

This period, characterized by rapid economic development, accelerated and sharpened class divisions and, as part and parcel of that, distinctions between women of different classes. Development in the United States was based on concentration of wealth and differential exploitation of labor. Among those who lacked access to wealth, differences of incorporation into the labor force, with minorities suffering greater exploitation, were rationalized by racism. It is only within this framework that the different experiences of women can be understood.

Perhaps the public/private dichotomy was most apparent among elite and middle-stratum women. These were the only women who could afford to remain outside the labor force throughout their life cycle. It is among these strata that the cult of "true womanhood" could be acted out and the separation of home and workplace maintained. Political disenfranchisement was more meaningful in these classes, where the men had power and wealth. True, most women had access to the fruit of these resources only as wives and daughters. Nevertheless, their class position gave them a lifestyle no other men or women could enjoy. Their responsibility for household, then, meant the supervision of household workers.

Ironically, it was gender role symbolism that helped to rationalize the hierarchical socioeconomic system. The celebration and glorification of "southern womanhood"—the celebration and "protection" of upper-class Euro-American women—was a major theme in the symbolic motif that rationalized a reign of terror against African Americans after the Civil War (see Davis 1981 for an excellent discussion of the connection between sex role ideology and lynchings). Elite women reaped the benefits of an unequal social order, and to the extent that they "bought into" the privileges the system generated, they accepted its structure.

For Euro-American working-class women, the public/private division was less clear. Unmarried women worked in the public sphere, and married women probably participated in wage labor more frequently than has been documented. For working-class women, the sexual division of labor meant gender-segregated (and lower-paying) jobs. Yet, particularly during the emergence of industrialization, the extent to which industries were dominated by men or women at a given point in time shifted with ecological and technological conditions and decisions of employers. While it was certainly true that working-class men participated in encouraging segregation of the workplace by gender, we need to look further at the role of employers in initiating conditions that encouraged these developments. Certainly recent studies have documented the active participation of employers in segmenting labor markets.

Working-class women utilized the ideology of women's place to demand a family wage (see, for example, Baxandall, Gordon, and Reverby 1976, 17) that would allow them to withdraw from the labor force at the same time that middle-class women's-rights activists were condemning that ideology. Working-class Euro-American women were also responsible for the household, but this generally required performing household tasks themselves. They too were politically disenfranchised relative to the men of their class once ownership of property ceased to be a condition for suffrage; however, in the absence of access to property and to real political power, the significance of relative disenfranchisement is not as great as for middle-class women.

African American women were perhaps least affected by the public/private dichotomy, as the prohibitions against employment of women never extended to them. As I have discussed, during slavery they often did men's tasks, and after emancipation job segregation developed more slowly. In the initial postemancipation period, both men and women worked as field hands in the South, domestic servants in the North. Gender segregation was experienced as wage differentials. Because racism facilitates the rationalization of a superexploited labor force (Mullings 1978), African Americans have rarely had access to a family wage, and both men and women have worked throughout their life cycle.

The double burden of women is most apparent in this population, where married women have historically worked in the public sphere and cared for their household without outside help. The fact that African American women must work but are forced to do so in race and gender-segregated jobs has been expressed dramatically by Bonnie Dill (1983): "Minority women do not have the protection of private patriarchy, but are exploited through public patriarchy." Ironically, the conditions African American women and men have encountered seem to have resulted in more independence in household relationships.

Conclusion

An exploration of class and race differences among women before 1900 raises intriguing issues. In all classes there was a gender-based division of labor. But what gives any division of labor significance is its link to a structure of differential and unequal rewards. In this sense, the gender-ordered division of labor may have been greatest in the property-owning class and least among African Americans, among whom the gender division of labor was relatively circumscribed for much of this period. When we examine the concrete outcomes of the division of labor—access to resources and consequent ability to control one's life—the difference is perhaps greater among women (and men) of different classes than between men and women of the same class.

It seems clear that production relations—that is, where women and their men stood in relationship to the process of production—influenced the significance of reproductive relations. Women of the privileged classes, while confined to the household sphere, were guaranteed certain protections and possessed options within the household, based on resources that no other class could command. At the other extreme, we find that African American women had neither the protections of the household nor the conditions that allowed them choice about labor force participation. Yet within their households they may have possessed the greatest degree of equality in their relationships with their own men.

The class position of women, then, was central to the way in which they experienced the events of this period. Race was intertwined with class as populations from various parts of the world were incorporated at different levels of the labor force. Racial differences were utilized to rationalize greater exploitation of African American men and women, producing a distinct experience for women of color. Although the gender-ordered division of labor ideology was universal, the manner in which it was manifested in a given class was, to a great extent, determined by the interests of the class in power.

This is not to suggest that gender role behavior is mechanically imposed from the top down. As is evident from the material discussed in this chapter, men and women actively participated in defining and redefining gender roles. But the ways in which women understood and participated in the struggle against gender oppression differed according to class and race. As numerous scholars have pointed out, most middle-stratum women of this period emphasized the struggle for political enfranchisement and the abolition of the private/public dichotomy within the limits of the socioeconomic system (see Lerner 1971; Davis 1981). To the extent that the source of injustice was perceived merely as the gendered division of labor, the perpetrators were judged to be men of various classes, and discussion of class and race was deemed unnecessary and divisive. The political perspectives expressed by these women, to some extent, prefigured those of contemporary moderate as well as radical feminists.

Working-class Euro-American and African American women confronted a system in which exploitation was not only a consequence of gender. For these women, who were linked to the men of their own class by the racist and class oppression that benefited men and women of the dominant class, struggles rarely took the form of attacks against patriarchy. For Euro-American women, the issue of equality was embedded in labor struggles; for African American women, it was part of the struggle for emancipation and for political and economic rights, campaigns they waged in unity with men of their class. The implications of these different orientations, arising out of divergent class experiences, are evident in contemporary proposals to gain women's equality in the United States, ranging from the demand of some Euro-American feminists for a "bedroom-to-bedroom struggle" to Angela Davis's (1981) call for socialist transformation.

Notes

1. Periodization is used somewhat broadly in this chapter. Difficulties arise in comparing African American women, for whom emancipation resulted in a major change of status, with Euro-American women, for whom it was industrialization that signaled significant transformations.

2. Herbert Aptheker analyzes raw data collected by Lathan A. Windley in *Runaway Slave Advertisements: A Documentary History from the 1730s to 1790*. Both Aptheker and Windley caution that these advertisements by no means reflected the totality of runaways. I would like to thank Dr. Aptheker for making his then unpublished paper available to me.

3. The extent to which women of this class had access to financial resources only through men is not at all clear. For example, Griffen and Griffen's (1977) study of Poughkeepsie, New York, between 1850 and 1800 indicates that wives had considerable control over financial resources and commercial ventures. Between 1869 and 1887, thirty-three states gave property rights to married women (Degler 1980, 332).

4. In New England, the unmarried daughters of farmers often became mill workers for a few years before retiring to marry or pursue other careers. The initial conditions under which they worked in such areas as Lowell, Massachusetts, lasted only for a few years, after which factory conditions deteriorated and the workforce became primarily foreign-born. For an account of the Lowell mill workers, see Dublin 1979.

5. Between the 1790s and the Civil War, the number of free African Americans grew to five hundred thousand.

6. There are some discrepancies, generally having to do with the definition of the labor force and the way in which populations are delineated (see Goldin 1977, 88n.), but the basic trend remains clear.

References

Aptheker, Herbert. 1984. "We Will Be Free: Advertisements for Runaways and the Reality of American Slavery." Occasional Paper no. 1. Santa Clara: Ethnic Studies Program, University of California.

Baxandall, Rosalyn, Linda Gordon, and Susan Reverby, eds. 1976. *America's Working Women.* New York: Vintage.

Blau, Francine. 1978. "Data on Women Workers: Past, Present, and Future." In A. Stromberg and S. Harkess, eds., *Women Working.* Palo Alto, CA: Mayfield.

Carr, Lois, and Lorena Walsh. 1979. "The Planter's Wife." In N. Cott and E. Pleck, eds., *A Heritage of Her Own.* New York: Simon and Schuster.

Davis, Angela Y. 1981. *Women, Race, and Class.* New York: Random House.

Degler, Carl. 1980. *At Odds: Women and the Family in America from the Revolution to the Present.* New York: Oxford University Press.

Dill, Bonnie Thornton. 1983. "Racial Ethnic Families in the Nineteenth Century." Paper presented at the Summer Institute on Women of Color. Center for Research on Women. Memphis: Memphis State University.

Dublin, Thomas. 1979. *Women at Work.* New York: Columbia University Press.

Farber, Bernard. 1973. "Family and Community Structure: Salem in 1880." In Michael Gordon, ed., *The American Family in Social-Historical Perspective.* New York: St. Martin's Press.

Foner, Philip. 1980. *Women and the American Labor Movement,* vol. 1. New York: Free Press.

Goldin, Claudia. 1977. "Female Labor Force Participation: The Origin of Black and White Differences, 1870–1880." *Journal of Economic History* 37: 87–108.

Griffen, Sally, and Clyde Griffen. 1977. "Family and Business in a Small City: Poughkeepsie, N.Y., 1850–1880." In Tamara A. Hareven, ed., *Family and Kin in Urban Communities, 1700–1930.* New York: New Viewpoints.

Groneman, Carol. 1977. "She Earns as a Child, She Pays as a Man: Women Workers in a Mid-Nineteenth-Century New York City Community." In Milton Canto and Bruce Laurie, eds., *Class, Sex, and the Women Worker.* Westport, CT: Greenwood Press.

Gutman, Herbert. 1976. *The Black Family in Slavery and Freedom, 1750–1925.* New York: Pantheon.

Harris, Barbara. 1978. *Beyond Her Sphere: Women and the Professions in American History.* Westport, CT: Greenwood Press.

Hartmann, Heidi. 1976. "Capitalism, Patriarchy, and Job Segregation by Sex." In M. Blaxall and B. Reagan, eds., *Women and the Workplace.* Chicago: University of Chicago Press.

Hershberg, Theodore. 1972. "Free Blacks in Antebellum Philadelphia: A Study of Ex-Slaves, Freeborn, and Socioeconomic Decline." *Journal of Social History* 5: 183–209.

Kennedy, Susan. 1979. *If All We Did Was to Weep at Home.* Bloomington: Indiana University Press.

Lerner, Gerda. 1979. "The Lady and the Mill Girl: Changes in the Status of Women in the Age of Jackson, 1800–1840." In N. Cott and E. Pleck, eds., *A Heritage of Her Own.* New York: Simon and Schuster.

Mullings, Leith. 1978. "Ethnicity and Stratification in the Urban United States." *Annals of the New York Academy of Sciences* 318: 10–22.

Owens, Leslie. 1976. *This Species of Property.* New York: Oxford University Press.

Pleck, Elizabeth. 1972. "The Two-Parent Household: Black Family Structure in Late-Nineteenth-Century Boston." *Journal of Social History* 6(1): 3–31.

Ryan, Mary. 1983. *Womanhood in America.* New York: Franklin Watts.

Spruill, Julia. 1938. *Women's Life and Work in the Southern Colonies.* Chapel Hill: University of North Carolina Press.

Starobin, Robert S. 1970. *Industrial Slavery in the Old South.* New York: Oxford University Press.

Stowe, Charles Edward. 1889. *Life of Harriet Beecher Stowe.* Boston: Houghton Mifflin.

Windley, Lathan A. 1983. *Runaway Slave Advertisements: A Documentary History from the 1730s to 1790.* Westport, CT: Greenwood Press.

Yans-McLaughlin, Virginia. 1977. "Italian Women and Work: Experience and Perception." In Milton Cantor and Bruce Laurie, eds., *Class, Sex and the Woman Worker.* Westport, CT: Greenwood Press.

Yetman, Norman R. 1970. *Life Under the "Peculiar Institution."* New York: Holt, Rinehart and Winston.

3

Minority Women, Work, and Health

The health of minority women is conditioned by their status as workers, as members of a minority group, and as women. This chapter will discuss the way in which inequalities of class, race, and gender have resulted in a special oppression of minority women in the U.S., subjecting their health to the hazards of ethnic and gender discrimination in the workplace, to the pernicious effects of poverty, and to the negative effects of the stress entailed in the "double day." While I will be primarily concerned with African American women, other minorities share many of the same conditions. Thus the general outlines of this analysis may be applied to other minority women, keeping in mind the differences generated by their different histories of incorporation into the U.S. economy (Mullings 1978). That very little information exists on the subject of occupational health and minority women is itself an indication of the problem. This chapter therefore constitutes an introductory and exploratory discussion that I hope will stimulate further research.

African American men and women experience greater morbidity (illness) and mortality (death) from certain cancers, and from hypertension, diabetes, and other occupational and chronic diseases.[1] For example, if we look at diseases of the heart, the leading cause of death, statistics for 1977 show an overall age-adjusted heart disease rate of 322 per 100,000 for African American men, compared with a rate of 294 per 100,000 for Euro-American men; for African American women, we find an age-adjusted rate of 204 per 100,000, compared with 137 for Euro-American women. For cancer, the second-leading cause of death, African American men had an age-adjusted death rate of 222 per 100,000 in 1977, compared with a rate of 133 per 100,000 for Euro-American men; African American women had a rate of 130 deaths per 100,000, compared with a rate of 108 per 100,000 for Euro-American women (Markides 1983).

The picture for occupational injuries and illness is equally grim. As Morris Davis has stated:

> We enter the 1980s with the following statistics. Fifteen percent of the black work force (one to one and one-half million) are unable to work due to permanent or partial job-related disabilities. Black workers have a 37 percent greater chance than whites of suffering an occupational injury or illness. Black workers are one and one-half times more likely than whites to be severely disabled from job injuries and illness and face a 20 percent greater chance than whites of dying from job-related injuries and illnesses. (Davis 1980, 724)

For minority women there are special problems. The probability that an African American woman, for instance, will die of childbearing complications is five times that of Euro-American women (Christmas 1983). Hypertension, a disease in part related to stress, kills African American women between the ages of twenty-five and forty-four seventeen times more frequently than Euro-American women (West 1975, 36). Not surprisingly, in the 1975 Health Interview Survey, African American women reported the lowest level of emotional well-being across sex and race, with 63 percent reporting moderate to severe levels of distress (Christmas 1983).

Following the lead of the dominant social science interpretations of societal inequality, theories seeking to explain the incidence of illness among minorities and low-income groups have tended to focus on alleged biological or cultural differences, rather than on an analysis of the position that population occupies in society.[2] The astoundingly higher rates of cancer in the African American community, for instance, have been attributed to biological and genetic differences, on the one hand, and to lifestyle characteristics, such as smoking, diet, and cultural and personal practices, on the other. Genetic explanations are attractive despite the fact that the incidence of cancer mortality among African Americans exceeds that of Africans, with rates among African American men being three times those of men in Ibadan, Nigeria, for example. For African American women, the rate is twice that of the African women in the same study (Young et al. 1975). The precipitous rise of genetic screening of employees by industry is one indication of the policy ramifications of such genetic explanations. In 1982, fifty-nine major industrial companies had informed the Congressional Office of Technology Assessment that they intended to begin genetic screening of employees in the next five years; according to the agency, seventeen had begun carrying out such tests in the past five years, and more than five were in the process of doing so (*Women's Occupational Health Resource Center News* 1982).

Similarly, the growing emphasis on lifestyle explanations for cancer tends to exaggerate their role and minimize that of occupational carcinogens and involuntary exposure (Epstein and Swartz 1981). Further, such explanations frequently ignore analysis of the interrelationship of structural constraints and lifestyle or personal practices: The type of work one does or how much money one makes will have an impact on what one eats, how much one exercises, how often one sees the doctor, how much one smokes, and so on.

Both the biological and cultural or personal explanations shift attention from the environment to the individual; the emphasis is on removing the allegedly susceptible worker from a dangerous environment or changing her lifestyle rather than on cleaning up the workplace or removing structural barriers to equal opportunity. Yet there is much evidence to demonstrate that patterns of morbidity and mortality are directly conditioned by the structure of society. For example, we find a marked decline in mortality from tuberculosis in the United States during the first three decades of the twentieth century, although antibiotic therapy did not become widely available until the 1950s—suggesting that changing social conditions were the major factor. It has been clear since the Industrial Revolution that social relations mediate the incidence and prevalence of a disease by shaping the conditions for its emergence and by determining the distribution of risk. With industrialization, the radically transformed relations of production created an environment for the rise of diseases related to the new conditions of work. Most important were the new relations of production—the creation of a class of workers who were, by virtue of their position in the social division of labor, most susceptible to certain diseases.

In the United States workers have been differentially incorporated into the labor market along racial and ethnic lines. While Euro-Americans constituted a free, although exploited, labor force, captured Africans were enslaved. As time went on, African Americans (as well as Mexican Americans, Puerto Ricans, and Asian Americans) were restricted to the most dangerous jobs, receiving the lowest wages for their labor. They have frequently been denied legal and civil rights and have been excluded from social services such as health and education and from organizations such as trade unions through which their status might be improved (Lieberson 1980; Mullings 1978; Perlo 1975). Further, their more exploited status in the labor market has been explained and rationalized by the larger society on the basis of their biological or cultural inferiority (Mullings 1982).

To understand the differential patterns of certain types of diseases among minorities, we must first examine the health ramifications of their social conditions. The rest of this chapter will focus on these social conditions, arguing that the issue of occupational health among African American women can be understood only within the context of an analysis of their status as workers, as minorities, and as women.

Work, Compensation, and Health

African American women have always participated in the labor force as workers. During slavery they were often forced to do the same work as men, in the fields and in the factories (Davis 1981). Despite the defeat of slavery, African American men have rarely received wages sufficient to support their families, and the women have always had to work in order for their families to survive.

In 1890 the labor force participation rate of Euro-American women was 16.3 percent, compared to 39.7 percent for nonwhite women (Goldin 1977, 87). Since at that time it was the ideal that a woman leave the labor force after marriage, more telling is the difference in the participation of married women: for married Euro-American women the labor force participation rate was 2.5 percent, compared to 22.5 percent for married nonwhite women (Goldin 1977, 87). By 1980, the gap between groups had narrowed considerably, however, with official statistics reporting 54 percent of African American, 52 percent of Euro-American, and 47 percent of Spanish-origin women in the work force (Wilkerson 1982).

Despite historically high rates of labor force participation, work options for African American women have always been conditioned by gender and ethnicity. Bound by the confines of a sex-segregated market, minority women are further restricted by their ethnic status. Prior to World War I, African American women were generally barred from higher-paid jobs in factory employment, and later from the white collar positions in offices and stores that were open to Euro-American women; they were largely confined to domestic and laundry work.

As militant collective action forced the removal of some employment barriers, African American women gradually moved into jobs that had been previously segregated. Yet discrimination continues to limit minority women to the lowest-paid and most dangerous jobs in an already lower-paid sex-segregated market. The broad categories used by official statistics (e.g., clerical, professional and technical, operatives) often mask the real stratification within these categories and the fact that minorities are not evenly distributed from top to bottom in the wage hierarchy. This has implications for economic status which in turn has ramifications for health as well as for the hazards encountered on the job.

Restriction to badly remunerated, dead-end jobs means that minority women have a greater chance than others of being poor. For example, in 1977, 33 percent of African American women who worked year round were below the poverty line (Foner 1980). In 1983 the average full-time year-round female worker earned 59 percent of the average man's earnings; African American women earned only 54 percent, and Hispanic women only 49 percent, of what the average man made (*WREE Review* 1983). In 1981, 15.6 percent of African American women over the age of sixteen were unemployed, as compared to 6.9 percent of Euro-American women (Jones 1983).

When we examine family income, we see even greater discrepancies. Because of the discrimination against both men and women, African Americans as a group have incomes considerably lower than do whites, with this inequality growing in many regions of the country. In 1980 the median income for African American families was $12,674, as compared to $21,904 for Euro-American families (Swinton 1983). Since African American men working full time year round earn substantially less than Euro-American men ($13,874 compared to $19,719) (U.S. Department of Labor 1982), African American women continue to have a greater responsibility for providing subsistence for their families. The disproportionate unemployment rates affect family income. The October 1982 unemployment rate of 20 percent for African Americans does not even take account of those who were involuntarily working part time, discouraged workers, and labor force dropouts (Swinton 1983). The fact that African American men too are forced to work at the most dangerous jobs, subjecting them to higher rates of job-related death and disability, further affects family income. Morris Davis has pointed to the relationship of elevated cancer rates found among African American workers to the jobs in which they are concentrated in rubber, steel, chromate, and other industries (Davis 1980).

The high rates of unemployment, morbidity, and mortality combine with other factors to modify family structure, which itself bears on income. It is not surprising that the complex factors that have promoted a rise—for all races—in the number of families maintained by women have had a disproportionate impact on African Americans, where the rate is 45 percent.[3] The fact that approximately one half of these families were below the poverty line in 1979 (Jones 1983) has led some investigators to portray "family instability" as a major cause of poverty among African Americans.

When we look closely at the data, however, we find that although working-class households certainly fare better with two incomes, the following question remains unanswered: If single-parent families are the problem, why is poverty far less prevalent among households headed by Euro-American females and by unmarried white or black men? If, for instance, we look at all households headed by women who worked full time in 1976, we find that the incidence of poverty was four times greater for minorities than for whites (Wilkerson 1982).

Furthermore, in 1979, while 50 percent of households headed by black women had incomes above the poverty line, this was true for almost 80 percent of those headed by white women or unmarried black men, and for 90 percent of those headed by unmarried white men (Jones 1983). Since the majority of households with single parents are not in poverty, it would seem that the problem lies not with the fact that African American women are supporting families but with the limited options they have in the job market.

Numerous studies have demonstrated that in constraining the ability of people to purchase adequate housing, food, and medical care, poverty itself increases health risks. Poverty and discrimination often force minorities to live in more polluted environments. Thus the inability to procure safe housing, food, and so on may increase the risk of being exposed to occupational pollutants even where people are not directly exposed as workers. For example, a study of mothers in the Mississippi Delta who had not been directly exposed to DDT during most of the study period found residual levels highest among rural African American mothers and newborns; the study suggests that the differences were related not to metabolism but to degree of exposure, determined by quality of housing, availability of running water, and sources of food and water (D'Ercole et al. 1976).

In a fee-for-service health system such as that in the United States, employment and income bear directly on the ability to purchase adequate medical care. With the soaring cost of health care, third-party payment becomes the only means by which most people can afford to use the system. Because people generally acquire insurance coverage through the workplace, discrimination in employment has serious ramifications for access to adequate medical care. A 1982 study by the U.S. Commission on Human Rights found that because minorities and women have greater rates of unemployment, have lower-paying jobs, and are more likely to be employed in part-time, seasonal, or "poor-risk" jobs such as private household service or agriculture, they are severely disadvantaged in obtaining health insurance. While unemployment increases the risk of being without health insurance coverage for everyone, unemployed minority women lack health insurance to a greater degree than unemployed Euro-American women. Further, minority children are less likely than others to be covered by medical insurance (U.S. Commission on Civil Rights 1982).

In addition to the health vulnerabilities that result from inadequate compensation for work, minority women also face direct dangers to their health in the jobs at which they work. We will turn now to a brief examination of some of the industries in which minority women are concentrated.

The largest proportion of African American women workers—34.4 percent—are employed in cleaning, food, health, and personal and protective services (Jones 1983). If we look at the health industry, for example, we find that minorities constitute a disproportionately large number of health service workers. The health industry is rigorously stratified by race and gender. The top echelon of physicians, administrators, and scientists remains overwhelmingly male and Euro-American. In 1970, 9 percent of the predominantly female paraprofessionals (nurses, therapists, and technicians) were African American, while 30 percent of the auxiliary, ancillary, and service personnel (also predominantly female) were African American (Navarro 1976). In 1980, 21 percent of all health service workers were African American women (Jones 1983). The 1970 median income of the auxiliary, ancillary, and service personnel in the health industry was $4,000, as compared to $6,000 for paraprofessionals and $40,000 for professionals (Navarro 1976).

Studies have shown that hospital workers have a generally high level of occupational diseases (Coleman and Dickinson 1984; *Women's Occupational Health Resource Center News* 1982; Tabor 1982). For some illnesses, such as hepatitis infection (which is three to six times higher among medical personnel than the general population), disadvantaged socioeconomic status interacts with job category to influence the incidence of disease (Maynard Pattison, Bergquist, and Webster 1975). A recent study of mortality among nonprofessional hospital workers in New York City, where minority workers make up the bulk of the lower echelons of health service workers, suggests that nonprofessional workers may be at elevated risk for certain types of cancers. The study found particularly high rates of liver cancer among African American men and breast cancer among African American women. While it was difficult to ascribe specific cancers to specific chemicals, the investigators noted that hospital workers are constantly exposed to ionizing radiation, anesthetic gases, benzene, ethylene oxide, formaldehyde, and alkylating agents—substances that have been linked to cancer. The study also raised the question of whether the excess of liver cancer among health service workers is associated with exposure to the hepatitis B virus through cleaning, handling of patients' laundry, and so on (Schnorr and Stellman 1982).

A National Institute for Occupational Safety and Health report based on Health Interview Surveys of 498,580 people between 1969 and 1974 found elevated morbidity rates for a range of diseases, among persons in private household service as compared to workers in other job categories (Kaminski and Spirtas 1980). These findings no doubt partially reflect the advanced age of these workers. More important, however, are the hazards of housework, aggravated by the stress of performing it for someone else, in conditions where the wages are low, and there is often no limit to the working day, no medical coverage, and no benefits such as sick pay and vacations.

As a result of the expansion of the service and clerical sectors, along with the struggle against discrimination, African American women have moved out of private household work, an occupational niche in which they had long been concentrated. While in 1967, 24.5 percent of all African American women workers were in private household service, by 1980 only 7.5 percent placed themselves in this occupational category, and these were primarily older women (Jones 1983). However, this is not a dying occupation. As unemployment rises among all minority women, more and more, of all ages, will be forced to turn to "day work." And for many immigrants from the Caribbean, for instance, private household work is in any case one of the few occupational options—and an important way to regularize their status in this country. A year after the 1965 liberalization of the immigration laws, more live-in maids had been approved for entry than any other category. Many others come in without documents, and, as I shall show below, undocumented status further threatens the health of the worker.

Thirty percent of African American women workers are clerical workers (Jones 1983). The hazards of clerical work include muscular and circulatory disorders, fatigue, and exposure to dangerous chemicals such as benzene, toluene, and other organic solvents (Fleishman 1984). Clerical workers also seem to be particularly vulnerable to stress-related diseases. A major study examining the relationship of employment status and employment-related behaviors to the incidence of coronary heart disease found that women clerical workers with children experienced coronary heart disease at a rate twice as great as those of other comparable nonclerical workers or housewives. Increased risk of coronary heart disease among clerical workers appears to be related to features of the work environment, including the lack of control and autonomy, nonsupportive relationships, and limited physical mobility (Haynes and Feinleib 1980).

These conditions may have a particular impact on minority women, who are concentrated at the lowest levels of the office hierarchy. African American women, for example, tend to be underrepresented among the higher-paid legal and medical secretaries (Malveaux 1982), and among other secretaries and receptionists but overrepresented among file clerks, mail handlers, keypunch operators, and telephone clerks (Westcott 1982)—jobs that are often subject to speed-up, isolation, and lack of job mobility. A study of the psychological health effects (including anxiety, depression, and isolation) of the new office technology concluded that clerical workers at the lower end of the office hierarchy were subject to health risks similar to those of assembly-line workers. Such conditions as job insecurity, low utilization of skills, low participation in decision-making, and low levels of social support in the workplace caused them to exhibit signs of psychological strain (Gordon et al. 1982). Given the high rate of hypertension among African American women, these relationships warrant further study.

Among operatives, minority women workers hold jobs that put them at particular risk. In 1980, 40.4 percent of all clothing ironers and pressers and 23.3

percent of all laundry and dry cleaning operators were African American women (Westcott 1982, 32). A study conducted by the National Cancer Institute compared the death rates of laundry and dry cleaning workers to those of the general population, using records kept by a St. Louis trade union local from 1957 to 1977. Analysis of the distribution of deaths found a predominance of women—particularly nonwhite women—and excessive rates of cancer among the workers, particularly cancers of the lungs, cervix, uterus, and skin. Most significant, the death rate for African American males and females was *double* that for Euro-American males and females. The study suggests that elevated cancer risks result from multiple exposures to various dry cleaning fluids, including tetrachloroethylene, carbon tetrachloride, and trichloroethylene (Blair et al. 1979).[4]

Minority women also work in health-threatening jobs in the textile and apparel industries. In 1980 57 percent of the 240,000 textile workers were women (*Women's Occupational Health Resource Center Fact Sheet* 1980), while 20.7 percent of all operatives and 13.8 percent of all sewers and stitchers were African American women (Westcott 1982, 32). In New York City, where much of the garment industry is located, the bulk of workers are minority women. Puerto Rican women, for example, constitute almost 25 percent of those employed in apparel industries (Gray 1975). The International Ladies' Garment Workers' Union (ILGWU) estimates that in 1983 there were approximately 20,000 unionized workers in New York Chinatown garment factories, the vast majority of whom were Asian women (Abeles et al. 1983). Although accurate statistics are difficult to obtain, it has been estimated that undocumented workers, most of whom are people of color, constitute over 30 percent of the workers in New York City's apparel industry (Safa 1981).

The apparel industry increasingly relies on sweatshop labor and piecework. According to federal government and ILGWU statistics, there are at least five hundred sweatshops in New York City alone (Foner 1980). Conditions in these shops are unsafe and unhealthy, reminiscent of sweatshops at the turn of the century—crowded, poorly lit, badly ventilated, and vulnerable to accidents and fires. The tenuous legal position of these workers often discourages them from filing complaints (Conference on Undocumented Workers in New York City 1982). The *New York Times* described these shops as

> situated in dank cellars and broiling lofts, in barricaded store-fronts and back-alley garages, in dingy attics and rundown apartments. They exploit minorities and illegal aliens, paying wages below the Federal minimum of $2.90 an hour, often operating from sunrise to sunset but not paying for overtime and sending out cut fabric for illegal sewing at home. They prey on fears of workers who worry about losing their jobs or being deported as illegal aliens. (Cited in Foner 1980, 554)

In addition to the miserable work conditions, the compensation is minimal. In 1974 the average hourly wage in the apparel industry was $2.99—the lowest in any industry, comparing unfavorably to manufacturing as a whole, where the average hourly wage was $4.40 (Safa 1979). For undocumented workers, the wages are even lower. A report to the New York State Assembly estimated the undocumented workers' average rate of pay in 1981 to be less than $2.00 an hour ($15.00 a day) outside Chinatown and even lower in Chinatown itself (Leichter 1981). In order to care for their children at home, some workers do piecework, which brings in even less; for sewing together an entire dress, a woman may earn between 75¢ and $1.00 (Foner 1980; Leichter 1981).

In the textile industry, byssinosis (brown lung) and other respiratory ailments (such as chronic bronchitis, asthma, and breathlessness) that result from inhaling the dust of cotton or other fibers constitute a major health hazard. Minority workers tend to be concentrated in high-dust areas, such as opening, picking, and carding operations, and have disproportionate rates of respiratory disease (Davis 1980). In both the textile and apparel industries, workers are constantly exposed to various chemicals—dyes, formaldehyde, arsenic—used to treat fabrics.

Of the estimated five million migrant and seasonal farm workers, 75 percent are Chicano and 20 percent African American (Women's Occupational Health Resource Center News 1981). There are many hazards in farm work (Jasso and Mazorra 1984), but the use of organophosphates in pesticides is a major one, and it is often minorities who are assigned to mix, formulate, and spray them; it is also minorities who have the highest rates of organochlorine pesticide residues and, in some areas, the highest rates of pesticide-induced liver and renal dysfunction (Kutz, Yobs, and Strassman 1977). Women (and children), who usually do the weeding, are often directly sprayed with pesticide.

In addition to the direct health hazards of the workplace, minority women also face special risks as members of households of minority men who themselves hold dangerous jobs. Studies of families of asbestos, lead, and beryllium workers have found that contamination of the home environment through such mechanisms as soiled work clothes may be associated with elevated disease levels in the families of the workers (see Anderson et al. 1974; Baker et al. 1977; Eisenbud et al. 1949).

One of the means by which the subordinate position of minorities has been maintained is the denial of legal and civil rights. This may take the form of special legislation directed against them, such as laws codifying legal segregation, or of formal or informal exclusion from the protection offered by existing laws. With reference to occupational health and safety, African Americans and other minorities often work in small shops (ten or fewer employees) that are not covered by federal accident and illness recordkeeping requirements. Even where shops are covered by federal regulations, threats to lay off or terminate workers who belong to groups that are already disproportionately unemployed and subject to job discrimination, or whose undocumented status makes them vulnerable to deportation, act to limit complaints about hazardous conditions and reports of violations.

The Double Day and the Triple Day

Given their history of forced participation in the labor market, African American women have generally escaped the psychological damage of confinement to their own homes, but instead have been subjected to the stress of the double-day syndrome. For most African American women, this means that in addition to a full day of work outside the home, they also have the responsibility of running the household,[5] a task made much more difficult by a limited budget. African American and other working-class groups have developed creative means for collectively addressing the situation, including extended family networks, fictive kin, and ritual kin—ways of sharing resources and responsibilities with a wider group of people than the nuclear family (see, for example, Stack 1974). But this becomes yet another task for women, who tend to be the nodes of these networks and who are in charge of organizing and maintaining them.

All these obligations become even more difficult in a situation where social services are being reduced by the government. The high rate of unemployment and inflation, the dismantling of the Occupational Safety and Health Administration, and the increasing wage differential between minorities and other workers disproportionately affect minorities and result in rising morbidity among minority children, deterioration of the educational system, teenage unemployment, and increasing poverty among the elderly. It often falls to women to deal with the serious problems caused by cuts in government support for health care, child care, education, social services, and food stamps.

Under these circumstances, childbearing brings additional problems and hazards. Compared to Euro-American women, a greater proportion of minority women work during their childbearing years, when the presence of children makes work more difficult but more necessary.[6] In 1976, 62 percent of minority women with children six to seventeen years of age were workers, as were 53 percent of those with children under six; the comparable figures for Euro-American women were 55 percent and 38 percent (United States Department of Labor 1977). Thus minority women are disproportionately affected by cutbacks in child care. The fact that minority women frequently work at low-wage jobs in small nonunion shops decreases the likelihood that they will receive adequate benefits for prenatal and postnatal care, or maternity leave. The conditions of work and household responsibilities influence the health of the fetus as well as the mother. A recent study analyzed data collected on 7,722 pregnancies of African American and Euro-American women in the following categories: (1) those who did not work outside the home; (2) those whose employment required sitting (students, clerical workers); and (3) those who had stand-up employment (retail sales workers, private household workers, service workers, and laborers). Of the women in the second and third categories taken together, 81 percent of the Euro-American women had sit-down jobs, compared to only 32 percent of the African American women. The study found lower birth weights among children of mothers who held employment outside the home during the last trimester of pregnancy than among those of mothers who remained at home during that time and concluded that the "growth retardation was most severe when mothers had stand-up jobs, continued working until near term, were hypertensive, or had children at home to care for when they returned from work" (Naeye and Peters 1982, 727). For most of these variables, African American and other minority women are more likely to be at risk.

The burdens of work and household, as well as limited access to adequate nutrition, housing, child care, and medical services, certainly have a bearing on the fact that minority women die in childbirth at five times the rate of Euro-American women and that the infant mortality rate among African Americans is nearly double that of Euro-Americans (Christmas 1983).

In attempting to juggle the commitments of work, household, and reproduction, sterilization may be an extreme and irreversible solution among a limited range of alternatives. The 1978 case of four female lead pigment workers at American Cyanide who charged that they were sterilized because they were given the choice of sterilization or being transferred to lower-paying jobs has dramatized the widespread policy among industries to exclude vulnerable women from jobs where they may be exposed to reproductive hazards rather than clean up the workplace (Shabecoff 1980; see also Scott 1984). The possibilities of losing a job and of being unable to support another child weigh heavily on minority women, who have fewer options to begin with. Outright abuse of sterilization, in addition to limited alternatives, have produced a situation where minority women continue to be sterilized in disproportionate numbers. Accurate statistics are hard to come by, but those that exist give some indication of the situation. According to a study by Princeton University's Office of Population Control, in 1970, 20 percent of all married African American women had been sterilized; other sources suggest that approximately 20 percent of Chicana women and over 35 percent of all Puerto Rican women of childbearing age had been surgically sterilized (cited in Davis 1981, 219).

African American women and men, and other minority women and men, have always been involved in efforts to resist the conditions foisted upon them—slavery, segregation, and discrimination. In this sense, many minority women may be said to have a triple day. Such struggles are carried out on a variety of levels, from individual actions, such as the everyday resistance to harassment, to collective mass struggles, such as the civil rights movement of 1960s. Actions may be directed toward the dominant structure of the victimized group; they may be aimed at changing the social organization of work, the legal restriction and denial of civil rights, or the ideologies of racism that rationalize such conditions (see Gilkes 1983). Rosa Parks is an example of the militant role played by a working-class African American woman. A seamstress and private household worker who had toiled all day, she refused to give up her seat on a bus to a white man. This action sparked the Montgomery bus boycott and an important phase of the massive civil rights movement of the 1960s.

Space does not permit a full discussion of the history of these struggles, but I want to briefly discuss those directed toward restructuring the social organization of work. After mass struggles brought about advances in overcoming discriminatory barriers in industry and the trade unions, African Americans became the ethnic group in the workforce with the highest proportion of unionized members—33 percent (Davis 1980). African American women have generally seen unionization as a necessary instrument for improving their conditions of work, and they have, often under dangerous and difficult circumstances, played an active part in the struggle to organize trade unions and in subsequent trade union actions.

Today, minority women are active in the leadership of such trade unions as District 1199 of the National Union of Health Care Employees, the United Food and Commercial Workers International Union, and the National Education Association, the largest union in the country. Recognizing that a number of unions have adopted the policies and practices of some corporations in accepting unequal treatment of women and minorities, African American women have become active participants in national organizations such as the Coalition of Labor Union Women and the Coalition of Black Trade Unionists, which press for equality in the trade union movement and in society at large.

This chapter has described the way in which the triple oppressions of class, race, and gender affect the health of minority women. Given these circumstances, it is appropriate to question those explanations and policies that focus primarily on alleged biological, cultural, and lifestyle differences and ignore structural constraints in explaining ethnic and class differences in rates of morbidity and mortality. Such explanations, which shift the responsibility to the victimized populations, are accepted as part of a long history of rationalizing slavery, gender, and race discrimination on the basis of biological and cultural inferiority. Refined in academic circles and disseminated by the mass media, these notions attempt to vindicate the corporate structure that profits from these conditions, to blame the victim, and therefore to undermine movement for social change. Yet, being triply oppressed, minority women are also a triple threat. With their consciousness shaped by their experiences as workers, as members of a minority group, and as women, they are at the core of resistance.

Notes

1. For example, see Radov and Santangelo 1979; U.S. Department of Health, Education, and Welfare 1975; Mettlen and Murphy 1980.

2. There is, however, a body of literature in epidemiology that describes class as a variable that overrides race and culture in most diseases.

3. The meaning of the term "female-headed household" continues to be in dispute. Studies such as Stack 1976 have demonstrated that although the residential unit may not include men for a variety of reasons, men often continue to contribute to the households of their sisters, mothers, and the mothers of their children.

4. A more recent study of women laundry and dry cleaning workers in Wisconsin (Katz and Jowett 1981) found that some of the elevated risks noted among these workers declined when compared to women workers in other low-wage occupation, pointing to the interaction of other socioeconomic variables. However, the small percentage of nonwhite females in the study group were "omitted for the sake of homogeneity."

5. While it is generally true that women bear major responsibility for the household, the extent to which working-class minority men share this responsibility needs more study.

6. If we look at the proportion of women in specific age groups who were working in 1973, the differences in the overall impact of work experience can be better understood. Among women age twenty-five to thirty-four—the principal childbearing years—there is a sharp decline in the participation in the labor market for Euro-Americans but an increase for African Americans. It is in this age range that the excess of African American women over Euro-American women in the workforce reaches its peak, with 61.1 percent of African American women working, as compared with 48.6 percent of Euro-American women. See Perlo 1975, 23.

References

Abeles, Schwartz, Haeckel, and Silverblatt, Inc. 1983. *The Chinatown Garment Industry Study.* Report submitted to Local 23–25, International Ladies' Garment Workers' Union. New York.

Anderson, H. A., et al. 1974. "Asbestos-Related Disease from Household Exposure to Occupational Dusts." Paper presented to the American Conference of Chest Physicians, New Orleans, October 2–4.

Baker, Edward, et al. 1977. "Lead Poisoning in Children of Lead Workers." *New England Journal of Medicine* 296(5): 260–61.

Blair, A., et al. 1979. "Causes of Death Among Laundry and Dry Cleaning Workers." *American Journal of Public Health* 69(5): 508–11.

Christmas, June J. 1983. "Black Women and Health in the 80s." Keynote address to the first National Conference on Black Women's Health Issues, Atlanta, Georgia, June 24.

Coleman, Linda and Cindy Dickinson. 1984. "The Risks of Healing: The Hazards of the Nursing Profession." In Wendy Chavkin, ed., *Double Exposure: Women's Health Hazards on the Job and at Home.* New York: Monthly Review Press.

Conference on Undocumented Workers in New York City. 1982. Center for the Study of Human Rights, Columbia University, New York, May 6–8.

Davis, Angela. 1981. *Women, Race, and Class.* New York: Random House.

Davis, Morris. 1980. "The Impact of Workplace Health and Safety on Black Workers: Assessment and Prognosis." *Labor Law Journal* 31 (12): 723–32.

D'Ercole, A. J., R. Arthur, J. Cain, and B. Barrentine. 1976. "Insecticide Exposure of Mothers and Newborns in a Rural Agricultural Area." *Pediatrics* 57(6): 869–74.

Eisenbud, M., et al. 1949. "Non-Occupational Berylliosis." *Journal of Industrial Hygiene Toxicology* 31: 282–94.

Epstein, Samuel, and Joel Swartz. 1981. "Fallacies of Lifestyle Cancer Theories." *Nature* 289: 127–30.

Fleishman, Janet. 1984. "The Health Hazards of Office Work." In Wendy Chavkin, ed., *Double Exposure: Women's Health Hazards on the Job and at Home.* New York: Monthly Review Press.

Foner, Philip. 1980. *Women and the American Labor Movement,* vol 2. New York: Free Press.

Gilkes, Cheryl. 1983. "The Community Work of Racial-Ethnic Women." Lecture presented at the Summer Institute on Women of Color, Center for Research on Women, Memphis State University, Memphis, Tennessee.

Goldin, Claudia. 1977. "Female Labor Force Participation: The Origin of Black and White Differences, 1870–1880." *Journal of Economic History* 37: 87–108.

Gordon, Gloria, et al. 1982. "Psychological Effects of Office Workers' Job Conditions." Paper presented at the annual convention of the American Psychological Association, Washington, DC, August 24.

Gray, Lois. 1975. "The Jobs Puerto Ricans Hold in New York City." *Monthly Labor Review* 98(10): 12–26.

Haynes, Suzanne, and Manning Feinleib. 1980. "Women, Work, and Coronary Heart Disease: Prospective Findings from the Framingham Heart Study." *American Journal of Public Health* 70(2): 133–41.

Jasso, Sonia, and Mazorra, Maria. 1984. "Following the Harvest: The Health Hazards of Migrant and Seasonal Farmworking Women." In Wendy Chavkin, ed., *Double Exposure: Women's Health Hazards on the Job and at Home.* New York: Monthly Review Press.

Jones, Barbara A. P. 1983. "The Economic Status of Black Women." In James D. Williams, ed., *The State of Black America.* New York: National Urban League.

Kaminski, Rose, and Robert Spirtas. 1980. "Industrial Characteristics of Persons Reporting Morbidity During the Health Interview Surveys Conducted in 1969–1974: An Exploratory Review." National Institute for Occupational Health and Safety, Research Report: Cincinnati: 115: 80-123.

Katz, Ronald, and D. Jowett. 1981. "Female Laundry and Dry Cleaning Workers in Wisconsin: A Mortality Analysis." *American Journal of Public Health* 71(3): 305–7.

Kutz, F. W., A. R. Yobs, and S. C. Strassman. 1977. "Racial Stratification of Organochlorine Insect Residues in Human Adipose Tissue." *Journal of Occupational Medicine* 19(9): 619–22.

Leichter, Franz S. 1981. "The Return of the Sweatshop." Report to the New York State Senate, February 26.

Lieberson, Stanley. 1980. *A Piece of the Pie.* Berkeley: University of California Press.

Malveaux, Julianne. 1982. "Shifts in the Occupational and Employment Status of Black Women." In *Black Working Women: Debunking the Myths.* Proceedings of a research conference to examine the status of black working women in the United States. Berkeley: Center for the Study, Education, and Advancement of Women, University of California.

Markides, Kyrialcos S. 1983. "Mortality Among Minority Populations: A Review of Recent Patterns and Trends." *Public Health Reports* 98(3): 253–55.

Maynard Pattison, C. J., K. Berquist, and H. Webster. 1975. "Epidemiology of Hepatitis B in Hospital Personnel." *American Journal of Epidemiology* 101(1): 59–64.

Mettlen, C., and G. Murphy. 1980. *Cancer Among Black Populations.* Buffalo, NY: Roswell Park Memorial Institute.

Mullings, Leith. 1978. "Ethnicity and Stratification in the Urban United States." *Annals of the New York Academy of Sciences* 318: 10–22.

———. 1982. "Rationalizing Inequality." *Journal of Academic Skills* 3(1): 6–17.

Naeye, Richard, and Ellen Peters. 1982. "Working During Pregnancy: Effects on the Fetus." *Pediatrics* 69(6): 724–27.

Navarro, Vicente. 1976. *Medicine Under Capitalism.* New York: Prodist.

Perlo, Victor. 1975. *Economics of Racism.* New York: International Publishers.

Radov, M., and N. Santangelo. 1979. "Health Status of Minorities and Low-Income Groups." Department of Health, Education, and Welfare Publication No. 79-627. Washington, DC: Government Printing Office.

Safa, Helen. 1981."The Differential Incorporation of Hispanic Women Migrants into the United States Labor Force." In D. M. Mortimer and R. S. Bryce-Laporte, eds., *Female Immigrants to the United States: Caribbean, Latin American and African Experiences.* Washington, DC: Research Institute on Immigration and Ethnic Studies, Smithsonian Institution.

Schnorr, Teresa, and J. Stellman. 1982. "The Health of Health Care Workers, A Proportionate Mortality Study." Unpublished study. Cited in *Women's Occupational Health Resource Center* 4(4): 1.

Scott, Judith. 1984. "Keeping Women in Their Place: Exclusionary Policies and Reproduction." In Wendy Chavkin ed., *Double Exposure: Women's Health Hazards on the Job and at Home.* New York: Monthly Review Press.

Shabecoff, Phillip. "U.S. Appeals Ruling on Women in Hazardous Jobs." *New York Times,* September 9, 1980, p. B9.

Stack, Carol. 1974. *All Our Kin: Strategies for Survival in the Black Community.* New York: Harper and Row.

Swinton, David. 1983. "The Economic Status of the Black Population. In James D. Williams, ed., *The State of Black America.* New York: National Urban League.

Tabor, Martha. 1982. "Health Care, Job Stress." *Occupational Health and Safety,* December: 20–35.

U.S. Commission on Civil Rights. 1982. *Health Insurance: Coverage and Employment Opportunities for Minorities and Women.* Clearinghouse Publication 72. Washington, DC: Government Printing Office.

U.S. Department of Health, Education, and Welfare. 1975. *Health, United States.* Washington, DC: Government Printing Office.

U.S. Department of Labor. 1982. *Equal Employment Opportunity for Women: U.S. Policies.* Washington, DC: Government Printing Office.

U.S. Department of Labor. 1977. *Minority Women Workers: A Statistical Overview.* Washington, DC: Government Printing Office.

West, William. 1975. "Drug Action in Management of Hypertension." *Urban Health* 4(3): 36–41.

Westcott, Diane. 1982. "Blacks in the 1970s: Did They Scale the Job Ladder?" *Monthly Labor Review* 105(6): 29–38.

Wilkerson, Margaret. 1982. "Working Women in the United States." In *Black Working Women: Debunking the Myths.* Proceedings of a research conference to examine the status of black working women in the United States. Berkeley: Center for the Study, Education, and Advancement of Women, University of California.

Women's Occupational Health Resource Center Fact Sheet. 1980. March.

Women's Occupational Health Resource Center News. 1981. Vol. 3, no. 4.

———. 1982. Vol. 4, no. 4.

WREE Review: Journal of Women for Racial and Economic Equality. 1983. Vol. 8, no. 1.

Young, John L., et al. 1975. "Incidence of Cancer in United States Blacks." *Cancer Research* 35: 35–36.

PART 2

KIN AND FAMILY

Introduction

Perspectives on the American Family

Today, more than ever, the family—its definition, character, history, and future—is a contentious battleground for politicians, policy analysts, and social theorists. Throughout the 1990s, in successive elections, the Republican Party has staked out a rigid definition of family, and "family values" became the vehicle through which they sought to undermine liberalism, the welfare state, multiculturalism, and women's rights. Manipulating the symbolism of the "normal" family, elements of their agenda included: ending welfare benefits after two years even if recipients cannot find jobs; relegating the destitute to the care of private charities; placing the children of impoverished mothers in orphanages; and denying aid to children of teenaged mothers.

Similar debates about the family abound at the level of social analysis. David Popenoe (1993) laments what he refers to as "end-of-the-line family decline" and its dire consequences for the future. Restricting the definition of family to a domestic group with at least one dependent, he chronicled the decline in family functions of reproduction, socialization, emotional support, economic cooperation, and sexual regulation. Popularized renditions of these themes have appeared in several national newspapers and magazines.

Taking a different approach, feminist scholars have questioned the apocalyptic predictions of doom resulting from transformations in family structure. Furthermore, studies of racial stratification and family life have contested the assumptions of a normative model, underscoring the social conditioning of household form and function.

71

Stepping back for a moment from the ideological debates, what can we say definitively, using the admittedly limited data provided by the U.S. Census Bureau and other surveys, about what we call the family? The data indicate that there has indeed been significant change in the last three decades.

By 1992 the normative, idealized family—a married couple with two children present in the home—had truly become nearly mythical, constituting only 10 percent of all households (Rawlings 1993, vi). Married couples now form slightly more than half (55 percent) of all households, but the majority of these do not have children under eighteen (ibid.) and, according to data collected through the 1990 census, only three in one hundred households "conform to the classic family headed by a working husband with a dutiful wife and two children at home" (Roberts 1993, 30).

Single-parent households are a rapidly growing segment of the household population, constituting roughly one third (30 percent) of the households with children under eighteen in 1992 (up from 13 percent in 1970) (Rawlings 1992, xiv). In 1991, only about half (51 percent) of all children in the United States lived in a nuclear family composed solely of both biological parents and full brothers and sisters; 15 percent lived in blended families, and 24 percent lived in single-parent households (Furukawa 1994, 1).

Everyone agrees that the composition of the American family has changed radically in the last three decades. What is being debated is the significance of these changes and their long-term implications for the welfare of the society. The various interpretations reflect dissimilar perspectives on the family and its evolution, but also speak to different ways of theorizing relationships among power, resources, and culture. As several anthropologists have observed, the family is an ideological construct. Contemporary events provide us with perhaps the clearest demonstration to date that "family" is the prism through which ideological battles are waged.

Conceptualizations of family are at the core of conservative ideologies about culture, society, and domination as the Right seeks to reestablish hegemony over our understanding of what the family is and its relationship to society. The genius of the right lies in their ability to conflate the very real decline in community resulting from the processes of global capitalism with the transformation—which they label a "decline"—in the structure and function of the household. The effects of deterioration of "community" and "civility" are felt by millions of Americans. Cornel West, for example, has described the severe constrictions in public space brought about by societal changes, suggesting that the boundaries of community may soon be defined by an individual and a television set (West 1995).

One could argue that a major factor in the decline of public space and civility, particularly in our urban areas, is the decrease in labor force participation rates among adults and the declining income of young families, and consequent reduction of social services. Declining standards of living create a context for the fragmentation of households and community, in which people indeed turn against and fear each other. The right then projects the root of this social disintegration as "family crisis"; specifically, the decline of community and sense of civility is blamed on the collapse of a mythical traditional family, helping to mystify the real causes of household fragmentation.

At the heart of this discourse is an obviously ahistoric concept of family. This perception of the traditional family is based on a model that is nuclear, conjugal, and patriarchal, with a male breadwinner, despite the projection that over the next twenty years only one in five people who join the labor force will be white males.

The "cult of the traditional family," similar to the cult of true womanhood, functions to reproduce, exacerbate, and reinforce class and race differences and to aggressively reframe and redefine old and new concepts of "otherness," anticipating the new ethnic and class transformations of the United States. The mythical construct of the traditional family draws heavily upon biological and cultural discourses. As I argue in chapter 9, in the United States biology and culture have functioned as parallel paradigms through which inequality is rationalized. These themes, mediated through the discourse of the family, help provide a framework for "stratified reproduction" (see chapter 5), whereby some populations are empowered to reproduce and others are not.

Cultural metaphors signifying behavioral dysfunction are familiar to all of us. Concepts of "the culture of poverty" and the "underclass" evoke the disintegration of family values as the primary cause of social and cultural decline. These cultural themes are supported by pseudobiological explanations for inequality, most recently expressed in *The Bell Curve* (Herrnstein and Murray 1994).

Biological discourses concerning the family draw their language and concepts from demography and population studies, disciplines that have frequently found themselves in an uneasy relationship with eugenics. Normative notions of fertility, sexuality, population decline, and demographic transition may appear as value-neutral concepts. However, they may also obscure fin de siècle anxieties that emerge in the context of the declining fertility of people of European descent, increasing immigration, and challenges to cultural and intellectual hegemony.

New York senator Daniel Patrick Moynihan, a sociologist wellknown for his depiction of a "tangle of pathology" and "matriarchy" among African Americans and his recommendations for "benign neglect," merged these themes during a 1994 hearing on welfare. Testifying that by the next decade half of all children will be born out of wedlock, he predicted this will bring about a change in the human condition—in his words, "speciation: the creation of a new species."[1]

Biological and cultural explanations for inequality mediated through the framework of "family" reinforce and mutually support each other to project a notion of family that becomes a metaphor for the reconstruction of a patriarchal past, a history characterized by more rigid racial domination. These discourses mask countervailing social and economic trends which indeed fragment households. These trends are manifested initially and also most profoundly among households of people of color and families of limited financial resources.

Though the constraints within which African Americans structure households reflect the hierarchies of class, race, and gender, in many ways African Americans are the harbinger of what is to come for the Euro-American working-class family, reflecting conditions developing in the other parts of the world as well as strategies for dealing with them. For example, the proportion of households headed by women in developed and less developed countries is rising rapidly, and there is a global trend toward an increasing proportion of mother-supported families (Bruce et al. 1995). Even in developed countries, there is a decline in the number of married-couple households, a rise in the number of consensual unions, and a rise in the number of single-parent families (Sorrentino 1990). Though the single-parent family form is found in disproportionately high numbers among African Americans, its frequency is increasing among all racial groups and kinds of communities in the United States, including Euro-American rural communities (Fitchen 1991).

But the African American family may also be seen as being in the vanguard of another phenomenon: the creation of familylike networks in the absence of blood kin. This is evident in the history of African Americans, who re-created familial structures when stripped of actual kin through enslavement or unemployment, as well as in contemporary African American communities.

For example, in Harlem in New York City, we find that increasingly women are the breadwinners and households are matrilocal. Yet to end the discussion here would yield only a partial view of a complicated picture of fluidity of household form and function. People activate various networks for different purposes. Networks for socialization, reproduction, consumption, emotional support, economic cooperation, and sexuality may overlap but not be coterminous. It is this disaggregation that policy analysts and social theorists label the "decline" of the family.

In this era of economic and social transformation, social scientists are challenged to analyze change without becoming enmeshed in their own moral and normative categories. It is particularly important for those who study families to continue to attend to how people perceive their own strategies and relationships, to privilege those people's knowledge of kinship and family, and to work with them in contesting dominant representations. We must continue to deconstruct essentialist frameworks; to problematize concepts of culture and race; to disaggregate reproduction, social reproduction, and sexuality; and to seek to analyze the historical circumstances in which they are linked. We must explore the social conditions in which household forms emerge and those that allow them to function. This will require a historically and cross-culturally informed vision of the variety of ways in which people organize themselves—an acceptance of domestic diversity without seeing it as pathology. However, it is equally important for scholars not to romanticize the difficult conditions within which people select among limited choices for themselves, their children, and their communities.

As I noted earlier, family is a social and historical product in a profound sense. People form affective bonds and associations to accomplish the tasks and share the joys involved in negotiating life. They do so in different ways at different points in history and in their own life cycle. We must stop blaming people for the "decline" of the family and explore and support the implementation of policies that allow people to form associations of their choice and facilitate their ability to assist each other in carrying out domestic functions.[2]

The chapters in this section incorporate the anthropological insight that family form is neither natural nor immutable, but a product of history and society. Their starting point is the need to demystify the ideology of family, to describe the real ways in which people organize themselves, to understand how they think about kinship and reciprocity, and to analyze the manner in which class and race structure the range of options and strategies available to them.

In "Anthropological Perspectives on the African American Family," I attempt to explore both culture and class as they influence the ways in which people organize themselves around gender and kinship, suggesting that these are not competing but rather intertwined concepts. I underscore the importance of including Africa as the starting point for any understanding of African American culture and history. Not to do so, to accept the assumption that for this group of Americans (unlike all others) memory and culture was entirely erased, is not only unscientific but also facilitates acceptance of models that incorporate ideas of "pathology" and "deficiency."

Chapter 4, delivered at the Black Task Force Conference, The Black Family: Mental Health Perspectives, at the University of San Francisco in 1984, closes with a description of some of the effects of Reaganomics on the African American family. The consequences of the economic trends described there are analyzed in chapter 5, written almost ten years later, and presented at a conference sponsored by the Wenner-Gren Foundation for Anthropological Research in Brazil in 1991.

Notes

1. *New York Times Magazine,* Sunday, August 7, 1994, p. 29.

2. This part of the introduction was based on a paper presented at a session entitled "Critical Perspectives on Emerging Family and Household Forms in the United States" at the 1994 annual meeting of the American Anthropological Association.

References

Bruce, Judith, Cynthia B. Lloyd, and Ann Leonard. 1995. *Families in Focus: New Perspectives on Mothers, Fathers, and Children.* New York: The Population Council.

Fitchen, Janet. 1991. *Endangered Spaces, Enduring Places: Change, Identity and Survival in Rural America.* Boulder, Colorado: Westview.

Furukawa, Stacy. 1994. "The Diverse Living Arrangements of Children: Summer 1991." Washington, D.C.: U.S. Department of Commerce, Economics and Statistics Administration, Bureau of the Census. *Current Population Reports.* Series P-70. Household Economic Studies, no. 38.

Herrnstein, Richard, and Charles Murray. 1994. *The Bell Curve: Intelligence and Class Structure in American Life.* New York: Free Press.

Popenoe, David. 1993. "American Family Decline, 1960–1990: A Review and Appraisal." *Journal of Marriage and the Family* 55(3): 527–41.

Rawlings, Stephen. 1993. "Household and Family Characteristics: March 1992." Washington, D.C.: U.S. Department of Commerce, Economics and Statistics Administration, Bureau of the Census. *Current Population Reports.* Series P-20, Population Characteristics, no. 467.

Roberts, Sam. 1993. *Who We Are: A Portrait of America Based on the Latest Census.* New York: Random House.

Sorrentino, Constance. 1990. "The Changing Family in International Perspective." *Monthly Labor Review* (March): 41–58.

West, Cornel. 1995. "Prophetic Alternatives: A Dialogue with Cornel West and Manning Marable." *Race and Reason* 2: 39–46.

4

Anthropological Perspectives on the African American Family

The study of kinship has always been central to anthropology, and, to my mind, one of the discipline's major contributions has been to demonstrate the cross-cultural relativity of kinship and family. Though all societies organize people to perform domestic functions, the manner in which they do so may differ. The structure, organization, and function of family and kin groups vary greatly: households and families may be extended or nuclear; descent may be patrilineal, matrilineal, or bilateral; marriage may be monogamous or polygamous. Hence to speak of a "natural" family form is meaningless; likewise, to label a family structure inherently "pathological" is problematic. Kinship is a social product, molded by class, culture, and society.

The contributions of the anthropological perspective have not been prominent in analyses of the African American family. The controversy surrounding this subject is not surprising. Science, including social science, is practiced in the context of society; it is influenced by the power relationships of a given society, and knowledge (or what passes for knowledge) may be used as an instrument for subjugation or liberation.

Perspectives on the African American Family

There are several good accounts of theoretical approaches to the African American family. I will not review them in detail here but will highlight some of the more important debates, particularly those concerning the structure and function of the family.

One major area of disagreement is the extent to which contemporary African American family structure reflects African culture or the conditions of the New World. Herksovits (1958), for example, became one of the best-known proponents of the view that African culture explained major features of the African American family. W.E.B. DuBois (1961) took a more dialectic approach, examining the "doubleness" of African American culture, woven with strands from both the African and American experiences. Recent works by such social scientists as Nobles (1974) and Sudarkasa (1981) have focused on African influences in African American family structure.

E. Franklin Frazier (1939) was one of the most influential representatives of the opposing view—that family form was primarily determined by conditions in the Americas. He maintained that African culture had been destroyed by slavery, which itself was the major influence on the African American family.

More recently, proponents of the adaptational approach have analyzed family form as a positive adaptation to social conditions. Gutman's (1976) historical study of African American families explores the utilization and transformation of African forms, while Stack (1974) demonstrates the formation of large kinship networks as an adaptation to conditions of poverty in the 1970s.

Controversies about the structure and function of the African American family have serious ramifications for social policy. Some social theorists and policymakers have suggested that family structure has a direct causative relationship to the socioeconomic status of African Americans in the United States and the model of the African American family as "pathological" or "deviant" is used to support this view.

Those who support this model often cite E. Franklin Frazier, who wrote at a time when the forces opposed to integration rationalized their position by claiming unresolvable differences between the races. In noting the destructive effects of slavery and poverty, Frazier suggested that differences in family form were not those of irreconcilable cultural traditions, but rather those resulting from oppression.

Many of those who followed Frazier were neither so benign nor progressive in their intentions. While Frazier emphasized the oppressive social conditions that affected the family, others attributed problems faced by African Americans to deficiencies in their culture. Many scholars have assumed the validity of the deficiency model, but Daniel Patrick Moynihan, as the most influential of these, deserves special attention. Moynihan's *The Negro Family* (1965) represents an early version of the "culture of poverty" school, asserting that the reasons for poverty lie not with racism or the inegalitarian economic system, but rather with the culture of the poor. For Moynihan, the focus of cultural deficiency was the family. While admitting that discrimination and unemployment were serious issues plaguing the African American community, he concluded that African American society was a tangle of pathology and at its center was the "pathological" and "matriarchal" African American family. (See chapter 8 for a full discussion of this thesis.)

Studies such as these became the theoretical rationale for a series of programs known as the War on Poverty. These programs, primarily concerned with attempting to modify the "culture" of the poor, were based on the assumption that by changing certain problematic aspects of lifestyle and behavior, the poor would be able to raise themselves out of poverty. While many of these policies were well-intentioned and assisted some individuals, they hardly constituted a major offensive against poverty. They have been perhaps more accurately described as a war against the culture of the poor. For example, Head Start programs sought to remove children from what were deemed to be inadequate home environments. While these programs did provide helpful early enrichment activities for some children, the War on Poverty did not include a full employment bill guaranteeing that employment at decent wages would be available to all those who wish to work. Not surprisingly, poverty was not eradicated and the War on Poverty failed. The failure to eliminate poverty was then attributed to the intractable culture of the poor, rather than to the absence of structural measures to combat poverty (Valentine 1971). The so-called pathological or deviant family structure of African Americans took much of the blame.

It is important to note that the resurgence of the pathology model—the emphasis on the African American family as deviant, abnormal, and somehow un-American—occurred at the time when African American women, men, and children, along with some Euro-Americans, were mobilizing against institutional racism and making significant gains in civil rights. Had such gains continued, they might have laid the foundation for fundamental and far-reaching changes in the basic socioeconomic structure of the society.

The reaction of scholars to the deficiency model was swift and extensive, although not nearly as well publicized as the model itself. Work by Billingsley (1968), Gutman (1976), Hill (1972), Ladner (1971), and Stack (1974), to name only a few, documented the many strengths of the African American family— strengths that allowed it to survive slavery, the enclosure of the South, and the depressions of the North.

Culture, Class, and Kinship

In the United States both ethnicity and class are salient principles of organization. People are categorized according to an allegedly common "culture history."

At the same time, the unequal distribution of resources, tasks, and rewards stratifies the population into classes. These principles of stratification may crosscut the class structure, as in the case of Euro-Americans, who are distributed throughout the classes (albeit not evenly); or they may coincide with it, as in the case of African Americans, Native Americans, Puerto Ricans, and Mexican Americans, whose opportunities are limited by racism and discrimination and who are disproportionately found among the working class and the poor.

One of the issues underlying the study of kinship in the United States has been posed as culture versus class: whether what determines family form and functioning is values, traditions, and norms handed down from generation to generation, or rather external socioeconomic constraints. Most frequently, as in the culture of poverty model, family organization is reduced to "culture," which is usually viewed as deficient. Vulgarization of the class model, on the other hand, usually underplays people's responses to the conditions imposed upon them. I will argue that class and culture are not dichotomous frames of reference, and that it is precisely their interrelationship that must be analyzed in any attempt to understand the structure and organization of the African American family, or any other.

In our quest to illuminate the family, it is useful to begin with the socioeconomic and political structure and the way in which it limits the range of choices for certain populations. It is also important to understand culture—the symbols and values that create the ideological frame of reference through which people attempt to deal with the circumstances in which they find themselves. Culture, in this sense, is not comprised of static, discrete traits transported from one locale to another. It is constantly changing and being transformed as new forms are created out of old ones. Thus culture is not *sui generis;* it is created and modified by material conditions.

In order to make these concepts more concrete, I would like to discuss two examples that demonstrate the complexity of the interrelationship of class and culture—family structure and gender roles. Both have been the focus of much controversy about African American families and stratification.

Family Structure

Most scholars agree that there were certain common principles of kinship in the African societies from which enslaved Africans were forcibly removed. In most of these societies kinship was the most important organizing principle. Everyone was born into a lineage—a long line of kin that situated the individual in the society and the universe. Lineage relationships allowed a range of people to cooperate in raising children. Hence, consanguinity (the ties of blood) was often more important than affinal (marriage) relationships. Reciprocity was generally a major feature of social relations.

When Africans were enslaved and brought to America, one would assume that they had not lost their ideas about what kinship should be, but it is also the case that they were not free to behave as they wished. Faced with one of the most oppressive political-economic structures in history, the extent to which African cultural values, norms, and ideas could be put into practice was limited. Slave systems varied in their degree of repression, and this variation was reflected in the degree to which Africans and African Americans had latitude to enact these ideas (cf. Mintz and Price 1976).

For example, Mintz and Price (1976) note that in the Para region of Suriname, it was the policy of the planters not to break up slave families by selling them to different masters. After several generations, kinship groups emerged that were attached to particular localities and imbued with ritual functions; these gradually assumed the broader function of regulating social relationships. The small island of Carriacou, in the southeastern Caribbean, presents a more striking example. Even today, we find a fully articulated system of unilineal descent there, with ancestor cults and localized patrilineages (Mintz and Price 1976).

In the United States, conditions of slavery were a great deal more repressive. Regardless of the cultural maps of lineage organization that people carried in their heads, a system of slavery wherein relatives were systematically sold away from each other, and mothers and children were frequently separated, limited the scope of kin relationships people were able to activate. Yet people continued to create culture, developing new forms out of old ones when necessary and possible. Gutman (1976) has documented the forms through which African Americans created and maintained kinship ties during slavery and emancipation. These include adopting and modifying African practices, such as the naming of children for particular relatives and alternate generation reciprocity, among others.[1]

Similarly, studies of working-class and poor African Americans in the 1970s revealed the use of extended families—networks that included fictive as well as blood kin (see, for example, Stack 1974; Aschenbrenner 1974). Such networks, activated in circumstances where unemployment was high and welfare regulations undermined the viability of the residential nuclear family, functioned to ensure the care of children. Although the frequency of these networks has not been well documented—one obvious problem being that survey methodologies often do not lend themselves to gathering this sort of data—the studies that do exist have demonstrated that relationships of blood were often more salient than those of marriage, that residential and domestic units were not necessarily coterminous (that is, people who did not reside together might still cooperate in raising children), and that a range of people shared resources, fostered children, and exchanged services, facilitating the survival of children in marginal economic circumstances.

Should these practices be attributed to class or culture? It is obvious that the socioeconomic constraints of slavery, unemployment, underemployment, and discrimination restrict available choices. The alternatives people select, within the limitations imposed by class relationships, are influenced by, among other factors, their cultural history. Undoubtedly, the strategies we have discussed above—consanguineous ties, the extended family network, child fostering, and so on—were found in African family structures. The issue of culture becomes more complex when we note that some of these strategies have also been described among working-class Euro-American groups. It is clear, however, that for African Americans the significance of the family in promoting individual survival has always been an important element of culture.

Gender Roles

The topic of gender roles in the African American family, much discussed of late, demonstrates similar complexities. Several investigators have remarked on the independence of contemporary West African market women, who frequently have their own income and are free to dispose of it as they wish (Mullings 1976). While it is problematic to extrapolate these findings to seventeenth- and eighteenth-century West African societies, it is probable that in many of the societies from which slaves were removed, the definition of masculinity was not based on the dependence of women (Mintz and Price 1976), that men and women frequently had independent arenas and occupations, and that men and women had asymmetrical but not necessarily unequal roles in society (Mullings 1976).

Ironically, the experience of the Africans in the New World supported the independence of their women, though the prevailing ideology denigrated such women. During slavery in the United States, the majority of women worked alongside men as field hands, often doing the same work. It was not unusual that advertisements for women slaves proclaimed their ability to work like men. It appears that under the circumstances of slavery, men and women had relatively egalitarian relationships within the household, with neither possessing the power to enforce relations of domination and subordination (Davis 1981).

After emancipation, the "cult of true womanhood" emphasized the separation of the domestic, private sphere from the public sphere of paid work and asserted that a woman's place was in the home. African American women in the South, on the other hand, were compelled to work in the fields, providing cheap labor to harvest the cotton crop. In the North, a large proportion of African American wives worked as laundresses and domestics—unlike Euro-American women, who for the most part left the labor force upon marriage. Their work facilitated the subsistence of the household in circumstances in which wage discrimination against both men and women necessitated that they both work (see chapter 2).

Pleck (1979) has compared the work experiences of African American wives to those of Euro-American immigrant wives in the 1880s, holding income constant. She found that African American wives worked in much greater proportions even when the income of their husbands was at a similar level. For example, while Italian American women were more likely to stay at home and send their children to work, African American wives were more likely to keep their children in school and themselves go out to work. She suggests that this difference can best be understood as a cultural one.

Again, to reduce the complexity of issues to culture is problematic. Although Pleck held income constant, how does one measure the effects of racism: the knowledge that African American workers are likely to be the last hired and the first fired, and the perception that African American children must have a better education than others to qualify for the same job?

It is perhaps true that African culture gave African Americans an orientation that did not denigrate the independence of women. It is, however, demonstrably true that in the New World, African American women were often forced to do the same work as men during slavery, and that married women always worked in greater proportions than their Euro-American counterparts. These circumstances probably resulted in more egalitarian relationships within the household.

To understand the family, then, one must analyze both the structure of restraints imposed by the socioeconomic system and the strategies—both positive and negative, informed by cultural history—that are created to address the circumstances. The relationships of class—of economic means and access to power—set limits on the cultural forms that may be mobilized. To underestimate class, to obfuscate the role of the constraints imposed by a hierarchical structure, leads to blaming the victim. At the same time, to ignore the way in which people create strategies to deal with their conditions is to underestimate the role of struggle.

The Contemporary African American Family

Before concluding, it is necessary to say a few words about fate of the African American family under the Reagan administration. Between 1980 and 1984, African Americans of all income groups suffered declines in their incomes and standards of living. The African American rate of poverty in 1983 was the highest in fifteen years, at 36 percent of the population, and in 1984 the official unemployment rate was 16 percent. Under the Reagan administration, long-term unemployment among African Americans rose 72 percent (as compared to a 1.5 percent increase among Euro-Americans) (Center on Budget Priorities 1984). While the number of female-headed households for families of all races increased, for African-Americans the proportion of such households rose to approximately 42 percent.

Though the average African American family in every economic stratum suffered a decline in disposable income and standard of living, the hardest hit were two-parent families in which one spouse works and the other takes care of children. These families, who represent the "ideal" American family, suffered an average loss of $2,000 in disposable income from 1980 to 1984.[2] Despite data such as those cited above, suggesting that it is not family structure but government policies that are wreaking economic havoc, we are confronted with a new series of ideological attacks on the African American family by scholars, government officials, and the mass media.

It will be necessary to explore the ways in which the crisis conditions currently affecting many African American families will influence family organization. It is possible that the coping mechanisms that served this population in the past are no longer adequate for the new situation and that the times will require the development of new strategies.

Conclusions

What all of this means for the individual is directly related to the question of why is there so much theorizing about the African American family and why reinterpretation and demythologizing have become so important. Because families are important to all people, symbols that concern the way we think about families—blood, love, and so on—are strongly felt. Through the language of family people are blamed for the status to which society consigns them; they are structurally denied equal access to resources and then told that their notion of family is what has prevented them from accumulating those resources (Rapp 1978). The society creates and maintains conditions in which African American women must work, but African Americans are told by scholars that their problems are a result of their women, whose labor renders them "matriarchal" and "unfeminine."

Family forms and gender roles, then, are topics fraught with emotional and cultural baggage. In our society, where the dominant ideology is projected by the media, the schools, and the practice disciplines, African Americans and other working-class people are constantly given the message that they are deviant. The discrepancy between what is projected as ideal and real-life experience may contribute to destructive behavior.

I would like to close with a brief mention of the implications of these issues for individual therapy. Anthropological approaches contribute the suggestion that it is often the inability to understand larger structural forces that may lead to aggression turned inward to the family or the self; that individual treatment is important, particularly as it allows people to better address their circumstances, but that at all times one must keep in the forefront the macrocircumstances that impinge on the lives of individuals and families.

Notes

1. While Gutman's work is very useful, in his commitment to demonstrating the use of "adaptive strategies" he sometimes misses the severity of the structure of oppression.

2. Although the two-parent family, with the father working and the mother at home, has long been projected as the ideal American family, according to 1980 census data it now accounts for only 16.3 percent of all U.S. families.

References

Aschenbrenner, J. 1971. *Lifelines: Black Families in Chicago.* New York: Simon and Schuster.

Billingsley, A. 1968. *Black Families in White America.* Englewood Cliffs, NJ: Prentice-Hall.

Center on Budget Priorities. 1984. *Falling Behind: A Report on How Blacks Have Fared Under the Reagan Policies.* Washington, DC: Center on Budget Priorities.

Davis, A. 1981. *Women, Race, and Class.* New York: Random House.

DuBois, W.E.B. 1961. *The Souls of Black Folk.* New York: Fawcett.

Frazier, E. F. 1939. *The Negro Family in the United States.* Chicago: University of Chicago Press.

Gutman, H. 1976. *The Black Family in Slavery and Freedom, 1750–1925.* New York: Pantheon.

Herskovits, M. J. 1958. *The Myth of the Negro Past.* Boston: Beacon Press.

Hill, R. 1972. *The Strengths of Black Families.* New York: Emerson-Hall.

Ladner, J. 1971. *Tomorrow's Tomorrow: The Black Woman.* New York: Doubleday.

Mintz, S., and R. Price. 1976. *An Anthropological Approach to the Afro-American Past: A Caribbean Perspective.* Philadelphia: Institute for the Study of Human Issues.

Moynihan, D. 1965. *The Negro Family: The Cause for National Action.* Washington DC: U.S. Department of Labor.

Mullings, L. 1976. "Women and Economic Change in Africa." In N. Hafkin and E. Bay, eds., *Women in Africa.* Stanford: Stanford University Press.

Nobles, W. W. 1974. "Africanity: Its Role in Black Families." *The Black Scholar* 5:10–17.

Pleck, E. 1979. "A Mother's Wages: Income Earning Among Married Italian and Black Women, 1886–1911." In N. Cott and E. Pleck, eds., *A Heritage of Her Own: Toward a New Social History of American Women.* New York: Simon and Schuster.

Rapp, R. 1978. "Family and Class in Contemporary America." *Science and Society* 42:278–300.

Stack, C. 1974. *All Our Kin: Strategies for Survival in the Black Community.* New York: Harper and Row.

Sudarkasa, N. 1981. "Interpreting the African Heritage in Afro-American Family Organization." In H. McAdoo, ed., *Black Families.* Beverly Hills: Sage.

Valentine, C. 1971. "'The Culture of Poverty': Its Scientific Significance and Its Implications for Action." In E. Leacock, ed., *The Culture of Poverty: A Critique.* New York: Simon and Schuster.

5

Households Headed by Women

The Politics of Race, Class, and Gender

In 1990, over 20 percent of all families in the United States with children under eighteen were headed by women (U.S. Bureau of the Census 1990a).[1] The precipitous increase in frequency in this household form—from 10.7 percent in 1970 to 21 percent in 1990 (U.S. Bureau of the Census 1973, 1990a)—has generated a great deal of academic debate. But perhaps more pertinent are those discussions that take place in the popular and political arenas: from former Vice President Dan Quayle's attack on *Murphy Brown,* a television portrayal of a professional Euro-American woman who chooses to have a child out of wedlock, to the more insidious and less contested demonization of "welfare mothers."

As people struggle over definitions of the normative family and control of reproduction, divisions of race and class are never far from the surface. For African Americans, the conflict over fertility has always been linked to the political economy, as their efforts to control the conditions of their reproduction clashed with the interests of the dominant class. During slavery, slaveowners encouraged fertility among enslaved women to increase the labor force. In the contemporary economy, as African Americans resist confinement to the low-wage jobs of their parents and grandparents (Collins 1991), they are increasingly considered a "redundant population," an underclass that must be contained. Reproduction is now regulated less directly and less personally than it was during slavery: The structure of the households of women seeking welfare benefits or admission to homeless shelters has come under increasing bureaucratic manipulation and regulation, and women who head households are increasingly stigmatized.

Today, with labor and capital moving around the globe, race, class, and gender, as well as nationality, define boundaries to be held, reclaimed, or challenged. In the global context of population policies, disease, and disasters of all kinds, local populations seek to envision continuity through children and act to ensure that continuity. Using low-income women in Harlem, New York City, as an example, this chapter describes the global and local socioeconomic relations that form the context for stratified reproduction, the power relations by which "some categories of people are empowered to nurture and reproduce, while others are disempowered" (Ginsburg and Rapp 1995, 3); explores the ways in which ideologies and social policies reinforce stratified reproduction; and discusses "transformative work," through which people seek to sustain themselves, their families, and their communities.

Global, National, and Local Intersections

That women increasingly raise children themselves is an international phenomenon, characteristic of both industrialized and developing nations. Various factors bear on the rise of these households in different parts of the world. A precipitous increase in the proportion of such households may be associated with war, as in Iraq; genocidal policies, as in Guatemala; neocolonial apartheid and separation, as in South Africa; labor migration, as landless peasants search for work in much of the world; or with increasing unemployment, as in parts of the industrialized world. The international labor diaspora places huge burdens on women, and in most areas households headed by women are associated with high rates of poverty as children become a cost particular to them.

Household structure in both developing and industrialized countries is shaped by global as well as local processes, as policies implemented at national or international levels increasingly mold reproductive experiences. The flight of industry from U.S. cities to areas with cheaper and less organized labor and the rapid movement of "hot money" around the world in search of speculative opportunities have local consequences: unemployment, destruction of social services, and infrastructural deterioration plague postindustrial cities in the United States.

In the United States, global processes interact with historical patterns of racism and discrimination, sharpening racial and gender disparities. Minority populations in inner cities are most severely affected by the increasing social and economic polarization. Since the 1980s the African American middle class has expanded. But at the same time a growing number of workers have been expelled from the labor force, and unemployment and underemployment among African American and Latino men has reached staggering proportions.

Because the growth of households headed by women is linked to unemployment and low earnings (see Ross and Sawhill 1975; Wilson 1987), it is not surprising that 50 percent of all African American households and 24.2 percent of all Latino households with children under 18, compared with 15.8 percent of all Euro-American households with children under 18, are headed by women (Bureau of the Census 1990a). While the rise of feminism, growing labor force participation (which increases women's economic independence), and changing attitudes toward marriage may be factors in the rising incidence of female headship among Euro-American women (England and Farkas 1986), for African Americans, male unemployment seems to be a major reason for the increase in the number of female-headed households (Wilson 1987). The disappearance of "marriageable" African American men—through disproportionate unemployment, consequent participation in an informal underground economy of which crime is only one aspect, and ensuing high levels of incarceration and "excess" death—means that African American women of all classes are less likely to marry or to remarry. But the consequences are greatest for low-income women, who must deal with poverty. In 1990 almost half (42 percent) of all households with children under 18 headed by women—including 34 percent of Euro-American, 53 percent of African American, and 55 percent of Latino households—fell below the poverty threshold (U.S. Bureau of the Census 1990b). Increasingly concentrated in the inner cities, these households become the subject of considerable critical scrutiny in the context of global discourses linking economic development with population control.

Local Communities: Women, Work, and Family in Central Harlem

Central Harlem, a predominantly African American community in northern Manhattan, presents an example of the havoc wreaked in local communities already disadvantaged by centuries of discrimination. But it is also a complex and variegated community, in which people struggle against increasingly difficult conditions. At the turn of the century, people of African descent began to migrate to Harlem from other parts of New York City, the South, and the Caribbean. Though shaped by segregation and discrimination, Harlem has been a vibrant social, political, and cultural center for African Americans of all classes. In the 1920s it was the hub of a cultural renaissance. Social movements ranging from

Marcus Garvey's Universal Negro Improvement Association to the election of Ben Davis as the first Communist city councilman have found fertile ground in Harlem.

Many of Central Harlem's residents are currently experiencing severe difficulties as the effects of global restructuring and the economic policies and cutbacks of the 1970s and 1980s interact with longstanding patterns of racism to produce rapidly deteriorating conditions.[2] Though there is a strong middle class in Harlem, poorer Harlemites' limited access to well-paying jobs is reflected in the low median income, which was $13,252 in 1989, compared with $29,823 for New York City as a whole, and in levels of unemployment more than double those of New York City (New York City Department of City Planning 1992a, 1992b). Almost half (42.2 percent) of Harlem youth between sixteen and nineteen were unemployed in 1989 (New York City Department of City Planning 1992c), and almost 40 percent of the residents of Central Harlem had incomes below the poverty line (New York City Department of City Planning 1992d).

As the conditions for poor people in the inner cities of the industrial world increasingly resemble those of people without resources in the developing world, it is not surprising that a study found that for men in Central Harlem "the rate of survival beyond the age of 40 is lower . . . than in Bangladesh" (McCord and Freeman 1990, 174). Less well publicized is the situation for women. "For women, overall survival to the age of 65 is somewhat better in Harlem [than in Bangladesh], but only because the death rate among girls under five is very high in Bangladesh" (McCord and Freeman 1990, 174).

Women find themselves in an increasingly difficult position. In Central Harlem, 69 percent of all families with children under eighteen are headed by women (New York City Department of City Planning 1992b). While some women have been immobilized by the crisis conditions, others succeed in raising their children without a stable income from men and are able to maintain their households despite adverse circumstances.

Historically, most African American women have been compelled—by slaveholders or by necessity—to work outside the home. With the devastating levels of unemployment of African American men, the labor force participation rate of African American women has become roughly equal to that of men. In 1990 women constituted 52.4 percent of the African American work force, though women made up only 45.3 percent of the Euro-American work force (U.S. Bureau of the Census 1992).

Though differences in work force participation rates between African American and Euro-American women are no longer dramatic, their history is. Euro-American women's aggregate participation in the work force has only recently approached that of African American women, who, as mothers, have always worked outside their homes in large numbers (see chapter 2). The obstacles that confront all working mothers are intensified for African American women, who find themselves in the ambiguous position of being primary wage earners in a society where the official ideology designates men as the principal breadwinners. In Central Harlem, 65 percent of women in the labor force have children under eighteen, and 43 percent of them have children under six (New York City Department of City Planning 1993). These difficulties are compounded for those with low-income jobs.

By the 1980s, as a result of the struggle for civil rights and an expanding service economy, African American women had moved into a variety of professions and occupations. But a large proportion of African American women continue to be concentrated in low-wage jobs, with little job security, few benefits, and difficult working conditions. The poorest women are excluded from the job market altogether. In Central Harlem in 1990, more than half (54.7 percent) of women eligible to work were not in the labor force (New York City Department of City Planning 1990b), with 28.9 percent of Harlem residents receiving Aid to Families with Dependent Children (New York City Department of City Planning 1991). Women may work entirely in the informal sector or may augment their income from welfare or low-wage work with such informal-sector jobs as child care and other domestic work, renting out living spaces, or selling various products. Some develop strategies that combine attending school to improve their job chances with one or more low-wage jobs. Nevertheless, 54.3 percent of all Harlem households headed by women that include children under eighteen have incomes below the poverty line (New York City Department of City Planning 1993). In short, many women work a triple shift—work outside the home, additional informal-sector work, and housework—which must be extended to fill the gap left by declining social services.

In addition to responsibility for supporting the household—often on marginal incomes—women must maintain the family in conditions exacerbated by the economic policies of the 1980s. As the federal government decreased its contribution to New York City's budget from 19.8 percent in 1978 to 10.9 percent in 1990 (New York City Office of the Budget 1991), women have had to cope with the problems caused by cutbacks not only in social services but also in education, housing, child care services, and health care.

For example, many African American mothers feel that they can no longer rely on the schools. Education has historically been of great importance to the African American struggle for equality. African Americans have fought for equal access to education, and since emancipation mothers' wages have often been applied to allowing children to continue in school (see Pleck 1979). This strategy has had some successes. Since the 1970s, African Americans have significantly narrowed the gap between themselves and Euro-Americans in the number of school years completed, although this improvement has not resulted in narrowing the income gap.

But the gains in education won during the civil rights era of the 1960s and 1970s have eroded since then, and racial inequality in access to education has increased (Kozol 1991). Children in New York City schools, for example, receive less funding per capita than children in suburban schools (Kozol 1991), and in Central Harlem children and schools receive less funding in almost every category than in other districts in New York City (Breslin and Stier 1987). The "survival rate" in these large, underfunded, understaffed schools is low: The two high schools to which the majority of students from junior high schools in Central Harlem are directed have a four-year graduation rate of approximately 27 percent (Mullings and Susser 1992), which does not include those who drop out between the eighth and ninth grades. There is, nonetheless, a belief in the efficacy of education. Parent and community organizations have been successful in instituting after-school programs and in persuading the Board of Education to establish several special schools and programs, including a high school to serve Central Harlem.

In addition to their concerns about education, women must raise their children in neighborhoods where poverty, neglect, drugs, and crime are threatening the social fabric. Since the 1970s, nearly ten thousand units of housing have been abandoned in Central Harlem (Harlem Urban Development Corporation 1990; Mullings and Susser 1992), and at the same time there has been a major reduction in federal funds for new housing units. Consequently, between 1970 and 1990 the number of available housing units in the community dropped by 27.1 percent (New York City Department of City Planning 1990a). The resulting overcrowding, homelessness, and destruction of neighborhoods have had a ripple effect: As families move away, networks that have historically sustained the community and that might control deviant behavior are destroyed, and deterioration and crime increase (see Wallace, Fullilove, and Wallace 1992).

Drugs are a case in point. With the inability (or unwillingness) of the federal government to halt the importation of drugs into the United States and with police effectiveness significantly curtailed by corruption, strategically located low-income neighborhoods become marketplaces for the sale of drugs to surrounding suburbs. Youth are drawn into the sale and distribution of drugs as meaningful economic or educational opportunities decline. The director of a substance-abuse program in Central Harlem pointed out: "The young people today don't have an anti-work ethic. . . . Those kids are out doing the crack thing, that's work. . . . They have a sophisticated understanding of management, organization, distribution, marketing, and competition. But it's all geared to the wrong thing" (cf. Williams 1989).

The depth of worry about children growing up in these conditions is difficult to convey. The epidemic of violence (the cost of which is borne by these neighborhoods), fueled by the ready availability of firearms, threatens everyone, but people worry most about the youth. Older relatives sometimes give teenage boys guns for protection, and violence spirals. In 1989 Central Harlem had a total of 3,175 violent crimes, ranking seventeenth among seventy-five community districts in New York City in number of violent crimes per person (New York City Office of Management Analysis and Planning 1989).

People are adamant about trying to keep children safe. Women spend an extraordinary amount of time escorting children, limiting their movement, and trying by any means to keep them away from the violence of the streets. There are building-by-building and block-by-block struggles (often unsuccessful) to expel drug dealers. At the same time, proceeds from the sale of illegal drugs may be the only source of income for some families. As I interviewed residents of Central Harlem, people repeatedly expressed acute concern about losing the children—to the drug culture, to early death as a result of substance abuse, to the often random violence associated with illegal drugs in poor neighborhoods. Today, the leap of faith to envision continuity through children must be as great as it was during the days of slavery.

In these circumstances, it might be argued that women are making adaptive reproductive decisions in a situation where the population is endangered by excessive morbidity and mortality. As with unemployment rates, infant mortality rates among African Americans are over twice the national average. In Central Harlem, the infant mortality rate in 1988 was approximately three times the national rate; between 1985 and 1988, children up to the age of four were dying at three times the expected rate for the United States as a whole (Health and Hospitals Corporation 1991). Indeed, in all age groups except for those between the ages of five and fourteen and those over sixty-five, residents of Central Harlem die at higher rates than the general U.S. population (Mullings and Susser 1992; Health and Hospital Corporation 1991).

It is not surprising that among pregnant young women I interviewed in Central Harlem, the death of family members was not an unusual occurrence. For example, one unmarried nineteen-year-old stated that her mother had urged her to carry this pregnancy to term, though she had terminated a previous pregnancy by abortion. In the course of the discussion, it became clear that in the last two years several family members had died unexpectedly: her brother had been killed by a stray bullet, a cousin had died of AIDS, and another cousin had died of respiratory distress in a hospital.

Though women through their childbearing behavior may, in a sense, replace people lost to early death (cf. Sharff 1987), it is important not to underestimate the cost of all these burdens to women themselves. Between 1985 and 1988, the annual excess death rate (see Mullings and Susser 1992 for an explanation of this index) of women in Central Harlem was ten times that of New York City as a whole, with heart disease being the leading cause (Mullings and Susser 1992), no doubt reflecting the stresses to which these women are subject. One might conclude that while excess death among men reflects direct confrontation with the social system, women die of indirect effects.

As conditions in these communities decline, the potential for violence directed at the larger society escalates. While AIDS and illegal drugs function as forms of population control, the public discussion of fertility escalates. As women attempt to raise children in crisis conditions, they find themselves the focus of representations that in effect obscure and even blame them for those conditions.

Ideology and Public Policy

Elements of strongly held ideologies concerning race, class, and gender are reflected in the public discussion of women who head households. Ideologies of race portray them as promiscuous women and inadequate mothers; ideologies of class blame them for their poverty; and ideologies of patriarchy label nontraditional family forms as "pathological." The convergence of these beliefs and their reproduction at so many locations render the representation of women who head households particularly deleterious.

Race, Motherhood, and Sexuality

Stratified reproduction is reinforced and reproduced by gender constructions that have emphasized motherhood for Euro-American women (Davin 1978; Laslett and Brenner 1989) but sexuality for African American women. Both sides of this fractured imagery have implications for reproduction, as motherhood, womanhood, and race are symbolically intertwined and contested.

For elite Euro-American women, motherhood has been a major defining element of gender identity. Women as mothers—who are involved in both biological and cultural reproduction—become master symbols of family, race, and civility, and are central to the authorized definition of the national community (cf. Stoler 1989). When boundaries are threatened, rhetoric about fertility and population control escalates, and native Euro-American women, preferably those of the dominant class, are exhorted to have children. Deviation from traditional roles is presumed to promote race suicide, and women who do not or cannot conform are censured as contributing to the decline of civilization. For example, abolitionists were labeled "shameless amazons" and "unsexed females" (Scott 1970, 20); suffragists were accused of contributing to race suicide by concerning themselves with matters outside the home (Rosen 1982, 45).

In the face of rising discontent with the widening division of wealth and challenges to cultural hegemony, and as international migrations again modify the face of the United States, the oratory of the 1992 Republican National Convention bore a striking resemblance to Nazi rhetoric, which demanded motherhood for the "mothers of the master race" versus compulsory sterilization for others and "race hygienic sterilization . . . [as] a prelude to mass murder" (Bock 1983, 408). "Family values" became a ringing slogan, but not just any family would do. The model was the (Euro-American) nuclear family with the father working and the mother at home, characteristic of less than one sixth of U.S. families. Not surprisingly, traditional gender roles, antiabortion laws, attacks on households headed by women, and defense of the traditional educational curriculum were linked to the preservation of the nation.

The dominant class's construction of gender has throughout history portrayed African American women as inadequate mothers and promiscuous women. Not only were enslaved women vulnerable to sexual exploitation, but slavery required fertility without motherhood:[3] children could be and were sold away from them.

When slavery ended, segregation and discrimination dictated that African American women work outside the home, but their opportunities were initially limited to domestic work. Representations of African American women as sexually provocative, which had rationalized the vulnerability of slaves to the sexual advances of Euro-American men, continued to excuse advances toward African American domestic workers.

Images of African Americans as bad mothers, ineffective mothers, and matriarchs (see Collins 1991, Morton 1991, and chapter 6 for a discussion of these notions in popular culture and scholarly literature) also conceal and justify the difficult conditions in which they work and raise children. But, oddly enough, these same women, who are said to run amok in their own communities, are thought to be entirely competent at parenting the children of the elite—as mammies during slavery, as domestic workers during segregation, or as child care workers today. Thus the popular images of low-income African American women who head households emphasize not mothering but sexuality. They are not portrayed as mothers with limited resources struggling to care for children. Their public image as nurturers depends entirely on the care they "offer" to the children of Euro-American families. At the same time the problem of endangered African American manhood is laid at the door of these "weak" mothers, who cannot adequately "discipline" their children.

Class and Patriarchy

Ideologies of class come into play in depicting these women and their children as the crystallization of the urban underclass. Several works (see, for example, Lemman 1986; Murray 1984; Jenks 1991) attribute contemporary poverty in minority communities to the growth of households headed by women. This literature has been reviewed and critiqued elsewhere (for example, chapter 8; Williams 1992; Reed 1992), but these views persist despite the work demonstrating the relationship between unemployment and the rising numbers of female-headed families.[4] By blaming these women for their own poverty and, indeed, for the economic ills of the entire nation, attention is diverted from the injustice of the racial and gendered labor market and from the "savage inequalities" (Kozol 1991) increasingly characterizing U.S. society.

Notions of normative gender roles continue to pervade those works that attempt to analyze the structural conditions that give rise to these households (for example, Wilson 1987). Despite the lack of significant evidence that single-parent households are in themselves harmful, these households are invariably described as inherently pathological (for discussion of these concepts in the social-policy literature, see Schorr and Moen 1979, Schlesinger 1986). One might conclude that the intensity of affect and scrutiny to which these households are subject at some level reflects "a fear of women without men" (cf. Tiffany and Adams 1985 on the "matriarch fixation"); households headed by women are seen as the "other" of the patriarchal family (Sands and Nuccio 1989), just as the underclass is the "other" to the middle class.

Limiting Options Through Policies and Representation

Powerful ideas of class, race, and gender are central to social policies, which, by imposing constraints on reproduction according to race and class, replicate and reinforce structural inequality. Public policies regarding child care, women's work, and compensation, rationalized by notions about appropriate gender roles, promote the male-headed nuclear family by reinforcing the dependence on women (see chapter 8). For the working class, and increasingly for middle-stratum women who must work, these policies make their lives difficult.

For poor women, however, state policies that structure access to social benefits often reinforce and encourage matrifocality. As the lack of employment and educational opportunities constrains women's access to men's income and they are forced to rely on the state, social policies then function to further encourage matrilocality. Benefits such as income support (Stack 1974) or Medicaid (Davis and Rowland 1983) are virtually unavailable to men or to households that include men (Stack 1974). Susser's (1989) ethnographic study of shelters for the homeless in New York graphically documents the role of the state in structuring the composition of households through its regulation of who may sleep where and with whom and whether parents may stay with children. As low-income housing becomes increasingly unavailable and the homeless population grows, the shelter system routinely separates men from their children and the mothers of their children. In some facilities boys over the age of nine are not permitted to stay in the shelters with their mothers. Families are defined as women and young children, and men are considered irrelevant and even dangerous.

These public policies combine with popular perceptions to further limit already limited options. Images of the promiscuous welfare mother deflect attention from the role of the society in producing African American mothers and children who are dependent on the state. Harrington suggested that the image of "a welfare mother with a large family, pregnant once again (the poor as promiscuous and lazy) . . . [has] done more to set back the struggle against poverty than have all efforts of reactionary politicians" (Harrington 1984, 179). These representations are then deployed to rationalize policies ranging from forcing Norplant birth control implants on welfare recipients to cutting welfare benefits of parents whose number of children exceed a designated limit (Reed 1992, 36). The limitations on educational and occupational opportunities, which create the conditions in which young women are likely to have children, are then reinforced.

Some feminists (for example, Hartmann 1987) suggest that households headed by women may be a positive development, contributing to women's autonomy and control. We do need to "denaturalize" (Rapp 1987) the family: to understand the nuclear family as a historically particular form characteristic of a minority of humankind for a relatively small proportion of time. We do need to point out that male or female "headship" in and of itself does not determine the consequences widely attributed to it, but that the social context of the family (whatever its form), especially access to material and social resources, seems to be crucial.

Nevertheless, feminist analyses emphasizing increased independence tend to underplay its costs to women, children, and the community and to verge on adopting the conservative view that these women are making an unrestricted lifestyle choice. While this is a complex issue, I think it reasonable to assume that for a majority of African American women who head households, their situation is both imposed and chosen (cf. Lebsock 1984). To the extent that they choose, they do so within a range of options severely limited by hierarchies of race, class, and gender. The task, then, is to transform the structure that limits options for both men and women.

Women, Reproduction, and Resistance: Transformative Work

As described above, women work outside the home and in the home, rearing children in difficult circumstances. But they also engage in what we might call *transformative work.* I use transformative work in two senses: efforts to sustain continuity under transformed circumstances, and efforts to transform circumstances in order to maintain continuity. These efforts have spanned the domains of work, household, and community.

A History of Struggle

In their efforts to sustain continuity under transformed circumstances, women in Harlem have a long tradition to draw on. In slavery, some women resisted increasing the property of slavers through their fertility by using various contraceptive and abortion techniques that southern medical journals referred to as "medicine," "violent exercise," and "external and internal manipulation" (Gutman 1976, 81). Others imagined their continuity through children even within the "peculiar" institution of slavery. To bear children who became the property of the slave owner must have given an especially poignant meaning to the concept of alienation; nevertheless, women bore and raised children, creating families in which woman-centered networks figured prominently (Gutman 1976; Mintz and Price 1976; chapters 2 and 4).

Within the constraints of segregation, African American men and women attempted to maintain some control over the conditions under which they bore children. Though planters (Gutman 1976) and poverty forced many married women to work, they often chose to work as laundresses rather than as live-in domestics, increasing the time they could spend with their families and limiting as best they could their vulnerability to sexual exploitation.

In their effort to maintain continuity and support survival through the conditions of slavery, segregation, and deindustrialization, African American women have often utilized woman-centered networks. These "blood mothers and other mothers" (Collins 1991) embedded in larger networks have a long history in the African American community as an alternative family form (see Omolade 1987). They have sustained and supported survival, caring for children and adults when immediate relatives were unable to do so. In Harlem these networks continue, often supported by community-based organizations.

Efforts to sustain the family have always been inseparable from efforts to assist the community. African American women have a long history of community work (see Gilkes 1988). Inevitably, the attempt to sustain the community requires measures to transform the larger society. Most African American women and men have been actively involved in individual and collective efforts that foster resistance and empowerment.

Conditions and Constraints

African American women, and particularly poor women in communities such as Harlem, now face one of the greatest challenges since slavery. In the face of deteriorating conditions, many women in Harlem continue to engage in efforts directed at both sustaining continuity and transforming conditions. Kin and nonkin networks continue to be important in raising children, but the extent to which these networks are threatened by the crisis conditions (DeHavenon 1988) is indicated by the record number of children in foster care. These networks and other institutions are particularly weakened by the spread of illegal drug use among African American women.

Though the decline of working-class movements has undercut a major area of potential advance, women in Central Harlem, many of whom head households, are the backbone of militant unions, such as Local 1199 of the Hospital Workers Union, and they continue to try to change the workplace. They are active in community efforts to build associations and tenant organizations, to improve housing and schools, and to eliminate drugs from buildings and neighborhoods. Community-based activities such as the church-led movement to protest extensive billboard advertisement of cigarettes and alcohol and two environmental movements focusing attention on pollution in low-income neighborhoods have been highly publicized. These local struggles have sometimes been the building blocks of larger, citywide political actions, such as the election of the first African American mayor of New York City in 1989 and the formation of the New Majority Coalition, a multiracial organization that was active in voter registration, supporting progressive candidates for election to the city council, and organizing for a civilian review board.

However, with the failures of liberal integration (Marable 1992) and the destruction of the left movement (Horne 1993), the political context for collective movements for empowerment and basic social reform has become severely restricted. The current repressive environment, which has a negative impact on efforts for collective empowerment, lends itself to the resurgence of ethnically based political and cultural movements. This development is immediately evident to the casual observer in the rise of various Afrocentrisms; the adoption of neo-African hair styles, jewelry, and clothing; the growing influence of the Nation of Islam; and expressions of concern about loss of history, culture, and community. Explanations such as "We need to return to our values" and "We need to build our own cultural and moral base for our children" were typically given by people I interviewed in Central Harlem. On one hand, this concern with culture may represent an attempt to contest hegemonic constructs of race and culture, to repossess history and to create new definitions of community. On the other hand, fundamentalist nationalist movements are frequently patriarchal and authoritarian. In these cases, the status of women, who are often seen as culture-bearers, becomes highly problematic (see chapters 6 and 7).

In doing transformative work, then, women seek to construct a space in which they can ensure continuity for themselves, their children, and their communities. We need to increase our understanding of the conditions in which these efforts are successful and the circumstances in which they develop into larger social movements. But what is perhaps unique about the experience of African American women is the dramatic way in which their experience has linked the domains of household, community, and the larger society. For women of color, working-class women, and increasingly for middle-stratum women, protection of their children, which mobilizes their activism, requires the protection and transformation of their households, their communities, and the larger society. For this reason, efforts to sustain and maintain continuity inevitably involve significant social transformations.

Notes

1. Nearly one third (28.7 percent) of all households were headed by women (U.S. Bureau of the Census 1990a).

2. Health, employment, housing, education, and social services in Central Harlem are described in greater detail in Mullings and Susser 1992. Some of the findings on Harlem appeared in an earlier version in this unpublished report.

3. In some cases interest in adding to property seemed to mandate easing the burdens of pregnant women (Fox-Genovese 1988), and demonstrated high fertility might bring privileges to a woman and perhaps decrease the likelihood of sale and separation from her kin (Gutman 1976, 75–77). Yet we have numerous accounts of pregnant and nursing women being subjected to grueling working conditions. Jones points to the brutal whipping of pregnant and nursing mothers "so that blood and milk flew mingled from their

breasts" and to the special trenches found throughout the South, designed for adminis-tering a beating to a pregnant slave while minimizing harm to the fetus. "They were made to lie face down in a specially dug depression in the ground" (1985, 20). The condi-tions under which African American women conceived, bore, and raised children varied with historical periods, geographic area, plantation size, and the disposition of the planter. But in no case was the slave family legal.

4. Wilson demonstrates that, despite popular beliefs, the rate of childbearing among African American women decreased 40 percent between 1960 and 1983. But because there are fewer employed men to marry, there are higher statistical rates of out-of-wed-lock births for African American teenagers (Wilson 1987, 194). Other analyses point to the lack of evidence that family structure causes poverty—indeed, for people of color, the two-parent family is no guarantee against poverty (see Baca Zinn 1989 for a review of such studies.) More recently, a Census Bureau study concluded that poverty is a major factor contributing to the dissolution of families in the United States (Hernandez 1992).

References

Baca Zinn, Maxine. 1989. "Family, Race, and Poverty in the Eighties." *Signs* 14: 856–74.

Bock, Gisela. 1983. "Racism and Sexism in Nazi Germany: Motherhood, Compulsory Sterilization and the State." *Signs* 8: 400–21.

Breslin, Susan, and Eleanor Stier. 1987. *Promoting Poverty: The Shift of Resources Away from Low Income New York City School Districts.* New York: Community Service Society of New York.

Collins, Patricia Hill. 1991. *Black Feminist Thought: Knowledge, Consciousness, and the Politics of Empowerment.* New York: Routledge.

Davin, Anna. 1978. "Imperialism and Motherhood." *History Workshop* 5: 9–65.

Davis, Karen, and Diane Rowland. 1983. "Uninsured and Underserved: Inequities in Health Care in the United States." In Peter Conrad and Rochelle Kern, eds., *The Sociology of Health and Illness: Critical Perspectives.* New York: St. Martin's Press.

DeHavenon, Anna Lou. 1988. "Where Did All the Men Go?: An Etic Model for the Cross-Cultural Study of the Causes of Matrifocality." Paper presented at the symposium Female-Headed/Female-Supported Households, Twelfth International Congress of Anthropological and Ethnological Sciences, July 21–31, Zagreb, Yugoslavia.

England, Paula, and George Farkas. 1986. *Households, Employment, and Gender: A Social, Economic, and Demographic View.* New York: Holt, Rinehart, and Winston.

Fox-Genovese, Elizabeth. 1988. *Within the Plantation Household: Black and White Women of the Old South.* Chapel Hill: University of North Carolina Press.

Gilkes, Cheryl. 1988. "Building in Many Places: Multiple Commitments and Ideologies in Black Women's Community Work." In Ann Bookman and Sandra Morgen, eds., *Women and the Politics of Empowerment.* Cambridge: Harvard University Press.

Ginsburg, Faye, and Rayna Rapp. 1995. "Introduction." In Faye Ginsburg and Rayna Rapp, eds., *Conceiving the New World Order: The Global Politics of Reproduction.* Los Angeles: University of California Press.

Gutman, Herbert G. 1976. *The Black Family in Slavery and Freedom, 1750–1925.* New York: Pantheon.

Harlem Urban Development Corporation. 1990. *Bradhurst Revitalization Planning Document.* New York: Harlem Urban Development Corporation.

Harrington, Michael. 1984. *The New American Poverty.* New York: Holt, Rinehart, and Winston.

Hartmann, Heidi I. 1987. "Changes in Women's Economic and Family Roles in Post–World War II United States." In Lourdes Beneria and Catherine R. Stimpson, eds., *Women, Households, and the Economy.* New Brunswick, NJ: Rutgers University Press.

Health and Hospitals Corporation. 1991. *A Summary Examination of Excess Mortality in Central Harlem and New York City.* New York: Office of Strategic Planning, Health and Hospitals Corporation.

Hernandez, Donald J. 1992. *When Households Continue, Discontinue, and Form: Studies on Household and Family Formation.* Current Population Reports, series P23179. Washington, DC: U.S. Bureau of the Census.

Horne, Gerald. 1993. "Myth and the Making of Malcolm X." *American Historical Review* 98: 440–50.

Jenks, Christopher. 1991. "Is the American Underclass Growing?" In Christopher Jenks and D. Peterson, eds., *The Urban Underclass.* Washington, DC: Brookings Institute.

Jones, Jacqueline. 1985. *Labor of Love, Labor of Sorrow: Black Women, Work, and the Family from Slavery to the Present.* New York: Basic Books.

Kozol, Jonathan. 1991. *Savage Inequalities: Children in America's Schools.* New York: Crown.

Laslett, Barbara, and Johanna Brenner. 1989. "Gender and Social Reproduction: Historical Perspectives." *Annual Review of Sociology* 15: 381–404.

Lebsock, Suzanne. 1984. *The Free Women of Petersburg: Status and Culture in a Southern Town, 1784–1860.* New York: W. W. Norton.

Lemman, Nicolas. 1986. "The Origins of the Underclass," Parts 1 and 2. *Atlantic Monthly* (June): 31–35, (July): 54–68.

McCord, Colin, and Harold P. Freeman. 1990. "Excess Mortality in Harlem." *New England Journal of Medicine* 322(3): 173–77.

Marable, Manning. 1992. "Race, Identity and Political Culture." In Gina Dent, ed., *Black Popular Culture.* Seattle: Bay Press.

Mintz, Sidney W., and Richard Price. 1976. *An Anthropological Approach to the Afro-American Past: A Caribbean Perspective.* Philadelphia: Institute for the Study of Human Issues.

Morton, Patricia. 1991. *Disfigured Images: The Historical Assault on Afro-American Women.* New York: Praeger.

Mullings, Leith, and Ida Susser. 1992. *Harlem Research and Development: An Analysis of Unequal Opportunity in Central Harlem and Recommendations for an Opportunity Zone.* New York: Office of the Borough President of Manhattan.

Murray, Charles. 1984. *Losing Ground.* New York: Basic Books.

New York City Department of City Planning. 1990a. *Community District 10.* New York: Department of City Planning.

————. 1990b. *Persons 16 Years and Over by Labor Force Status and Sex, New York City, Boroughs and Community Districts.* DCP 1990, no. 317. New York: Department of City Planning.

————. 1991. *Community District Needs, FY 1993.* DCP no. 91-14. New York: Department of City Planning.

————. 1992a. *Civilian Labor Force 16 Years and Over by Employment Status and Sex, New York City, Boroughs and Community Districts.* DCP 1990, no. 315. New York: Department of City Planning.

————. 1992b. *Demographic Profiles: A Portrait of New York City's Community Districts from the 1980 and 1990 Censuses of Population and Housing.* New York: Department of City Planning.

————. 1992c. *Persons 16–19 Years, Enrollment, Education, and Labor Force/Employment, New York City, Boroughs and Community Districts.* DCP 1990, no. 321. New York: Department of City Planning.

————. 1992d. *Selected Poverty Tabulations in 1989, New York City, Boroughs and Community Districts.* DCP 1990, no. 310. New York: Department of City Planning.

————. 1993. *Socioeconomic Profiles: A Portrait of New York City's Community Districts from the 1980 and 1990 Censuses of Population and Housing.* New York: Department of City Planning.

New York City Office of Management Analysis and Planning. 1989. *Statistical Report: Complaints and Arrests.* New York: Crime Analysis Unit, Office of Management Analysis and Planning.

New York City Office of the Budget. 1991. *1990 Annual Average Labor Force Data Disaggregated by Community District.* New York: New York State Department of Labor.

Omolade, Barbara. 1987. "The Unbroken Circle: A Historical and Contemporary Study of Black Single Mothers and Their Families." *Wisconsin Women's Law Journal* 3: 239–74.

Pleck, Elizabeth. 1979. "A Mother's Wages." In N. Cott and Elizabeth Pleck, eds., *A Heritage of Her Own.* New York: Simon and Schuster.

Rapp, Rayna. 1987. "Toward a Nuclear Freeze? The Gender Politics of Euro-American Kinship Analysis." In Jane Collier and Sylvia Yanagisako, eds., *Gender and Kinship: Essays Toward a Unified Analysis.* Stanford: Stanford University Press.

Reed, Adolph. 1992. "The Underclass as Myth and Symbol: The Poverty of Discourse About Poverty." *Radical America* 24(1): 21–40.

Rosen, Ruth. 1982. *The Lost Sisterhood: Prostitution in America, 1900–1918.* Baltimore: Johns Hopkins University Press.

Ross, Heather L., and Isabel V. Sawhill. 1975. *Time of Transition: The Growth of Families Headed by Women.* Washington, DC: Urban Institute.

Sands, Roberta, and Kathleen Nuccio. 1989. "Mother-Headed Single Parent Families: A Feminist Perspective." *Affilia* 4(3): 25–41.

Schlesinger, Benjamin. 1986. "Single-Parent Families: A Bookshelf, 1978–1985." *Family Relations* 35(1): 199–204.

Schorr, Alvin L., and Phyllis Moen. 1979. "The Single Parent and Public Policy." *Social Policy* 9(5): 15–21.

Scott, Ann Firor. 1970. *The Southern Lady.* Chicago: University of Chicago Press.

Sharff, Jagna. 1987. "The Underground Economy of a Poor Neighborhood." In Leith Mullings, ed., *Cities of the United States: Studies in Urban Anthropology.* New York: Columbia University Press.

Stack, Carol. 1974. *All Our Kin: Strategies for Survival in a Black Community.* New York: Harper and Row.

Stoler, Ann. 1989. "Making Empire Respectable: The Politics of Race and Sexual Morality in Twentieth-Century Colonial Cultures." *American Ethnologist* 16(4): 634–60.

Susser, Ida. 1989. "The Structuring of Homeless Families: New York City, 1980–1990." Paper presented at the annual meeting of the American Anthropological Association, November, Washington, DC.

Tiffany, Sharon, and Kathleen Adams. 1985. *The Wild Woman: An Inquiry into the Anthropology of an Idea.* Cambridge, MA: Schenkman.

U.S. Bureau of the Census. 1973. *1970 Census of Population and Housing, Characteristics of Population, U.S. Summary.* Washington, DC: Government Printing Office.

———. 1990a. *1990 Census of Population and Housing, Summary Tape File 1C.* Washington, DC: Government Printing Office.

———. 1990b. *1990 Census of Population and Housing, Summary Tape File 3C. Poverty Status in 1989 by Family Type and Presence and Age of Children.* Washington, DC: Government Printing Office.

———. 1992. *Detailed Occupation and Other Characteristics from the EEO File for the United States. 1990 Census of Population and Housing, Supplementary Report.* Washington, DC: Government Printing Office.

Wallace, Rodrick, M. Fullilove, and D. Wallace. 1992. "Family Systems and Deurbanization: Implications for Substance Abuse." In Joyce Lowinson, ed., *Substance Abuse: A Comprehensive Textbook.* Baltimore: Williams and Wilkins.

Williams, Brett. 1992. "Poverty Among African Americans in the Urban United States." *Human Organization* 51(2): 164–74.

Williams, Terry. 1989. *The Cocaine Kids.* New York: Columbia University Press.

Wilson, William J. 1987. *The Truly Disadvantaged: The Inner City, the Underclass and Public Policy.* Chicago: University of Chicago Press.

PART 3

✻

REPRESENTATION, RESISTANCE, AND TRANSFORMATION

*Theory and Practice in Politics
and in the Academy*

Introduction

Today, as throughout history, subaltern groups attempt to redefine the structuring of reality and their representation within it. For embedded within definitions of reality are competing presumptions about how to understand the world, the nature of institutions, the past, and, most important, the possibilities of the present and a vision for the future. Because, as Gramsci has so eloquently demonstrated, the reality of hegemonic representation rests on institutions of inequality, the struggle of these groups to reshape the boundaries of the present requires challenging the foundations of societal institutions. They must project alternative assumptions about community, family, and identity, and redefine notions of class, race, and gender.

As people seek to reclaim history, they do not passively accept images presented to them, but engage in active struggles—in the household, on the picket line, in schools, in communities, in the halls of Congress—that range from day-to-day resistance to militant confrontation. The academy is perhaps a less dramatic arena in which ideology, knowledge, and culture are generated and contested. The debates about multiculturalism and the intellectual canon are not merely about which books to read, but about power and privilege and how they are to be distributed. The struggle to define what knowledge is and its relationship to institutions of learning and their curricula is directly linked to conflicts over how power is deployed in the society.

"Images, Ideology, and Women of Color" explores some of the popular representations of African American women, how these are related to their historical experience as workers, and how this imagery has been contested by the African American community. An earlier draft was delivered as the keynote address at the 1990 workshop Integrating Race and Gender into the Curriculum, sponsored by the Center for Research on Women at Memphis State University, and was published in their series of working papers.

"Mapping Gender in African American Political Strategies" assesses alternative paradigms contemporary African Americans have constructed to envision gender relationships and probes their implications for women. The ideas in this paper were first presented as part of a series of lectures to a seminar at the Ecole des Hautes Etudes en Sciences Sociales in Paris, April 1993. Earlier versions were presented in papers delivered at the Institute for African American Studies, Columbia University, New York, September 1994, and at a conference entitled Africa in the World, held in Manchester, England, October 1995. The theoretical model of inclusion, autonomy, and transformation was developed in collaboration with Manning Marable and first appeared in the essay "The Divided Mind of Black America," published in *Race and Class* 36, no. 1 (1994): 61–72. "Mapping Gender in African American Political Strategies," which was written for this volume, employs that model to illuminate the subject of gender relationships in the African American community.

While the first two chapters in this section address society, the next three examine the contestation of knowledge in the academy. "Gender and the Application of Anthropological Knowledge to Public Policy in the United States" was originally written for *Gender and Anthropology: Critical Reviews for Reading and Teaching,* a volume that challenged gender representation in anthropology by demonstrating the manner in which knowledge is transformed by considering the relationships of gender. Each article reviewed new scholarship and presented concrete suggestions for integrating this material into an introductory anthropology course. This chapter applies the theoretical issues discussed in previous chapters to teaching.

"Race, Inequality, and Transformation: Building on the Work of Eleanor Leacock" was originally a speech given at the presentation of the first Eleanor Leacock Award to Stephen Gregory at the Thirteenth International Congress of Anthropological and Ethnological Sciences, July 1993, in Mexico City.

"Reclaiming Culture: The Dialectics of Identity" was originally published under the title "Culture and Afrocentrism" in *Race and Reason* (1994) as part of an exchange among African American scholars about the academic current of Afrocentrism.

6

Images, Ideology, and Women of Color

So some few women are born free, and some amid insult and scarlet letters achieve freedom; but our women in black had freedom thrust contemptuously upon them. With that freedom they are buying an untrammeled independence and dear as the price they pay for it, it will in the end be worth every taunt and groan.

—W.E.B. DuBois

In wondering at the way in which class and race mediate gender for African American women, W.E.B. DuBois, who so eloquently portrayed the double consciousness characterizing the "souls of black folk," described another conflicting duality: the freedom and constraint that mark the experience of gender for African Americans. The fetters of racism leave them bereft of the "protection of private patriarchy" (Dill 1994, 149) but also mitigate some of the constraints of gender, inadvertently creating a small measure of freedom.

But this window of freedom, narrow and equivocal as it is, poses a problem, a threat to the dominant society's rationalizations of gender hierarchy. One solution, the representation of African American women as inappropriate women—images of them as sexually provocative, as mammies, matriarchs, castrators, as the reason for the plight of the African American community— becomes a small part of "the price they pay."

Women of color, and particularly African American women, are the focus of well-elaborated, strongly held, highly contested ideologies concerning race, class, and gender. The images, representations, and symbols that form ideologies often have complex meanings and associations that are not always easily or readily articulated, making them difficult to challenge. Appearing in scholarly literature as well as popular culture, they take the form of accepted truths, constructing the nature of personhood.

How ideologies—the term *ideology* is used here in the sense of production of meanings—are generated, maintained, and deployed is intimately related to the distribution of power (see, for example, Williams 1977; Wolf 1982; Abercrombie and Turner 1978). Dominant ideologies often justify, support, and rationalize the interests of those in power: They tell a story about why things are the way they are, setting out a framework through which hierarchy is explained and mediating contradictions between classes and between beliefs and experiences. But dominant ideologies are also resisted and contested as people develop alternative and oppositional views of the world.

Taking African American women as an example, this chapter will examine some of the dominant representations of African American women, looking specifically at how they emerge in the context of class and race relations in the United States, how they function, and how they are contested. Though various writers have discussed stereotypes as they relate to sexuality and conquest, a thorough analysis must also take account of the African American woman's relationship to work. Throughout history African American women have been forced to work outside their homes, first by slaveholders and then by economic necessity. In a society in which the dominant ideology has held that a woman's place is in the home, the African American woman's status as a worker becomes a point of departure for representations that function first to mobilize her labor and then to stigmatize the measure of independence gained from her relationship to work. Her historical relationship to work may be a source of discord in the African American community, but it can also become the basis for subversion of negative ideologies. The chapter concludes with a consideration of how this analysis might apply to other women of color.

Women as mothers, virgins, and whores have been major archetypical symbols in Western thought. However, the problem of similarity and difference presents itself as we attempt to deconstruct the images, symbols, and representations of women in the United States. Although many of the images that rationalize the structuring of gender extend to all women, we need to deepen our understanding of how race and class mediate both the experience of gender and its imagery.

Representations of Women in the Antebellum South

Some of the most enduring representations of African American women took hold during slavery. These images, drawn from science, literature, and historical and popular accounts as well as from the practices of the planter class, were not always consciously articulated or uniformly applied. Nevertheless, the exercise of drawing them out gives us some insight into how the planter class "made sense" of the contradictions of slavery and the postemancipation caste system.

As the United States became a highly stratified society, hegemonic models of womanhood accentuated the distance between races and classes. Among the planter class of the antebellum South, where women were subordinate in the gender hierarchy but reaped the benefits of race and class asymmetry, the image of the ideal woman was a highly romanticized and extreme version of what has been called the "cult of true womanhood." The model woman was portrayed as incontrovertibly identified with the home; as the ideal wife and mother; as good, passive, delicate, pure, submissive, calm, frail, small, and dependent (Atkinson and Boles 1985; Boles and Atkinson 1986).

If this model did not fit the real experiences of Euro-American working-class women, most certainly the constructions of gender were very different for enslaved women of African descent. For these women, the asymmetries of race, class, and gender gave rise to a series of images and stereotypes influenced by the universal archetypes of gender but qualitatively transformed by ideologies of race, which themselves largely grew out of the class relationships of slavery.

Historians have described two images that reflect dominant Euro-American views of African American women during this period: the "Jezebel," the sexually aggressive, provocative woman governed entirely by libido; and the "mammy," the religious, loyal, motherly slave devoted to the care of the slave owner's family (see, for example, King 1973; White 1985; Simms-Wood 1988; Christian 1985; Sundquist 1987; Fox-Genovese 1988). To this I would add the underlying theme of defeminization—the African American woman as being without a clearly ascribed gender identity, that is, as being unfeminine in the sense of not possessing those traits, alleged to be biological, that defined, constrained, but also protected women of the time.

"Ain't I a Woman?"

While the Jezebel and mammy stereotypes may be seen as variations of universal female archetypes, as I will discuss below, the defeminization of African American women was more closely related to the ideologies of race that rationalized and perpetuated the brutal conditions of slavery. The belief that Africans and African Americans constituted a distinct, possibly nonhuman, and definitely inferior species, for which slavery was the most appropriate condition, not only was found in popular thought but also was elevated to "science" in the doctrine of polygenesis (see Harris 1968). Medical science, for example, marshaled evidence to demonstrate that African Americans had smaller lungs and brains and larger genitals, supposedly constituting irrefutable proof that the enslaved were of a different species.

Sojourner Truth's haunting address to the Akron Convention for Women's Suffrage in 1851 underscored the contradiction between the model of gender in which Euro-American women were both imprisoned and protected and the conditions of life for African American women: "I have plowed, and planted, and gathered into barns, and no man could head me! Ain't I a woman?" The place of women was said to be in the home, but enslaved women worked outside the home at jobs traditionally defined as men's work—sawing wood, plowing, repairing roads, digging ditches, pitching hay, building post-and-rail fences, and whatever else was necessary. While the particular tasks assigned to women were influenced by the historical period and the size of the plantation as well as the labor needs of the owner, the division of labor seems to have had more to do with the principle of division than the tasks considered appropriate for women (Fox-Genovese 1988, 172–77).[1] Just as denying enslaved African Americans human status rationalized their inhuman treatment, so the defeminization of African American women served to mediate the contradiction between beliefs about women's abilities and limitations, on the one hand, and the intense labor exploitation of African American women, on the other.

"I have borne thirteen children, and seen them most all sold off to slavery, and when I cried out with my mother's grief, none but Jesus heard me! And ain't I a woman?" Motherhood was a powerful and central symbol of gender definition for Euro-American women. But for African American mothers it offered few rights—not even that of keeping their children, who could be, and often were, sold away from them. In a model of femininity based on dependence as a defining characteristic, enslaved women became "defeminized"—excluded from the protections offered by womanhood, motherhood, and femininity.

Jezebel and Mammy

The mammy and Jezebel stereotypes, evoked at different historical periods and applied to women of different ages and phenotypes, are variations of the madonna/whore dualism. But race puts a peculiar cast on how these archetypes are applied.

The "otherness" of race—the notion that African Americans represented a distinct species—justified the attribution of excessive sexuality to people of African descent. Representations of the libidinous, sexually aggressive African American woman sanctioned rape and sexual exploitation by arguing that the enslaved women were the initiators, that their sexuality elicited a "natural" response in Euro-American men. Constructing African American women as "bad" women who were inappropriate for marriage served to allow interracial sexual activity but to discourage interracial marriage, thereby maintaining the caste system (see King 1973; Stoler and Cooper 1989) by drawing the boundaries along lines of race rather than of class. But as Angela Davis (1981) was the first to argue, rape of African American women was not simply an expression of the lust of Euro-American men. Rape was primarily an instrument of control, utilized to discipline the labor force and to keep African American men and women in line.[2]

Mammy—the servile, loyal, obedient woman who nurtures and protects the Euro-American family—was a prevalent image in nineteenth-century literature (Sundquist 1987) and in other popular forms (Simms-Woods 1988), and is familiar to generations of Americans through *Gone with the Wind*. But once again, race puts a peculiar cast on the maternal archetype, as the virtues of motherhood emerge only for the purpose of caring for elite Euro-American children. Deborah White (1985) argues that this stereotype, applied to some older women, personified the ideal slave and appeared later when southerners were forced to defend slavery. While the Jezebel image functioned to excuse miscegenation and sexual assault, the mammy image functioned to endorse, rationalize, and justify slavery.

The exploitation of African American women in the spheres of production and reproduction prevailed over notions of gender differentiation. The dilemma created by the distance between the patriarchal model and the real experience of African American women, who were denied the protection of private patriarchy, and whose men were stripped of all the attributes of male power, is in part addressed through representations of African American women as defeminized, inappropriate, or bad. Such images serve not only to rationalize labor and sexual exploitation but also to reinforce race solidarity across gender and class lines.

Gender, Race, and Class

Tensions of gender seem to have been subordinated to the benefits of class position, as elite Euro-American women, though dependent on men in this highly patriarchal system, clearly reaped significant material benefits from their partnership with these men. Ann Scott's curious portrayal of the planters' wives as passive, powerless, hardworking victims of the patriarchal system, humiliated by their partners' sexual access to enslaved women and burdened by the "difficult, demanding, frustrating and above all never-ending labor" (Scott 1970, 36) of supervising slaves, does not give sufficient attention to why "most southern women accepted, with a few nagging questions, the racial assumptions of their time and place" (Scott 1974, 61). Elizabeth Fox-Genovese (1988), on the other hand, demonstrates that the labor of the enslaved supported the leisured and advantaged life of the planters' wives. While slavery strengthened patriarchy, elite women certainly stood to gain from the labor of African Americans (see Wertz 1984 for cross-cultural comparisons).

But what of nonelite Euro-American women? As the standards of elite women became the model for all women, class differences in gender role behavior became yet another means of strengthening social control and emphasizing the distance between classes. The model of the "lady" certainly did not fit the experience of women who projected alternative standards, such as the "farm wife," a model that placed more emphasis on the work ethic (Hagler 1980).

In a peculiarly American fashion, however, ideologies of race often obscured contradictions of class and gender. The hierarchical system is held in place not only by force but also by the ideological unification of disparate segments of the population. Euro-American women gained not only materially but also symbolically, as the dualism inherent in Western imagery of women—good women versus bad women—was split into racial categories (Palmer 1983). These mutually defining images were the foundation for a set of beliefs about the protection of white womanhood that became a hegemonic ideology, uniting Euro-Americans across gender and class lines and justifying violence against African Americans during slavery and in the postemancipation period (see Leslie 1986).[3]

Shifting Realities, Changing Images

Emancipation brought freedom from slavery, but political, social, and economic discrimination prevented African American men from earning an adequate family wage. African Americans resisted pressure for married women to work outside the home (Gutman 1976), often using the dominant gender role model to demand a family wage, but need propelled women into the workforce. While the majority of Euro-American women did not work outside the home, African American women worked as sharecroppers, domestics, and laundresses in order for their families to survive (see chapter 2).

At the same time, gender role expectations dictated that African American women carry the bulk of the responsibility for household tasks. In short, in their struggle to maintain the family, the African American woman attempted to fulfill gender expectations without the protection of private patriarchy and while being exploited by public patriarchy (Dill 1994). In the postslavery period, the dissonance between the dominant ideology of equal opportunity and the reality of a society structured by class, race, and gender; between the dominant ideology of a woman's place and the reality of African American women's experiences as workers—again set the stage for the emergence of stereotypes and images.

Once again the representation of the African American woman as sexually provocative sought, as Roland Barthes suggests, to transform "history into nature" (1972, 129). Because African American women worked outside the home, often in servant roles, they were vulnerable to sexual exploitation. These conditions nourished the stereotyping of them as "bad" women, as work outside the home became symbolic of "whorish behavior" for Euro-American working-class women as well (see Palmer 1983; Rosen 1982, 46). As White (1985, 164) reminds us, perhaps the most graphic demonstration of the persistence of the "hot woman" image is the fact that through two thirds of this century, no white man was ever convicted of raping an African American woman. Recent rape cases suggest that this stereotype continues (Mullings 1992).

Throughout the history of the representation of African Americans in the United States, images that concern sexuality have been particularly compelling. The dialectically intertwined images of the pure and vulnerable white woman in need of protection, the primitive, sexually aggressive African American man, and the sexually provocative African American woman came together to rationalize the rape of African American women and the lynching of African American men (Burton 1985, 272; Hall 1983).

Although the protection of white women was the rallying cry, Hall notes that of the approximately five thousand people murdered by lynching between 1882 and 1946, less than one fourth were actually accused, let alone found guilty, of rape.[4] Violence, organized and rationalized through the motif of white woman-hood, was primarily directed toward restricting the civil and economic rights of African Americans. The ideology of white womanhood helped preclude class unity among working-class Euro-Americans and African Americans that might have extended the gains of reconstruction, forcing redistribution of land and implementation of broad-based reforms that might have benefited both groups.[5]

Although sexuality continues to be a major theme in discourse about race, compliance with the dominant ideology is not always assured (Abercrombie and Turner 1978). For example, the Association of Southern Women for the Prevention of Lynching, formed in 1930—in the context of a broader interracial struggle for reform—rejected the mythology of southern womanhood as a rationale for the epidemic of lynching. By 1943, forty-three thousand predominantly middle-stratum Euro-American women had repudiated lynching, stating, "Public opinion has accepted too easily the claim of lynchers and mobsters that they were attacking solely in defense of womanhood. In light of facts this claim can no longer be used as a protection to those who lynch" (quoted in Laue and McCorkle 1965, 83). The association noted and rejected the split image of the pure Euro-American woman and the promiscuous African American woman, claiming that both images served the interests of white men (Hall 1983).

Mammies to Matriarchs

Images of African American women as mammies continued in media and popular and material cultural forms. The mammy as Aunt Jemima (see Campbell 1989 for an interesting history of Aunt Jemima), for example, has graced cereal, pancake, and syrup containers since 1889. Although she has shed her bandanna for a curly Afro-like effect and lost some weight (Campbell 1989), this symbol continues to convey images of the faithful, obedient domestic servant. So attached were some southerners to this stereotype that in 1923 they petitioned to erect a monument in Washington, DC, to "the Black Mammy of the South" (White 1985). These representations reflected, but also helped to rationalize and reproduce, conditions in which job opportunities for African American women were largely confined to domestic work. And the image of the happy servant served, of course, to mask the economic exploitation of the domestic worker.

Despite formidable obstacles, and with exceptionally high rates of labor force participation, African American women gradually moved out of private household work as the expansion of the service and clerical sectors, along with the struggle against discrimination, presented new opportunities. In 1940, 60 percent of all African American women workers were domestic servants; by 1967 the number had declined to 24.5 percent (Jones 1982); and by 1980 only 7.5 percent placed themselves in this occupational category (Jones 1983). In the post–World War II revival of the cult of true womanhood and the establishment of the gender hierarchy, the "independence" created by the relationships of slavery and discrimination became particularly problematic.

In the context of these changing conditions, the imagery of African American women shifted from that of a nurturing servant to that of the emasculating matriarch. As Barbara Christian (1985) and others have pointed out, the emergence of the matriarch is a shift of emphasis rather than a radical departure. The Mammy, who gave tender care to the massa's family, was always portrayed as uncompromisingly severe with her own. The matriarchy image is most dramatically represented by the post–World War II stereotype of Sapphire, projected on radio and television as the "bossy," "emasculating" wife of Kingfish of the *Amos and Andy* show.

In the 1960s this representation gained a new scientific stature and became the basis for national policy decisions. *The Negro Family: The Case for National Action*, popularly known as the Moynihan Report, went beyond images projected by radio, television, movies, and literature. Like the rise of scientific racism at the turn of the century, this influential account gave popular stereotypes scientific status. For Daniel Patrick Moynihan (a Harvard sociologist who was elected to the U.S. Senate from New York in 1977), the African American family is "the principal source of most of the aberrant, inadequate, or antisocial behavior that did not establish, but now serves to perpetuate the cycle of poverty and deprivation" (1965, 76). The major weakness of the family is its "matriarchal structure," which is deviant. The term *matriarchy,* as used here, seems to refer to the fact that a greater proportion of African American than Euro-American women work outside the home and presumably enjoy relatively more independence within the household. The imagery shifted as the nurturing caretaker of the children of the elite became a "matriarch" in her own family—a bad mother responsible for low educational attainment, crime, and delinquency (Moynihan 1965).

This thesis, using elements of the stereotypes fostered in slavery to place the blame for the conditions of the African American community on the family structure and the roles played by women, arose precisely when the civil rights movement was mounting a serious challenge to the system of racial oppression and the women's movement was challenging the structure of patriarchy. As such, it was part of a broader ideological thrust—the "culture of poverty" perspective— that displaced concern from such issues as unemployment and discrimination to family structure and gender roles. But as attention shifted from relations between Euro-Americans and African Americans to relations within the African American community, the image of the warm mammy was no longer congruent with the idea of the "dysfunctional" African American family as the cause of poverty.

Ideology and Social Control

These images, then, are elements in ideological systems that are not unchanging but are continually re-created, modified, and defended (Williams 1977). The circumstances that force African American women to work outside the home also give them a greater degree of freedom from dependence on men than that of Euro-American women, although at a considerable cost. However, this independence, limited as it is, creates a dilemma that is resolved by placing sanctions on inappropriate independence through the use of negative imagery.

The "matriarch" label is used to represent a deviation from a class- and race-based model of gender roles that reflects neither the reality of African American women nor that of most Euro-American women. It brands independence as negative. Cheryl Gilkes (1983, 294) points out how such labeling seeks to transform "the model of insurgency"—African American women acting independently on behalf of their communities—into a "model of pathology." Stigmatizing the subordinate but more independent African American woman, she suggests, functions to constrain women of the dominant group, keeping them in their place. Women who, by accident or design, threaten the hierarchy of the social order are labeled "bad women." As I noted in chapter 5, suffragists (Rosen 1982, 45) and abolitionist women (Scott 1970, 20) were maligned through negative gender imagery.

Sanctions on behavior deviating from that deemed appropriate by the dominant class may take a more direct form. Based on her fieldwork with incarcerated African American women, Diane Lewis (1981) suggests that in deciding guilt or innocence and determining punishment, the police, the courts, and other criminal justice personnel sanction women as much for violating gender role expectations as for illegal behavior. African American women and, consequently, African American women offenders tend to be assertive, not to be married, to head households, to have an independent demeanor, and to be on their own. Citing the variety of gender role constraints correctional institutions employ in order to "demasculinize" deviant women, Lewis concludes that the greater number of incarcerated African American women "may simply reflect society's view that they are in greater need of demasculinization" (Lewis 1981, 102). As novelists (French 1977, 238) as well as social scientists (Hurtado 1989) have observed, rebellion against gender roles by Euro-American women may lead to psychiatric treatment, while for women of color who rebel, prison is the more likely consequence.

These constructions, then, seek to define the categories through which reality is to be understood and thereby to define the limits of social action. The stereotypes are grounded in enough reality to make them credible. They are not fully articulated, which makes them difficult to confront and contest; at the same time they arouse strong affect on many levels, some not always accessible to conscious reasoning. Of particular importance is the way these symbols and images, which speak to a basic aspect of identity—gender attributes—move us back and forth between society and nature (cf. Barthes 1972; Turner 1967). The matriarch image, for example, transforms social relations into cultural preference, constructing matrifocality as an attribute of personality. By placing the cause in nature rather than history, it obscures the role of unemployment, racism, and state policies in undermining the African-American family.

The Struggle Continues

Today, African American women have high rates of labor force participation. They have made impressive gains in educational attainment and significant inroads into professions and occupations previously dominated by Euro-American women (Almquist 1989, 419) and have recently begun to have a significant impact on the political process. Yet at the same time, the economic policies of the 1980s produced massive unemployment among men and women and the consequent rapid increase in the number of households headed by women.

African American women now have high visibility in many fields, including media, the arts, and politics. Although there are a range of images, some of the same themes persist in the representation of African American women of all strata. For example, the inappropriate independence of the "matriarch" is found in the portrayal of the middle-class "superwoman,"[6] who is depicted as inappropriately independent of men because of her access to work (often seen as one of the unfortunate results of affirmative action), as well as in the image of the "welfare mother," who is not properly dependent on men because of welfare payments by the state.

While African American women of all strata are affected by this imagery, the cost is greatest for poor women. The themes of promiscuous sexuality and inappropriate role fulfillment converge in discourse on women who head households. The precipitous rise in the number of African American women who head households is directly related to the economic policies of the last decades that have resulted in the decline of educational and employment opportunities and astounding levels of unemployment (see Wilson 1987). Yet images of the promiscuous, irresponsible welfare mother burdening society with her children serve to deflect attention from the role of society in producing dependent African American mothers and children. In doing so, these images reinforce racism and thus help to reproduce the conditions from which the stereotypes emerge (see chapter 5).

Most important, perhaps, these representations help to mitigate class conflict and support the status quo. As wealth becomes more and more concentrated, real wages decline, and income inequality grows, economic disarray increasingly affects most Americans. In the face of massive voter discontent, politicians and the mass media stigmatize poor women who head households. They are projected as responsible not only for their own poverty but also for the national deficit.

Ideologies Contested: Accommodation, Resistance, and Transformation

These representations, projected through education, religious institutions, and the mass media, are also resisted, challenged, and altered in social struggle. Despite minimal control of the institutions that produce and reproduce these images, people develop alternative beliefs that grow out of their own experience. In varying measures they contest both the gender imagery imposed upon them and the normative gender roles of the dominant group. In their everyday lives, people accommodate, resist, and transform hegemonic models.

Models are abstractions, however, and are always mediated at particular historical moments. Further, people may hold one set of beliefs and live according to another, and they may under some circumstances articulate a different ideal model. It is this process, involving experiences, relationships, and beliefs expressed at a given historical moment, that is difficult to capture.

As African Americans imagine gender roles, they have before them the dominant Euro-American model, which has historically emphasized male dominance and female dependence. This model is supported by education, law, religion, and the other major institutions of society. But they also draw on their own experience in a world informed by African traditions (see chapter 4), a world in which gender roles, domination, dependency, and work are not so strictly partitioned.

Although African Americans have resisted negative characterizations of African American women, they also have often accepted the hierarchical model of ideal gender relations. To the extent that the model is accepted as ideal, it must lead to the devalorization of African American women. Because their life circumstances preclude the same sort of dependence, because they must protect themselves, their men, and their children and be assertive on behalf of their community (see Gilkes 1983), they become "unfeminine." Uncritical acceptance of the dominant gender role model and the consequent negative characterization of African American women by African Americans themselves contribute to divisions within the African American community, diminishing the potential for united struggle.[7]

But the complexities of accommodation and resistance (cf. Anyon 1984) to class, race, and gender oppression are not easily sorted out. For example, during slavery there was masculinization of female roles but little feminization of male roles; that is, women did men's work but men did not do women's work. One could dispute the claim that slave households were more egalitarian and argue that sharecropping further reinforced patriarchy by reinstating hegemonic gender roles (cf. Mann 1989). But appropriating gender roles during slavery and sharecropping may also be seen as an attempt to resist the planters' imposition of degenderization, as an assertion of family relationships, and as a protest against the planters' tendency to ignore gender and family roles (see chapter 2; Jones 1982; Davis 1981; Harley 1978). Resistance and accommodation were similarly intertwined in some of the social, nationalist, and religious movements of the late 1960s and 1970s. Women were often expected to play traditional roles, and noncompliant women were labeled "Sapphires" (Christian 1985) or "matriarchs" (see Giddings 1984, 319–24).

But these relationships also involved a protest against the society that denied African American men and women the means to fulfill ideal gender expectations. They constituted an attempt to extend the protection of private patriarchy to African American women, those most exploited by public patriarchy. As such, appealing to the dominant gender role model may have served as a means of making demands—for a family wage and protection from the high personal cost of the double day, or as defense against the predatory sexual advances of Euro-American men.

What appears as accommodation may be resistance, but it does not lead to transformation. Resisting one set of oppressions may produce or reproduce another; dominant ideology may be replaced with alternative rather than oppositional forms (cf. Williams 1977). Without a critique of the hegemonic gender role model, the distance between the real and the ideal will always be a source of division in the public sphere and of tension and pain in the private sphere. The foundation for this critique lies in the real experience of African Americans. As Patricia Hill Collins (1989, 1990) and Mary Field Belenky et al. (1986) argue, community is essential for reconstructing ideology, as it may provide the context and validation for rejecting negative stereotypes and developing new ways of knowing.

These new ways of knowing are often much more difficult to document than stereotypes are, because they do not always appear in sources to which scholars traditionally turn. People often evolve, share, and pass along ways of knowing through folk tales and institutions such as the church, family (see Collins 1989, 1990), and other social organizations. For example, in the slave narratives we find a very different version of the mammy—one who is "cook, housekeeper, nurse-maid, seamstress, always nurturing and caring for her folk. But, unlike the white southern image of mammy, she is cunning, prone to poisoning her master, and not at all content with her lot" (Christian 1985, 5). Christian reminds us that Sojourner Truth was this type of mammy. Antebellum and postbellum writers such as Anna Julia Cooper, Ida B. Wells, Pauline Hopkins, Frederick Douglass, and others challenged the prevailing notions of gender.

Throughout their history, African American women have been involved not only in work outside the home but also in transformative work: individual and collective action to improve social conditions. In the course of this, they have attempted to address negative images. The National Association of Colored Women's Clubs, for example, formed in 1896, attacked the negative stereotypes of African American women's sexuality and opened boardinghouses to protect domestic workers from living conditions that made them vulnerable to the advances of employers (Hine 1989).

Though African American self-help organizations were characterized by some traditional gender role differentiation (Horton 1986; Neverdon-Morton 1978), they generally included both men and women and seem to have been considerably less sexist than comparable Euro-American organizations (Terborg-Penn 1978), with greater acceptance of women in activist roles (Giddings 1984, 59). Emphasis on "uplifting" the race meant that education of both boys and girls was of top priority (Perkins 1983; Horton 1986, 62). Thus while gender expectations among African Americans may have been comparable to those of the dominant society, objective conditions mediated the way in which people lived them, and there was some recognition that their historical experiences challenged the prevalent model.

It is perhaps in the course of attempting to effect institutional change that there is the greatest opening for transformation: the possibility of articulating new models of gender relations. Along with the struggle for civil rights, African Americans have contested the dominant class's construction of reality. As a result of struggle in everyday life, community organizations, trade unions, the media, literature, the arts, and academia, and as a result of contestation in both the political-economic and ideological arenas, there are today a variety of images of African American women. But as the "black is beautiful" movement demonstrated, without control over the social relations that generate ideology, the revision of ideologies cannot be sustained.

Women of Color: Identity, Gender, and National Liberation

To what extent are there similarities in the gender imagery of other women of color in the United States? Such a comparison would require a finely tuned historical analysis, examining transformations of gender imagery as these populations interact with each other as well as with Euro-Americans. In this context I will briefly note a few possible points of comparison. While different peoples of color have varied histories as a result of the dominant group encountering and exploiting them in different modes of production (Mullings 1978), they have all been subject to the exploitation of their labor and the denial of their economic, legal, and civil rights. As a result, there are many similarities in the way in which the dominant group has imaged their personhood.

For all people of color, an aspect of their exploitation centers on being defined as the "other" (see Said 1979). Representations of gender figure strongly in this process. Men from these groups are generally depicted as irresponsible and dangerous—a threat to European women (see Stoler 1989). Women are portrayed as "wild women of other worlds" (Tiffany and Adams 1985), that is, not deserving of the social and sexual protection enjoyed by the women of the conquerors' race and class.

Thus while men are constructed as sexually aggressive, women are depicted as sexually available. Native American women were portrayed as sexually excessive (Green 1975); Chicana women as erotic and exotic (Mirande 1980); Puerto Rican and Cuban women as "tropical bombshells . . . sexy, sexed, and interested" (Tafolla 1985, 39); Asian American women as cheap sexpots, prostitutes, and geisha girls (Chow 1987). Sexual domination may, as in the African American case, serve to reinforce labor exploitation as well as figure as a metaphor and representation of European supremacy.

Where there is stratification in the exploited population, the madonna/whore dichotomy may be applied differentially by class. Some of the gender constructions and protection bestowed on the women of the dominant class may be extended to elite women of the subordinated population. For example, representations of Native Americans include the "revered princess" Pocahontas but also the "savage squaw," a sexually acquiescent beast of burden (Green 1975; Albers 1989). Similarly, the imagery applied to Hispanic women incorporates a class distinction between the "hot-blooded working girl" and the "fervent, religious, faithful Spanish noblewoman" (Tafolla 1985, 38). For African American women, class distinctions do not seem to have been systematically applied, except perhaps by middle-class African American women themselves.

Given the emphasis on deleterious gender role stereotypes, it is not surprising that for people of color the family becomes the focus of negative imagery. Because the family is often experienced as a source of support and refuge from oppression as well as a powerful archetypal symbol, denigrating the family structure of people of color becomes a compelling form of victim-blaming. For example, sociological literature depicts the Mexican American family as "totally patriarchal, pathological and unstable," with a male who is overly dominant, violent, and obsessed with sexual fantasies, and a submissive and subordinate woman (Ybarra 1983, 92). Chicanas are portrayed as "long-suffering mothers who are subject to the brutality of insecure husbands and whose only function is to produce children—as women, who themselves are childlike, simple, and completely dependent on fathers, brothers, and husbands" (Baca Zinn 1982, 259). The root of family pathology, and therefore of poverty, for African Americans is matriarchy (castrating women and emasculated men), while for Mexican Americans pathology stems from machismo, the exaggerated masculinity of the men, and the docility of the women.

Images and symbols associated with gender roles, family, and race are particularly powerful. They evoke strong affect; they denote principles of social organization (social reproduction), on the one hand, and "facts" of nature (biological reproduction) on the other (cf. Turner 1967). By transforming social categories into biological ones, they effectively perpetuate the view that these distinctions are part of a natural order, not a social order; that they are grounded in nature, not in the class structure of the society.

As women of color challenge dominant representations—generally within the context of collective action to transform economic, legal, and political constraints on both men and women—they must negotiate the difficult terrain of gender identity and national liberation (see, for example, Garcia 1989; Medicine 1983). Feminist perspectives that do not take account of national and racial oppression are untenable. At the same time, the struggle for gender equality may be constrained by group pressure to conform to hierarchical gender roles, and women seeking to assert their rights are seen as undermining the struggle. For example, active Asian American women have been criticized for weakening male ego and group solidarity (Chow 1987, 288). Among the Lakota Sioux, Beatrice Medicine notes that, similar to the African American experience in the 1960s, nationalist movements have often called for women to play subordinate roles and to be sexually acquiescent (Medicine 1983, 71–72).

In the absence of a broader vision of human liberation, both traditional movements for equality of opportunity and cultural nationalist movements may push women toward subordinate roles. In the struggle for equal rights, concepts of equality are often explicitly or implicitly circumscribed by the gender models of the dominant group. Thus the call to be "treated like a man" is based on extending to men of color the full "rights" of manhood in the United States, including those of gender privilege. Because the relations of oppression often involve "feminization" of men (cf. Said 1979), that is, stripping them of the privileges of masculinity, women of color are caught between the need to assert their equality and the desire to restore the prerogatives of masculinity denied to their men. For women, then, the struggle for racial or national equality may involve acceding to the limitations, as well as the protections, of private patriarchy.

Women often eventually lose out where there are calls for reclamation of culture. Regaining culture is an important aspect of national liberation (see Fanon 1963; Cabral 1973), and women are often seen as culture-bearers. Christian writes of the idealization of African American women in some nationalist poetry, where they are portrayed as the keepers of the moral condition, and are "exhorted to change their ways (i.e. stop being Sapphires or loose women) in order to deserve these titles" (Christian 1985, 16). Tafolla (1985, 45) describes the "Guadalupe complex," in which Chicana women are seen as guardians of tradition. But again the end result may be subordination, whether the intent is to extend the "privileges" of gender roles in the dominant society or in a real or fictive traditional culture. The material base and productive, kinship, and political relations that may have given women real independence in traditional cultures (e.g., African, Native American) no longer exist. What is reconstructed, then, is role asymmetry, which, when combined with contemporary capitalist relations, may lead to gender inequality often surpassing that of traditional cultures. Furthermore, as Amilcar Cabral cautions, reclaiming and developing a national culture is a process that involves criticism of negative elements of traditional culture as well as the integration of the achievements of all humankind (Cabral 1973).

Women of color, for the most part, do not live with (or benefit from) partners who control, to any significant degree, societal resources and power. For this reason they tend to see the quest for women's rights not in individual terms but as linked to a broader struggle to transform economic, political, social, and legal constraints on both men and women. Collective actions, then, must be directed at changing the social conditions that both allow the dominant group to control the manufacture and dissemination of ideological constructions and lend strength and credibility to stereotypes.[8] By organizing to change the social relations that generate ideologies of inequality, collective action can make symbolic transformations meaningful.

From Within the Veil

Ideologies that stigmatize women of color have been central to maintaining class, race, and gender inequality. By masking social relations, by constructing them as "natural" rather than social and historical, these representations justify the continued oppression of African Americans and support gender subordination by stigmatizing women who would challenge the patriarchal model. Further, as part of a broader ideological thrust, they help to counter challenges to the class structure, deflecting attention from structured inequality by blaming African American women and poor people in general for poverty and economic decline.

But though "ideology may mediate contradictions . . . it cannot resolve them" (Wolf 1982, 390). African American women, and other women of color, find themselves in a narrow historical space, caught between ideal models and real social conditions, between the pressures of racial liberation and gender liberation.[9] But such conditions also create the potential for subverting the dominant ideology. For the position of women of color may engender a unique consciousness, informed not only by the double consciousness and second sight of the veil (DuBois 1973) but also by the triple consciousness of being at the forefront of race, class, and gender conflict. Their historical experience creates the basis for deconstructing ideologies (cf. Collins 1990); for a new vision of gender roles; for building, out of "untrammeled independence" (DuBois 1975), "standards for a new womanhood" (Davis 1981). Women of color face the major challenge of how to realize this potential in the context of a broad struggle to eliminate economic exploitation, racial oppression, and gender subordination.

Notes

I would like to thank Maxine Baca Zinn, Bonnie Thornton Dill, Carl Brown, Juan Flores, Sharon Harley, Aisha Khan, and Ida Susser for commenting on the manuscript.

1. The assignment of women's tasks to men and men's tasks to women seems to occur in many forms of slavery. The Nazis, too, sought out adolescent girls from among the incarcerated to move the heavy machinery in armament plants. Dorothy Wertz (1984) suggests that role reversal serves the purpose of degrading the enslaved population and demarcating the enslaved from the free.

2. Cross-cultural studies of slave systems support the view that rape functions to consolidate control of the enslaved population (Wertz 1984).

3. See Leslie 1986 for texts of antebellum apologies for slavery that employ these themes to justify violence in maintaining the social hierarchy.

4. Between 1891 and 1921 there were forty-five acknowledged lynchings of African American women. Several of these women were between fourteen and sixteen years old. A few were pregnant mothers, and one victim was in her eighth month of pregnancy (Katz 1965).

5. The protection of white womanhood seems to be a pervasive feature of racist ideology. In 1903 the Southern Rhodesian Immorality Act was enacted to protect white women but not black women (Hyam 1986). In 1926 the White Women's Protection Act imposed the death penalty in Papua New Guinea for raping a white woman (Inglis 1975). Describing similar measures in Asian colonies, Ann Stoler (1989, 641) notes that "the rhetoric of sexual assault and measures used to prevent it had virtually no correlation with the incidence of rape of European women by men of color. Just the contrary." Not surprisingly, nonwhite women were left unprotected by these measures, though the main threat of interracial rape was generally attacks by white men on women of color.

    The invocation of the theme of protection of white women, which surfaces all over the world as the banner to unite the white population and to justify violence against the colonized and otherwise oppressed, is a subject that requires further study. This will require an exploration of historically scientific definitions of whiteness and the symbolic association of reproduction, family, race, and nation.

6. Stein and Bailey's portrait of the superwoman, who "attempts to provide her husband and children with all the benefits that they would have if she were fully devoted to traditional feminine roles . . . a physically and emotionally exhausting way of living that may have considerable psychological costs" (cited in Palm and Brewer 1979, 6), does not do justice to the race and class issues.

7. That hegemony is not a meaningless concept is evident in the barrage of negative stereotypes of African American women that have penetrated the African American community through music, film, and popular handbooks.

8. For example, the early cohorts of Chinese women in the United States were prostitutes, but this occurred within the context of restrictive immigration laws and the subsequent gender imbalance. The Mexican American family structure is patriarchal, but women's rights were significantly undermined by the legislation that followed conquest.

9. The distance between ideal models of femininity and actual conditions of life does exist for working-class Euro-American women and increasingly for middle-stratum women as well. However, African Americans have historically experienced the sharpest edge of gender role contradictions, in the same manner that they have experienced the brunt of labor exploitation, economic decline, and unemployment.

References

Abercrombie, Nicholas, and Bryan S. Turner. 1978. "The Dominant Ideology Thesis." *British Journal of Sociology* 29(2): 149–70.

Albers, Patricia. 1989. "From Illusion to Illumination: Anthropological Studies of American Indian Women." In Sandra Morgen, ed., *Gender and Anthropology*. Washington, DC: American Anthropological Association.

Almquist, Elizabeth M. 1989. "The Experience of Minority Women in the United States: Intersections of Race, Gender, and Class" In Jo Freeman, ed., *Women: A Feminist Perspective.* 4th ed. Mountain View, CA: Mayfield.

Anyon, Jean. 1984. "Intersections of Gender and Class: Accommodation and Resistance by Working-Class and Affluent Females to Contradictory Sex Role Ideologies." *Journal of Education* 166(1): 25–48.

Atkinson, Maxine, and Jacqueline Boles. 1985. "The Shaky Pedestal: Southern Ladies Yesterday and Today." *Southern Studies* 34(4): 398–406.

Baca Zinn, Maxine. 1982. "Mexican American Women in the Social Sciences." *Signs* 8(2): 259–72.

Barthes, Roland. 1972 [1957]. *Mythologies.* New York: Hill and Wang.

Belenky, Mary Field, Blythe McVicker Clinchy, Nancy Rule Goldberger, and Jill Mattuck Tarule. 1986. *Women's Ways of Knowing: The Development of Self, Voice, and Mind.* New York: Basic Books.

Boles, Jacqueline, and Maxine P. Atkinson. 1986. "Ladies: South by Northwest." *Sociological Spectrum* 6(1): 63–81.

Burton, Orville V. 1985. *In My Father's House Are Many Mansions.* Chapel Hill: University of North Carolina Press.

Cabral, Amilcar. 1973. *Return to the Source.* New York: Africa Information Service.

Campbell, Cathy. 1989. "A Battered Woman Rises: Aunt Jemima's Corporate Makeover." *Village Voice* (November 7): 45–46.

Chow, Esther Ngan-Ling. 1987. "The Development of Feminist Consciousness Among Asian American Women." *Gender and Society* 1(3): 284–99.

Christian, Barbara. 1985. *Black Feminist Criticism: Perspectives on Black Women Writers.* New York: Pergamon.

Collins, Patricia Hill. 1989. "A Comparison of Two Works on Black Family Life." *Signs* 14(4): 875–84.

———.1990. *Black Feminist Thought: Knowledge, Consciousness, and the Politics of Empowerment*. Boston: Unwin Hyman.

Davis, Angela. 1981. *Women, Race, and Class*. New York: Random House.

Dill, Bonnie Thornton. 1994. "Fictive Kin, Paper Sons, and *Compadrazgo:* Women of Color and the Struggle for Family Survival." In Maxine Baca Zinn and Bonnie Thornton Dill, eds., *Women of Color in U.S. Society*. Philadelphia: Temple University Press.

DuBois, W.E.B. 1973 [1953]. *The Souls of Black Folks*. Millwood, NY: Kraus-Thomson Organization.

———. 1975 [1920]. *Dark Water: Voices from Within the Veil*. Millwood, NY: Krauss-Thomson Organization.

Fanon, Frantz. 1963. *The Wretched of the Earth*. New York: Grove Press.

Fox-Genovese, Elizabeth. 1988. *Within the Plantation Household: Black and White Women of the Old South*. Chapel Hill: University of North Carolina.

French, Marilyn. 1977. *The Women's Room*. New York: Summit Books.

Garcia, Alma M. 1989. "The Development of Chicana Feminist Discourse, 1970–1980." *Gender and Society* 3(2): 217–38.

Giddings, Paula. 1984. *When and Where I Enter: The Impact of Black Women on Race and Sex in America*. New York: William Morrow.

Gilkes, Cheryl. 1983. "From Slavery to Social Welfare: Racism and the Control of Black Women." In Amy Swerdlow and Hanna Lessinger, eds., *Class, Race, and Sex: The Dynamics of Control*. Boston: G. K. Hall.

Green, Rayna. 1975. "The Pocahontas Perplex: The Image of Indian Women in American Culture." *Massachusetts Review* 16(4): 698–714.

Gutman, Herbert. 1976. *The Black Family in Slavery and Freedom, 1750–1925*. New York: Pantheon Books.

Hagler, D. Harland. 1980. "The Ideal Woman in the Antebellum South: Lady or Farmwife?" *Journal of Southern History* 46: 405–18.

Hall, Jacquelyn Dowd. 1983. "The Mind that Burns in Each Body: Women, Rape, and Racial Violence." In Ann Snitow, Christie Stansell, and Sharon Thompson, eds., *Powers of Desire: The Politics of Sexuality*. New York: Monthly Review Press..

Harley, Sharon. 1978. "Northern Black Female Workers: 'Jackson Era.'" In Sharon Harley and Rosalyn Terborg-Penn, eds., *The Afro-American Woman: Struggles and Images*. Port Washington, NY: Kennikat Press.

Harris, Marvin. 1968. *The Rise of Anthropological Theory*. New York: Thomas Crowell.

Hine, Darlene Clark. 1989. "Rape and the Inner Lives of Black Women in the Middle West: Preliminary Thoughts on the Culture of Dissemblance." *Signs* 14(4): 912–20.

Horton, James Oliver. 1986. "Freedom's Yoke: Gender Conventions Among Antebellum Free Blacks." *Feminist Studies* 12: 51–76.

Hurtado, Aida. 1989. "Relating to Privilege: Seduction and Rejection in the Subordination of White Women and Women of Color." *Signs* 14(4): 833–55.

Hyam, Ronald. 1986. "Empire and Sexual Opportunity." *Journal of Imperial and Commonwealth History* 14(2): 34–90.

Inglis, Amirah. 1975. *The White Women's Protection Ordinance*. New York: St. Martin's Press.

Jones, Barbara. 1983. "The Economic Status of Black Women." In James Williams, ed., *The State of Black America*. New York: National Urban League.

Jones, Jacqueline. 1982. "My Mother Was Much of a Woman: Black Women, Work, and the Family Under Slavery." *Feminist Studies* 8(2): 235–69.

Katz, Maude White. 1965. "The Negro Woman and the Law." *Freedomways* 2(3): 278–86.

King, May C. 1973. "The Politics of Sexual Stereotypes." *Black Scholar* 4: 12–23.

Laue, James H., and Leon M. McCorkle Jr. 1965. "The Association of Southern Women for the Prevention of Lynching: A Commentary on the Role of the 'Moderate.'" *Sociological Inquiry* 35(1): 80–93.

Leslie, Kent Anderson. 1986. "A Myth of the Southern Lady: Antebellum Proslavery Rhetoric and the Proper Place of Woman." *Sociological Spectrum* 6: 31–49.

Lewis, Diane. 1981. "Black Women Offenders and Criminal Justice: Some Theoretical Considerations." In Marguerite Q. Warren, ed., *Comparing Female and Male Offenders*. Beverly Hills, CA: Sage.

Mann, Susan A. 1989. "Slavery, Sharecropping, and Sexual Inequality." *Signs* 14(4): 774–98.

Medicine, Beatrice. 1983. "Indian Women: Tribal Identity as Status Quo." In Marian Lowe and Ruth Hubbard, eds., *Woman's Nature: Rationalizations of Inequality*. New York: Pergamon Press.

Mirande, Alfredo. 1980. "The Chicano Family: A Reanalysis of Conflicting Views." In Arlene S. Skolnick and Jerome H. Skolnick, eds., *Rethinking Marriage, Sexuality, Child Rearing, and Family Organization*. Berkeley: University of California Press.

Moynihan, Daniel Patrick. 1965. "The Negro Family: The Case for National Action." Reprinted in Lee Rainwater and W. L. Yancey, *The Moynihan Report and the Politics of Controversy*. Cambridge, MA: MIT Press.

Mullings, Leith. 1978. "Ethnicity and Stratification in the Urban United States." *Annals of the New York Academy of Sciences* 318: 10–22.

———. 1992. *Race, Class and Gender: Representation and Reality*. Memphis: Center for Research on Women, Memphis State University.

Neverdon-Morton, Cynthia. 1978. "The Black Woman's Struggle for Equality in the South, 1895–1925." In Sharon Harley and Rosalyn Terborg-Penn, eds., *The Afro-American Woman: Struggles and Images*. Port Washington, NY: Kennikat Press.

Palm, Septima, and Ingrid Brewer. 1979. *The Cinderella Syndrome*. Sarasota, FL: Septima.

Palmer, Phyllis Marynick. 1983. "White Women/Black Women: The Duality of Female Identity and Experience in the United States." *Feminist Studies* 9(1): 151–70.

Perkins, Linda M. 1983. "The Impact of the 'Cult of True Womanhood' on the Education of Black Women." *Journal of Social Issues* 39(3): 17–28.

Rosen, Ruth. 1982. *The Lost Sisterhood: Prostitution in America, 1900–1918*. Baltimore: Johns Hopkins University Press.

Said, Edward. 1979. *Orientalism*. New York: Random House.

Scott, Ann Firor. 1970. *The Southern Lady*. Chicago: University of Chicago Press.

———. 1974. "Women's Perspective on the Patriarchy in the 1850s." *Journal of American History* 61(1): 52–64.

Simms-Wood, Janet. 1988. "The Black Female: Mammy, Jemima, Sapphire, and Other Images." In Jesse Carney Smith, ed., *Images of Blacks in American Culture: A Reference Guide to Information Sources*. Greenwich, CT: Greenwood Press.

Stoler, Ann. 1989. "Making Empire Respectable: The Politics of Race and Sexual Morality in Twentieth Century Colonial Cultures." *American Ethnologist* 16(4): 634–60.

Sundquist, Asebrit. 1987. *Pocahontas & Co.: The Fictional American Indian Woman in Nineteenth-Century Literature: A Study in Method*. Atlantic Highlands, NJ: Humanities Press International.

Tafolla, Carmen. 1985. *To Split a Human: Mitos, Machos, y la Mujer Chicana*. San Antonio: Mexican American Cultural Center.

Terborg-Penn, Rosalyn. 1978. "Black Male Perspectives on the Nineteenth-Century Woman." In Sharon Harley and Rosalyn Terborg-Penn, eds., *The Afro-American Woman: Struggles and Images*. Port Washington, NY: Kennikat Press.

Tiffany, Sharon, and Kathleen Adams. 1985. *The Wild Woman: An Inquiry into the Anthropology of an Idea*. Cambridge, MA: Schenkman.

Turner, Victor. 1967. *The Forest of Symbols*. Ithaca, NY: Cornell University Press.

Wertz, Dorothy C. 1984. "Women and Slavery: A Cross-Cultural Perspective." *International Journal of Women's Studies* 7(4): 373–84.

White, Deborah Gray. 1985. *Ar'n't I a Woman: Female Slaves in the Plantation South*. New York: W. W. Norton.

Williams, Raymond. 1977. *Marxism and Literature*. Oxford: Oxford University Press.

Wilson, William J. 1987. *The Truly Disadvantaged: The Inner City, the Underclass and Public Policy*. Chicago: University of Chicago Press.

Wolf, Eric. 1982. *Europe and the People Without History*. Berkeley: University of California Press.

Ybarra, Lea. 1983. "Empirical and Theoretical Developments in Study of Chicano Families." In Armando Valdez, Albert Camarillo and Tomas Almanguer, eds., *The State of Chicano Research on Family, Labor, and Migration*. Proceedings of the First Stanford Symposium on Chicano Research and Public Policy. Stanford: Stanford Center for Chicano Research.

7

Mapping Gender in African American Political Strategies

I n 1950 Claudia Jones, a Trinidadian immigrant woman who would be deported from the United States during the McCarthy era, wrote:

> An outstanding feature of the present stage of the Negro liberation movement is the growth in the militant participation of Negro women in all aspects of the struggle for peace, civil rights, and economic security. Symptomatic of this new militancy is the fact that Negro women have become symbols of many present-day struggles of the Negro people. This growth of militancy among Negro women has profound meaning, both for the Negro liberation movement and for the emerging anti-fascist, anti-imperialist coalition. (Cited in Busby 1992, 262)

Issues of gender have always been intertwined with national and ethnic processes (West 1992; Walby 1992), as women are involved in struggles of nations, ethnic groups, or national minorities against oppression (Anthias and Yuval-Davis 1989; Jayawardena 1986). For women of African descent in the United States, like their sisters around the world, efforts to challenge gender subordination have been integrally linked to the larger struggle for equality.

This has meant that for African American women, efforts at empowerment have differed fundamentally from those of many Euro-Americans—particularly middle-stratum and elite women—in their groundedness in national liberation struggles. Because African American women have been involved in the construction of an identity within a context of inequality defined by relations of race and class as well as gender, their efforts have been part of the larger struggle of African Americans to define their collective identity and to address the structure of hierarchy.

Given this distinct history, there is no doubt that common features of history and culture have produced an emerging identifiable African American women's consciousness and construction of gender. One scholar who speaks to this, charting the manner in which African Americans have constructed race, class and gender in opposition to the views of the dominant class and how this consciousness expresses itself in everyday life, is Patricia Hill Collins. But critics of her pioneering work *Black Feminist Thought* (1991) argue that her central paradigm is essentialist and even reductionist in its projection of an Afrocentric notion of gender (see White 1990; Thorne 1992).

There is some truth to this. As Collins herself admits, in emphasizing the commonalities she has muted variation, presenting a less nuanced account of the debate about roles of women. But even as we struggle together, we must consider the different ways in which African Americans have defined their collective identity and sought to empower themselves, and the implications of these differences for gender construction.

This chapter will suggest that there are distinct but overlapping paradigms through which African Americans have thought about the liberation project. I will first briefly discuss these approaches, their alternative solutions to the problem of gender, and their implications for issues such as reproduction and family and the participation of women in the liberation project. I will analyze several recent events, including the 1995 Million Man March and the 1991 appointment of Clarence Thomas to the Supreme Court, suggesting that these occasions, however diverse, speak to the central themes of the role of women in struggle and how gender is constructed in African American culture, society, and politics. Though conscious that I run the risk of overstating the differences in African Americans' constructions of race, class, and gender, as Collins may have overstated the commonalities, I would nevertheless argue that while gender has been constructed through common struggles for political empowerment in the African American community, it manifests itself in strikingly different ways.

I

The Deep Structure of African American Politics: Inclusion, Autonomy, or Transformation

Most political theorists have described two perspectives through which African Americans have organized their struggle for equality: integrationist versus nationalist.[1] While the bipolar approach has the elegance of symmetry, it fails to grasp the underlying structure of political culture among African Americans. Though there often appear to be two conflicting political ideologies and cultures, an analysis of the deep structure of African American politics suggests that there are three overlapping paradigms through which African Americans have understood the past and attempted to realize their future: inclusion, autonomy, and transformation. These three approaches, which are the subject of collaborative work I have done with Manning Marable, are discussed in more detail in earlier works (see Marable and Mullings 1994; Marable 1995). Before exploring constructions of gender, I will briefly summarize the contours of each tradition.

In posing this tripartite structure, I recognize that the use of models is inherently limited; that the process of struggle is not static but dynamic; and that these represent orientations within political culture and social development that are neither all-inclusive nor mutually exclusive. Nevertheless, these models reflect significant differences in underlying assumptions about identity—how African Americans define themselves, as well as strategies and goals of the liberation project.

Inclusion

The inclusionist vision assumes that African Americans are Americans who happen to be black. Its historical roots are found in the aspirations of the free Negro communities of the North before the Civil War, in the politics of the younger DuBois and the older A. Philip Randolph. It incorporates the traditional integrationist vision of sectors of the civil rights struggle as well as the neoliberal currents of the post-civil rights period.

The central strategic objective of the inclusionists is integration of African Americans into Euro-American civil society and the expansion of equal opportunities for minorities within the existing capitalist system. Equal opportunity or access is thereby generally sought through struggles within the confines of the social and legal system. The general order of the economic system is rarely questioned except as it relates to exclusion and the failure to live up to the "democratic principles" upon which the United States was allegedly founded.

But therein lie the seeds of a critique. Integrationists may be either conservative or militant; they may seek accommodation or change. Their attempts to change the system may lead to efforts to transform it; in the course of trying to reform the system, activists sometimes discover that hierarchical race relations are not an aberration but a fundamental aspect of the socioeconomic system. Martin Luther King Jr., for example, became very critical of capitalism as an economic system.

Autonomy

The second perspective is perhaps the most difficult to characterize. Popular usage usually designates this current as "black nationalist,"[2] but "autonomist" may be a more accurate label for those movements and people that seek free social space: autonomous geographic, institutional, or cultural space that allows them to participate as equals, either within the parameters of the state or in an altered political relationship with Euro-American civil society. Elements of nationalism can be found in empowerment strategies having to do with group identity, no matter what model they are part of. The back-to-Africa strategies of Martin Delaney in the nineteenth century and Marcus Garvey's Universal Negro Improvement Association in the early twentieth century are well-known historical examples of the call for territorial autonomy.

Given the deeply felt pessimism about the ability or willingness of white civil society to transform itself in order to accept the demands of people of color, nationalist strategies seek empowerment through autonomously controlled institutions that address the needs of African Americans and buffer them from the racism of Euro-Americans. There is often an unwillingness to engage in measures that challenge the basic economic and political system of the state; rather, nationalists often choose to demand autonomous space—hence the demand for territorial integrity, as in the Nation of Islam or the Republic of New Afrika; for economic space, as in the black capitalism of the Congress of Racial Equality; or for the substitution of cultural space for geographic separation, as expressed in the cultural nationalism of Maulana Karenga or in the cultural theory of Afrocentrism. For example, Molefi Asante, one of the major theorists of the academic current of Afrocentrism, says, "Without actually returning to Africa, the closest that African Americans can come to sanity in their relationships with one another is through an Afrocentric awakening rooted both in the African and American history of our people" (Asante 1981, 76).

Among nationalists there is a range of activities and philosophies. At one end of the spectrum one can find the black capitalism of the Congress of Racial Equality, and at the other the League of Revolutionary Black Workers or the Black Panther Party in its early stages, both of which include some form of class analysis (see Marable 1995, 76). What unites these various movements and perspectives is their emphasis on race as the fundamental variable in the distribution of power and consequently as the primary basis for mobilizing people, capital, markets, or politics. Like the inclusionist paradigm, racial categories are assumed to be largely fixed—African Americans are Africans who happen to live in

America. White racism is seen as a permanent reality of America's cultural and social landscape, one that will never change.

Transformation

Though relations between nationalists and the left are frequently fractious, African Americans holding a transformationalist perspective share key elements with autonomists in their identification with people of African descent and their desire to build black institutions and to oppose Euro-American cultural hegemony. However, they differ from both nationalists and inclusionists in their commitment to challenge the fundamental institutions of power, privilege, and ownership on which the contemporary state is based. The historical roots of this tradition may be found in the militancy of Nat Turner and Harriet Tubman, who sought to destroy slavery, as well as the radicalism of the older W.E.B. DuBois and the younger A. Philip Randolph. Other arenas for the enactment of this vision have been manifested, to varying extents, in African American participation in the radical elements of the labor movement, the Southern Youth Congress, the Communist Party, the Black Workers Congress, and recent political movements such as Harold Washington's mayoral campaigns in Chicago in 1983 and 1987, the radical tendency of the antiapartheid movement in the 1980s, and the left wing of Jesse Jackson's Rainbow Coalition.

The objective of this strategy is to dismantle all forms of inequality. Hence race is perceived not in biological or genetic terms but as an unequal relationship between collectivities, held in place by violence and power. African American liberation is simultaneously central to the larger struggle to reorganize power and resources on a global basis and dependent on changing the larger power relationships. Consequently, commitment to African American liberation is expressed not only through attempts to reorganize larger structures of power but also through transformative strategies directed toward specific class relationships that directly affect African Americans.

Interrelationships

It is extremely important not to oversimplify or reify what are in fact broad, overlapping traditions. First and foremost, each perspective is an attempt to address the problem of racism in American society, and each grapples with the question of empowerment of African Americans. All three traditions include both accommodationist and radical possibilities. Within each current we find individuals dedicated to the liberation of African Americans and who have been willing to die for this commitment.

Hence there have always been, and will always be, grounds for unity among those approaching the empowerment of African Americans from different perspectives. Indeed, political activists working within each of the three paradigms frequently utilize identical discourses, slogans, and forms of representation. For example, within each critical perspective, the empowerment of African Americans is phrased as the quest for "freedom." However, the meaning of freedom may differ significantly; those advocating inclusion into, autonomy from, and transformation of American society often work with very different strategic models about economics, politics, structure, culture, family life, and the role of women.

Real movements and real people frequently embody elements of various political directions, as was the case with the civil rights movement of the 1960s. Individuals may begin their activist careers with one set of perspectives and move to another. Today's inclusionist or nationalist may be tomorrow's transformationist. For example, Martin Luther King Jr. began his career by attempting to achieve integration through civil disobedience. By the final two years of his life, his confrontation with the machinery of the state had led him to question the basic premises of capitalism. He took an active stand in opposition to the Vietnam War and was assassinated as he was in the process of organizing the 1968 Poor People's March on Washington. From another direction, Malcolm X, as a young minister of the Nation of Islam, called for strict racial separation, noninvolvement in political affairs, and a solution to U.S. racial problems through creation of a black state. By the end of his life, he had acquired elements of a transformationist perspective. He was a staunch critic of capitalism, strongly opposed the war in Vietnam, and favored a strategy of African American empowerment that would ultimately make national and international alliances with forces outside of the African American community.

Furthermore, the majority of African Americans do not narrowly define themselves as belonging exclusively in one ideological camp or another, but may be influenced by the particular juncture of personal, political, historical, and economic forces in their lives at a given point in time. If we were to think of these currents as overlapping spheres, most African Americans, much of the time, might place themselves at the center—the nexus where all three ideologies overlap.

The Crucible of Gender

Each paradigm has very different implications for the construction of gender. Gender is not just about women; it is about the social *relationship* between men

and women and the dialectical, reciprocal, and cultural construction of femininity and masculinity.

Recognition of a unique historical experience concerning gender informs the
perspectives of African Americans of various political persuasions. This history
incorporates a land of origin with certain common principles about gender and
family (see chapter 4). It also encompasses the African American experience in
the United States where the denial of many "protections" offered by gender roles
and indeed sometimes inversion of such roles was a means of maintaining control (see chapter 6). Hence asserting the right to assume gender-based roles of
husband, father, wife and mother paradoxically was an act of resistance. The
manner in which African American people have envisioned relationships of gender in light of that history, has expressed itself in markedly different forms.

"I Am a Man"

For those who believe that African American empowerment is best achieved
through integration into U.S. society, the vision of ideal gender roles is generally
developed against the backdrop of the dominant Euro-American model, and the
struggle for inclusion in Euro-American civil society includes the "privileges" of
gender. Freedom is frequently identified with masculinity. Consequently the
right to be treated like a "man" was a recurrent theme in the civil rights movement. Slogans ("I am a man")[3] and songs ("How many roads must a man walk
down before you call him a man?") metaphorically equated manhood with
equality. While these examples in part reflect the semantics of generic usage, the
thrust of the inclusionist current has been to seek gender privileges within the
dominant paradigm: to claim for African American men the privileges of manhood and to seek for African American women the protections of patriarchy
denied to them by the dominant culture.

Historically, African American women, like other working women (see Laslett
and Brenner 1989), have used appeals to the traditional gender role model to
demand family wages for men. During the period of sharecropping or debt peon-
age, working women used the language of traditional gender roles (Gutman
1976, 167) to exert some control over their labor, emphasizing their roles as
homemakers rather than as workers. Similarly for middle-stratum African
American women, "gender-defined work and domestic responsibilities were
symbolic of their new status" (Harley 1978, 170), and women in organizations
such as the National Association of Colored Women strongly encouraged con-
formity to Euro-American models of womanhood (Higginbotham 1992, 271).

In the church, despite Brown's (1994) contention that Afro-Baptists, for example, perpetuate African cultural values of complementarity rather than the

androcentric bias of the Pauline scriptures, Christianity has helped to shape the representation of women primarily as mothers and helpmeets to men. Reverend Martin Luther King Jr. once wrote, "The primary obligation of the woman is motherhood" (quoted in Fairclough 1987, 50).

In keeping with the view that African Americans are Americans who happen to be black, the inclusionist strategy seeks for Americans of African descent the rights, obligations, and roles of Euro-American society as they are defined by gender. For many this is mediated by recognition of the special history of African American women. Furthermore, as traditional Euro-American gender roles are themselves challenged by the civil rights and women's movements, there is often a tendency to favor the extension of democratic rights to women, but generally within the parameters of the economic, political, and legal system of capitalism. However, the implicit acceptance of the foundations of capitalism inevitably reproduces patriarchal relationships.

Women, Men, and Nation

Patriarchal gender relationships are characteristic of many nationalist positions; the referent, however, is not Euro-American models of gender but "traditional" societies, religions, or philosophies. For those seeking territorial and/or cultural autonomy, the gender relations of a Eurocentric society are to be rejected as African Americans reestablish alternative gender relations that have their origins in a traditional "golden age" (see chapter 6). In this view, gender relations become an aspect of the larger project of building autonomous black institutions, culture, and society. In this construction of the past, men and women have complementary, harmonious roles.

Nationalist gender relationships, though phrased in terms of complementarity, tend to be largely patriarchal even when the discourse is gender-neutral. Women are thought to have different, but complementary, spheres of work, intellects, abilities, and sensitivities. Among the more enlightened who have tried to come to terms with gender, the woman's sphere may be considered as important as the man's. Molefi Asante, for example, emphasizes complementarity. Men and women, who

> are equally the source of our strength and indeed our genius . . . in a relation-
> ship must be attuned to the primary objective of all Afrocentric unions: the
> productive and creative maintenance of the collective cognitive imperative.
> (Asante 1981, 77–78)

Maulana Karenga, the inventor of Kwanza (and who appears to have significantly modified his view of gender over the years) states, "Black men and black women have always been equal. . . . The argument for sexual inequality is based on supposed biological differences" (Karenga 1978, 80).

While I have argued elsewhere that complementarity in and of itself need not result in inequality (Mullings 1976), assumptions about inferiority and superiority are usually implicit in frameworks of complementarity that operate within the context of a hierarchical society. This is more clearly expressed in a classic statement from *Mwanamke Mwananchi (The Nationalist Woman)*, a pamphlet published in the early 1970s:

> We understand that it is and has been traditional that the man is the head of the house. He is the leader of the house/nation because his knowledge of the world is broader, his awareness is greater, his understanding is fuller and his application of this information is wiser. . . . After all, it is only reasonable that the man be the head of the house because he is able to defend and protect the development of his home. . . . Women cannot do the same things as men— they are made by nature to function differently. Equality of men and women is something that cannot happen even in the abstract world. Men are not equal to other men, i.e., ability, experience, or even understanding. The value of men and women can be seen as in the value of gold and silver—they are not equal but both have great value. We must realize that men and women are a complement to each other because there is no house/family without a man and his wife. Both are essential to the development of any life. (Quoted in Combahee River Collective [1977] 1982, 19)

The perception of women as different and inferior is not merely a product of a prefeminist period. The recent diatribe by nationalist Shahrazad Ali (1989) in a widely publicized (though self-published) volume, *The Black Man's Guide to Understanding the Black Women*, holds women, whose "brain is smaller than the Blackman's" (p. 177), responsible for the problems of African American men and advocates physical violence against them if they are not acquiescent.

Whether "complementarity" is phrased frankly as superiority and inferiority or in more gender-neutral language, women are associated primarily with the domestic sphere. Their reproductive capacity is essentialized and becomes the primary aspect of their identity. Hence Molefi Asante refers to "a woman's time to create and a man's time to produce" (Asante 1981, 78). Nationalist scholar Nathan Hare expresses these assumptions in policy recommendations: "The most basic solution to the black or oppressed female's condition . . . will be unavoidably in the reproductive/sexual realm, while the solution to the male's condition will be notably in the sphere of productive/social instrumentality" (Hare 1989, 169).

Furthermore, the common denominator of most of these perspectives is an idealist approach to gender roles. The discourse about gender is generally not grounded in the material history of African American women but rather in metaphysical constructions of a traditional golden-age society. Women are essential to the ultimate and overriding project of building autonomous spaces—institutions, culture, society. But for this reason there is also an implicit need to control women.

Consequently the nexus between motherhood, family, and nationhood means that women may be seen as guardians of the nation and national culture and are granted an honored place in the national project. The attractions of the sense of dignity and protection inherent in this representation should not be lightly dismissed. In Iran, for example, Afshar describes women's positive reactions to the emotive nationalist projection of women's role in nation building, centered around concepts of home and dignity. Though there was widespread support for the Iranian revolution on the basis of nationalism, as the fundamentalists gained state power women were more directly limited to the domestic arena and designated as unequal before the law (for example, unable to give evidence unsupported by a male witness and "in many cases entitled to half as much justice as their male counterpart") (Afshar 1989, 124). To women of African descent, who have historically borne the double burdens of work and home, a language of complementarity, protection, or even frank patriarchy may be very seductive.

However, the other side of the coin of protection may be control. Hence, in *Message to the Blackman,* Elijah Muhammad, longtime patriarch of the Nation of Islam, asserts that the first step in self-knowledge is "the *control* [italics added] and the protection of our own women" (Muhammad 1965, 59). While protection may be suffused with benevolence and control associated with coercion, the two are linked by notions of women as property; Elijah Muhammad writes, "The woman is the man's field to reproduce his nation"(Muhammad 1965, 58).

Standards for a New Womanhood

Activists who represent the transformationalist approach have generally advocated dismantling relations of patriarchy as well as other structures of inequality, which are seen as inextricably linked.[4] For those within this tradition, gender is constructed, in the first instance, from the materiality of the experiences of African American women as workers and participants in the struggle as well as mothers.

For example, W.E.B. DuBois was, in his political and public life, if not in his intimate relationships, consistently committed to women's rights. He wrote several essays calling for "the emancipation of women" in *Crisis,* the journal he edited from 1910–1934. In 1912 he authored a pamphlet entitled *Disenfranchisement,* published by the National American Woman Suffrage Association, in which he asserted women's right to vote as a necessary precondition for the realization of democracy. He was an enthusiastic supporter of women workers, and he also urged African American husbands to "share housework" (Marable 1983, 82–83). Reviewing DuBois's sizeable body of work on African American women, Morton (1991, 64) notes, "In his own era DuBois was a pioneer in the transformation of even the most dehumanizing images of blackwomanhood into empowering symbols of worth."

Similarly, Angela Davis's work on women, race, and class attempts to examine the social construction of gender within the context of class and race relations. As a historical materialist analysis, it simultaneously addresses not only the reality of gender inequality and its meaning to African Americans but also issues of class and race. Exploring the material history of African American women, "the accumulated experiences of all those women who toiled under the lash for their masters, worked for and protected their families, fought against slavery, and who were beatened and raped, but never subdued," she suggests that they have passed on "a legacy spelling out standards for a new womanhood" (Davis 1981, 29).

But it is also true that among those who call for dismantling all forms of inequality, there have been sharp differences about how gender subordination is linked to other forms of inequality. Conflicts may take the form of romanticizing sexism in the working class or relegating various aspects of the struggle for women's rights to "bourgeois feminism." Efforts to gain equality for women may be seen as a diversion from the struggle against race and class oppression.

Notions of gender are fluid, and people modify their views in light of their experiences. For example, though Malcolm X never became an active advocate for women's equality, he struggled against the misogyny and patriarchal notions of his earlier years. In the latter years of his life, he appears to have changed his ideas about women, as he did about other things. Following his second African trip, he said,

> So one of the things I became thoroughly convinced of in my recent travels is the importance of giving freedom to the woman, giving her education, and giving her the incentive to get out there and put that same spirit and understanding in her children. And I frankly am proud of the contribution that our women have made in the struggle for freedom and I'm one person who's for giving them all the leeway possible because they've made a greater contribution than many of us men. (X 1970, 179)

II

Women's Place

The different approaches to gender outlined above may manifest themselves in policy alternatives. This may be illustrated by examining two salient issues: reproductive rights and the participation of women in the liberation project. For each of these, after noting areas of unity, I will indicate some of the differences in public positions of individuals and organizations associated with inclusionist, autonomist, and transformationist traditions.

Reproduction and Family

As people seek to reproduce themselves, they often do so within a context of "stratified reproduction," where some populations are empowered to reproduce and others are not (Ginsburg and Rapp 1995, 3). For African Americans, issues of reproduction have not been relegated to the private sphere, but have often been in the public arena.[5] Pressures to encourage or limit reproduction have varied with the historical moment: for example, during slavery African American women were often forcibly encouraged to reproduce the labor force, but in the contemporary period of deindustrialization and rising unemployment, their reproductive capacity has become a matter for national attention (see chapter 5). For many African Americans, regardless of their political orientation, issues about continuity and genocide have been real concerns.

Reproduction takes place within a complex set of social arrangements, and African Americans of most political persuasions would probably agree that the family has been a buffer from slavery and racism and that the struggle for family is part and parcel of the liberation struggle. But as Rapp (1987) reminds us, people mean different things by "family."

It is not surprising that questions of reproductive choice are strongly debated. The disagreements we find in the general population are reflected in microcosm in those who favor the strategy of integration. For example, there is a national organization of African Americans opposed to abortion, and African American clergymen have often been conservative on this issue. African American politicians, however, have generally supported reproductive rights.

While many inclusionists favor reproductive rights, often attending to the theoretical and tactical relationship between civil rights and women's rights, this concession does not necessarily extend to rethinking the premises of the patriarchal family. Though recognizing the variety of family forms and the strains on such families, inclusionists have generally supported the patriarchal nuclear family as ideal. They are frequently uncritical of the right-wing call for "family values," implicit in which is the notion that the decline of the "traditional" nuclear family is at the heart of increasing poverty among African Americans.

Uncritical acceptance of the dominant society's model of gender and family roles is perhaps most clearly evident in the work of sociologist William Julius Wilson (1987). While Wilson's analysis of conditions that produce increasing rates of households headed by women is very useful, he does not problematize the normative gender roles underlying his analysis. Documenting the relationship between the rising numbers of households headed by women and skyrocketing male unemployment among African Americans, his policy proposals are directed toward increasing the number of marriageable black males by giving priority to employment and education opportunities for African American men. While few would deny the importance of addressing male joblessness, Wilson's proposals accept and reinforce the traditional model of gender roles as an effective solution to the social problems facing African American households (see chapter 8).

Given the centrality of reproduction in the nationalist project, it is not surprising that their position on a reproductive rights is often conservative. Historically, nationalists have not been supportive of a woman's right to choose. For example, in 1934 Marcus Garvey's Universal Negro Improvement Association issued a resolution condemning the use of birth control for African Americans (Marable 1983, 83). The pronouncement of Louis Farrakhan, national leader of the Nation of Islam, that "when the black woman kills her unborn child she is murdering the advancement of her nation" (quoted in Marable 1983, 84–85) is a logical consequence of Elijah Muhammad's view that "the woman is man's field to reproduce his nation" (Muhammad 1965, 58).

Reproductive functions are ideally organized in the context of the patriarchal, perhaps polygynous, family. For nationalist groups that practice polygyny, it may be seen as both a return to African traditions and a response to the scarcity of African American men. Black poet and cultural critic Haki Madhubuti, for example, calls for "the quality of sharing" in the wake of the shortage of black men. His extension of this "choice" to women as well is perhaps somewhat disingenuous, given that the actual constraints of demography would insure that the "sharing" is done almost exclusively by women. Despite what appears to be balance in his discussion, women are nonetheless viewed as markers of ethnic boundaries and the property of the African American community: black women forming families with white men (in the absence of available black men) results in "a very serious consequence in terms of Black genocide" (Madhubuti 1978, 144).

A woman's rights over her own body need not always be juxtaposed to racial genocide. At the same time that Marcus Garvey condemned African American women's right to use birth control, DuBois strongly endorsed Planned Parenthood and invited Margaret Sanger to contribute articles on birth control to *Crisis*. Similarly, Manning Marable ([1991] and in press) presents a very nuanced view of reproductive rights, noting that in light of African American history, the fear of genocide is not unreasonable. Nonetheless, he insists on women's right to choose in the context of freedom and responsibility. Reverend Jesse Jackson has also supported reproductive rights, appearing at rallies and marches in support of choice in reproductive matters.

For those who seek to undermine patriarchal relations, the traditional family may be an arena in which these relationships are produced and reproduced. Contemporary family organization and function is seen not as "natural" or given but as historically determined. As Johnnetta Cole suggests:

> The nature and state of "the American family" cannot be understood without a recognition of the diversity of the groupings which bear the label "family" and the varied, complex, and often contradictory place of women within them. (Cole 1986, 116)

In this view public policy need not be based on reproducing the "traditional" patriarchal family.

Women's Roles in the Liberation Project

African Americans across the political spectrum would agree that three themes have been characteristic of the liberation project historically. First, for most women as well as men, the struggle for African American liberation took priority over struggles around gender. Furthermore, most recognize the unprecedented role played by women in the liberation project and simultaneously the denial of traditional Euro-American masculine roles to African American men. Though African Americans have different takes on how this history should inform contemporary relationships, in most inclusionist and autonomist organizations this experience, as well as the dominant ideology, has become part of the rationale for limiting the participation of women.

In the African American church, for example, though women often constitute the bulk of the congregations, the ministry is a vehicle of social mobility for men. In the mainstream denominations, biblical ideology promotes the subordination of women, who are not proportionally represented in leadership. A survey of the clergy of 2,150 African American "mainline" congregations in 1990 revealed that only 66, or 3.7 percent, were women (Baer 1993, 67). Even among the Afro-Baptists, where women are most active, women pastors, preachers, or evangelists are rare. Indeed, Brown suggests, "With the active complicity of women, men monopolize corporate leadership in the home and church" (Brown 1994, 173).

Similarly, if we examine the involvement of women in inclusionist political organizations, women have played more significant roles than in comparable Euro-American organizations and have generally unhesitatingly supported men and the struggle for the greater good of African Americans (see, for example, Jones 1985). But though they often constituted the shock troops in voter registration, boycotts, and civil disobedience and played major roles in initiating the militant actions around the Montgomery bus boycott, women rarely hold leadership positions in traditional civil rights organizations such as the Southern Christian Leadership Conference (SCLC), the Congress of Racial Equality (CORE), and the Student Noviolent Coordinating Committee (SNCC) (see Giddings 1984, 313–14; Jones 1985). For example, the two women who served on the executive staff of the SCLC both complained of the ways in which male chauvinism limited their leadership (Fairclough 1987, 49–50). Though women were represented in leadership and decision making in SNCC, Stokely Carmichael's infamous (and, it is to be hoped, joking) 1964 rebuttal to a position paper criticizing SNCC's treatment of women—"The only position for women in SNCC is prone" (Giddings 1984, 302; Jones 1985, 283)—did little to advance the issue of gender equality.

The traditional civil rights organizations have not made much progress in this area. For example, in the National Association for the Advancement of Colored People (NAACP) in 1994, ten of the twelve top executive positions were held by men, despite the fact that approximately two thirds of the membership are female. Similarly, in 1994 the SCLC and the Urban League were both led by men.

In many autonomist projects women's roles are circumscribed. In the 1970s Amiri Baraka, for example, insisted that women should not be involved in men's discussions. (He has since changed his position.) The Republic of New Afrika called for a return to a male patriarchal system where men made decisions (Giddings 1984). Angela Davis described her encounters with Karenga's organization US while organizing for a rally in San Diego in 1967:

> I was criticized very heavily, especially by male members of Karenga's organization, for doing a man's job. Women should not play a leadership roles, they insisted. A woman was supposed to "inspire" her man and educate his children. The irony of their complaint was that much of what I was doing had fallen to me by default. (Davis 1974, 161)

Today, with some notable exceptions (such as Shahrazad Ali's suggestion that women who defy men's leadership should be offered "a sound open-handed slap in the mouth" [1989, 170]), the public representation of women's roles in the liberation struggle is usually phrased in terms of complementarity and protection, as participants seek to reclaim leadership roles for men that existed in an ancestral society.

One of the most significant expressions of public activism around representations of gender in contemporary African American politics was the Million Man March. On October 16, 1995, perhaps as many as 1,000,000 African Americans went to Washington, D.C. for a day of racial unity and "atonement."[6]

The process of organization leading up to the march embodied the twin themes of protection and control of women and demonstrated points of unity in the nationalist and inclusionist perspectives on gender. The overwhelmingly male march was called by Minister Louis Farrakhan, the national leader of the Nation of Islam, after holding mass meetings of African American men in major cities across the United States at which women were often turned away at the door. Reverend Benjamin Chavis, after being stripped of his position as national secretary of the NAACP ostensibly for using organizational funds for the settlement of a sexual harrassment lawsuit, became national director of the march.

The Nation of Islam requested that the march be confined to men only; women were to stay at home, watch the children and pray. According to Farrakhan,

> We are asking the Black woman, particularly our mothers, to be with our children, teaching them the value of home, self-esteem, family and unity; and to work with us to ensure the success of the March and our mission to improve the quality of life for our people. We take this historical moment to recognize the major contributions that the Black woman has made and continues to make, toward the advancement of our people.[7]

> The march is not against females, it's not to say we don't love our women. But we must do something to atone for what we have done to our women and atone for the abuse we have heaped on our women.[8]

To questions about why women would not be participating in the march, Chavis replied:

> In the 1960s as a tactic in the civil rights movement, we put our women and children on the front line. We were under the false assumption that there was some humanity in the power structure that would respect women and chil-

dren. But they were beaten down, murdered, maimed, cattle prodded, fire hosed and bitten by police dogs.[9]

Conrad Muhammad, leader of the Nation of Islam's Harlem temple, explained:

> We are going to Washington because we have not been what we should be to black women. . . . We ask them to respect our need to walk shoulder to shoulder to reconcile with each other and atone to our God.

When asked about the participation of women in the African National Congress and Frelimo, he stated,

> The Honorable Minister Louis Farrakhan and the Nation of Islam genuinely believe it's a sad man that sends his women into battle before himself . . . we believe as men it is our duty to go out on the front line.[10]

While the public discourse of the march leaders emphasized the protection of women, others seemed more concerned with control. A. Asadullah Samad, in a column in the *Los Angeles Sentinel,* defended the male-only composition of the march:

> Sisters gotta stay home on this one. I know you ain't used to anybody telling you what you can do or where you can go. That might be part of the problem (more on this later). . . . Now correct me if I'm wrong, but I don't remember reading anywhere where Moses or any of the other prophets had to deal with women running up to them talking about, "Can I go? I wanna go see Pharaoh, too?" . . . Until the black man regains the respect *(and control)* of his women, he will never regain the respect of the larger society. (Samad 1995, italics added)

The march was supported by a wide spectrum of the African American community. Many African American women, including elected officials, officials of civil rights organizations, and members of sororities, enthusiastically supported the male-only march. This is not surprising given the historical burden of work and family carried by African American women throughout their history. To many women, the call for men to take responsibility was a welcome one. In an op-ed piece that appeared as a letter to the editor in *The Final Call,* the newspaper of the Nation of Islam, a CEO of a marketing firm and board member of the Baltimore chapter of the NAACP explained why she supported the all-man march:

> I say to them [African American men], you are not only worthy, but capable of assuming your rightful place as the "Kings of the Village." For women to

attempt to deny these brothers the right to claim this day would only affirm the European influence in our lives. No, I have no problem with "staying home" and going into prayer for these men, the mission and Black America.[11]

Progressives argued that while there is no inherent contradiction in single-sex movements, the march perpetuated divisions based on gender. As criticism mounted, the march leaders modified their stand on gender, and the widows of Martin Luther King Jr., Medgar Evers, and Malcolm X were asked to "represent" women in the march. Rosa Parks, the catalyst of the Montgomery bus boycott, poet Maya Angelou, and a few other women were added to the speakers' platform. Nevertheless, the underlying paradigm of the march, based on the patriarchal world view of the Nation of Islam, was not significantly transformed.

In a national context of mounting racism, the call for a march struck a chord among the majority of African Americans. The march was a massive demonstration against the demonization of African American men and was successful in promoting and renewing feelings of solidarity, unity, and purpose among those who participated. It is nevertheless true that the organizers conceived of the Million Man March in terms of a patriarchal vision—a collective statement of manhood and self-assertion on the part of African American men, with women deliberately relegated to arenas outside political and social confrontation. This framework is compatible with the patriarchy of both the inclusionist and autonomist perspectives. Hugh Price, the president of the National Urban League, referred to the Million Man March as "the largest family-values rally in the history of the United States" (Gates 1996, 128).

Those organizations seeking to radically alter the structure of hierarchical relationships have not been immune from the influence of the "Moynihan thesis"—that the activist roles played by African American women have emasculated African American men. The Black Panther Party, for example, presents a complex case. Though the party was certainly characterized by serious problems of misogyny and sexism, women were integrated into the party leadership, and party members were influenced by leftist liberation movements that projected progressive views about the participation of women. For example, a Black Panther woman leader stated: "We feel that the example given us by the Vietnamese women is a prime example of the role women can play in the revolution" (Black Panther Party 1969, 22). At the founding of the party, one of the "Eight Points of Attention" was "Do not take liberties with women."

In the more traditional leftist movements, certainly ideology (if not always practice) supported the participation of women in political projects. Though practice was often inconsistent, leftist organizations with significant African American membership, such as the Communist Party, could boast of an array of

African American women leaders, including Claudia Jones, Charlene Mitchell, and Angela Davis. Though the Marxist paradigm presented some limitations for the analysis of gender and gender oppression, these organizations differ significantly from the others discussed here in placing women in leadership positions as well as in giving ideological support to the deconstruction of patriarchy.

What preliminary conclusions can we draw from this? One aspect of inequality has been the dominant class's attempt to deny the humanity of Africans and African Americans by refusing them the attributes of gender. Within each political tradition, African Americans have challenged this by imagining and constructing gender relationships in distinct ways.

Literally coming from different places, those seeking inclusion and autonomy appear to construct very different models of gender relationships. Inclusionists seek equal opportunity and access to the gender privileges of the dominant Euro-American society, and many would support an expansion of women's rights within the confines of the existing legal system. Autonomists, on the other hand, reject the Eurocentric framework and seek to establish or reestablish gender relationships based on an ancestral tradition. Phrased in the language of complementarity (which easily shades into inequality), the division of labor, in which women's primary sphere is the domestic arena, is not a result of mutual agreement but rather is assumed to be a natural consequence of women's reproductive capacities. By reifying the cultural alternative, the material conditions of African American women's experiences and struggles as workers are often obscured.

Dissimilar as they seem, there are underlying continuities between the inclusionist and autonomist perspectives. The final product of both strategic visions is a patriarchal model of gender roles in which masculinity is defined by the dependence of women. Within both currents, gender, like race, appears to be essentialized and fixed rather than historically and socially constructed. Though each attempts to grant women the protection and respect that was not forthcoming in the dominant society, this form of resistance accommodates and reproduces gender inequality. Thus the patriarchal theme put forward by the organizers of the Million Man March, for example, contradicted neither the Eurocentric patriarchy of the inclusionists nor the traditional model of patriarchy subscribed to by many nationalists, including the Nation of Islam.

While the nationalists pose an alternative model of gender roles, those within the transformationist perspective pose an oppositional model. However unsuccessful they may be in implementing it, they seek to deconstruct a definition of masculinity defined by the dependence of women. In this sense gender, like race, is seen as a social construction, based on historically unequal social relationships.

III

The Nomination of Clarence Thomas: Race and Gender

In addition to the Million Man March, several recent public controversies have clearly demonstrated both the tensions around race and gender for African American women and the varied approaches to configuring these relationships. One of the most momentous events—one with profound implications for the future—was the national debate concerning the nomination of Clarence Thomas to the U.S. Supreme Court. Though this topic has been analyzed in tedious detail (see, for example, Morrison 1992; Hill and Jordan 1995), it is a good example of how the different constructions of gender can play themselves out in a situation that has repercussions for millions of people.

On July 1, 1991, Clarence Thomas, a black conservative Republican, was nominated by then-President Bush to replace Thurgood Marshall on the Supreme Court. After being contacted by staff members of the congressional Judiciary Committee, Anita Hill, an African American attorney who had worked with Thomas, confirmed that Clarence Thomas had sexually harassed her. Congressional hearings on the nomination were carried live on several television networks. Thomas denied any sexual misconduct, labeling the hearings a "high-tech lynching for uppity blacks." Despite several corroborating witnesses and a lie detector test passed by Hill, the Senate voted 52–48 to confirm Clarence Thomas as an associate justice of the Supreme Court on October 16, 1991.

The nomination of Clarence Thomas to the Supreme Court highlighted tensions around race and gender. Most African Americans of various political stripes—with the exception of the sociologist Orlando Patterson, who suggested that the televised hearings "reconfirmed" the democratic process and won African Americans "unambiguous inclusion; unquestioned belonging" in American society (Patterson 1991, 79)—were concerned about the manner in which the televised spectacle could be used against African Americans. An unwillingness to publicly demonstrate disunity was one of the central factors responsible for the majority support Thomas received in the African American community.

Though divided, a wide spectrum from inclusionists to nationalists embraced the notion that Clarence Thomas's elevation to the Supreme Court was a necessary evil. This included scholars such as Jacquelyne Johnson Jackson, who stated, "I supported Thomas' confirmation . . . because he was George Bush's *only* black star" (Jackson 1991–92, 49).

The inclusionist organizations, particularly the traditional civil rights organizations, either voted to confirm or did not effectively oppose the nomination. Though the Congressional Black Caucus Foundation eventually voted to oppose the nomination, the NAACP, while finally coming out against Thomas, issued an equivocal statement and did not take the lead in mobilizing opposition.

Inclusionist organizations supported Thomas on the basis of what Marable (1995) has termed "symbolic representation," the underlying assumption that the appointment of one of their own would inevitably work for the benefit of all African Americans. Hence the Southern Christian Leadership Conference voted to confirm the nomination, claiming that Thomas's experience as a black man "has subjected him to the 'Black Experience' that will help him to continue to grow more and more sensitive to the responsibility of the Supreme Court to insure justice for all" (Lowery 1991–92, 152). The Urban League voted neither to support nor to oppose him, expressing the hope that Thomas's "life experiences will lead him to closer identification with those in America who are victimized by poverty and discrimination" (Jacobs 1991–92, 153).

Nationalists supported Thomas on the basis of racial solidarity. Niara Sudarkasa, the president of Lincoln University, testified before the Senate Judiciary Committee on Thomas's behalf, closing with the plea that "we must not rest until Dr. King's dream becomes a reality" (Sudarkasa 1991–2, 102). For both inclusionists and autonomists, race outweighed other considerations, and the acceptance of a patriarchal model rationalized the disregard for issues of gender discrimination. Karenga, for example, neither strongly indicted Thomas's politics nor gave sufficient attention to gender, painting Clarence Thomas and Anita Hill as "a pathetic pair of seduced, opposing surrogates" of white conservatives and feminists (Karenga 1991–92, 68). Counterposing race and gender, he asked whether women should make a claim that will result in "collateral and devastating damage to African people" (p. 60), calling for unity "for a house divided among itself is a gift to the enemy" (p. 62) and asserting that the African American movement must continue to give weight to gender issues, but not at the expense of the African American struggle (p. 64).

In general, those holding a transformationist perspective challenged the nomination of Clarence Thomas. Reverend Jesse Jackson opposed it. Scholars such as Gerald Horne (1991–92) and Barbara Ransby urged consideration of class and gender as well as race. For Ransby the "hearings highlighted . . . the increasing hostility toward and scapegoating of black women . . . [and] the rise . . . of black neo-conservatives" (Ransby 1991–92, 82). Ransby and others organized a statement, signed by 1,603 women of African descent, entitled "African American Women in Defense of Ourselves," which appeared in the *New York Times* on

November 17, 1991. The text indicted the Bush administration for the nomination and addressed the interrelationship of class, race, and gender issues, noting:

> The consolidation of a conservative majority on the Supreme Court seriously endangers the rights of all women, poor and working class people and the elderly. The seating of Clarence Thomas is an affront not only to African American women and men, but to all people concerned with social justice.[12]

Clarence Thomas was confirmed by the Senate committee on October 16, nearly a month before this statement appeared. I suggest that what Karenga described as "devastating damage" to African Americans lay not in Anita Hill's accusations but rather in the uncritical view of racial unity adopted by many inclusionists and nationalists and their failure to address gender issues (or, frankly, sexism), which has helped to produce a disaster of unmitigated proportions. In less than four years on the court, Thomas had supported—indeed sometimes as the swing vote—measures that undercut democratic rights and opportunities for African Americans, women, poor and working people, and all Americans.

Thomas has voted with the majority to refuse to stay the deportation of Haitian refugees; to limit the scope of the Voting Rights Act in an Alabama case in which newly elected black representatives were stripped of power by white commissioners before they could take their seats; and to weaken the National Labor Relations Board act that allowed union organizers to leaflet in parking lots adjacent to stores they are trying to organize.

When this conservative court has been too liberal for his tastes, he has issued dissenting opinions. He signed onto the dissenting opinion in *Planned Parenthood v. Casey*, asserting that the *Roe v. Wade* decision should be overruled and that states should be free to permit or ban abortion. At a point in history when one in three African American men between the ages of twenty and twenty-nine are involved in the criminal justice system[13] and prisons serve as warehouses for unemployed African American and Latino youth, Thomas was one of two Supreme Court justices to dissent when the court held that the use of excessive physical force against a prisoner can violate the Eighth Amendment ban on cruel and unusual punishment. His dissent on this issue prompted a *New York Times* editorial entitled "The Youngest, Cruelest Justice" (Rosenthal, 1992) and Justice Sandra O'Connor to write in her majority opinion that Thomas's dissent ignored "concepts of dignity, civilized standards, humanity and decency that animate the Eighth Amendment" (quoted in Coyle 1992, 40).

Most significant in retarding the gains of the civil rights movement, Thomas was the swing vote in 5–4 decisions that curbed affirmative action programs allowing federal benefits to members of minority groups and invalidated

Georgia's 11th Congressional District, a majority black voting district, laying the groundwork for eliminating several majority black districts and decreasing the number of African Americans in Congress. Thomas was the swing vote in the decision holding that lower federal courts acted improperly in ordering the state to pay for a school desegregation plan in Kansas City, which is expected to open the door for decreasing federal involvement in school desegregation and even the rethinking of *Brown v. Board of Education.* According to the *National Law Journal,* Thomas has proven "more than willing to join those justices pushing hardest to the right" (Coyle 1992, 40).

The Thomas fiasco illustrates the theoretical and practical limitations inherent in some autonomist and inclusionist perspectives as they relate to gender. In both instances, those adopting these positions failed to understand how Thomas's elevation to the Supreme Court directly contradicted efforts to improve the status of African American women and by extension undermined the entire struggle for freedom for all African Americans. Inherent in an essentialist view of race and an uncritical vision of racial solidarity is the necessity to exercise power over women. However, by failing to give attention to issues of gender and class, the larger project of African American liberation is endangered.

Where Are We Going? A Personal Postscript

What are the implications of this exploration, and where do we go from here? Historically African Americans, as individuals and as a people, have moved between various political visions and strategies. What are the conditions that produce the dominance of one or the other strategy, and what are the consequences for gender?

The 1960s and 1970s saw the rise of the civil rights movement, which employed various forms of civil disobedience to force changes in the state structure. This was a heroic—indeed in some instances revolutionary—movement, including streams of transformationist, inclusionist, and nationalist strategies. Its successes in democratizing access to and opportunity in housing, education, health care, immigration, and employment redounded to the benefit of all Americans. African American women were major participants in the struggle, if not in the leadership, and heroines such as Fannie Lou Hamer and Rosa Parks were pivotal to the movement.

With the Civil Rights Act of 1964 and the Voting Rights Act of 1965, the struggle took an inclusionist direction, emphasizing change through legal channels and electoral strategies. In many of the civil rights and black power organizations, capitulation to the representation of "emasculating" African American women led to increased identification of the struggle for equality with masculine privilege.

The 1970s brought with a vengeance the consequences of growing inequality, deindustrialization, and cutbacks in government services. As income inequality has increased, the middle class has expanded, but so has the number of those living below poverty, particularly poor women heading households. In addition, these conditions have given birth to a population of urban youth who have never seen successful struggle for change and have few job prospects in an economy where black youth unemployment is as high as 50 percent in some cities. The growth of a "ghettocentric" culture, including the musical form of hiphop, in part reflects and expresses this experience. Initially embodying a serious critique of contemporary society, rap music quickly developed various currents that differ in their representation of politics and gender. But there is a major trend that is clearly politically conservative and misogynist. In gangsta rap, for example, women are frequently referred to as "bitches" and "hos."

In light of contemporary conditions, the inclusionist vision has proven unrealizable. An inherently unequal system cannot be expanded to produce opportunities for everyone, including African Americans. In an international context characterized by serious (if temporary) reversals for the left, the return of ethnic fundamentalism and racial essentialist explanations of social reality, and the consolidation of international capitalism, those individuals and organizations calling for transformationist strategies have been for the moment weakened.

In this void, there is a rising popularity of nationalist approaches, with the call for turning inward. Tempting as it may seem to shake the sand off our feet and turn our backs on Sodom and Gomorrah, this strategy is unlikely to succeed. The problems of the "skin strategy" are evident on the local level in the rise of a small but actively promoted group of conservative African Americans such as economist Thomas Sowell, Clarence Thomas, and Republican politician Alan Keyes, who clearly cannot be trusted to promote the interests of African American liberation. On the international level, the consolidation of globalized capitalism, with new forces of technology, renders narrow national struggles obsolete.

Furthermore, inherent in the nationalist project, in its essentialization of race and its prioritization of the black social order, is the necessity to "control" women, who reproduce the social order and mark its boundaries. Our historical struggle has clearly demonstrated that the pursuit of African American liberation is inextricably connected to realizing the full potential of African American women. The struggle against class exploitation, racial discrimination, and gender subordination must be integrated in theory and practice in order for any one element to be realized. As a people, we cannot afford to exclude women from full and equal participation in our struggle. Or, as an African brother said to me, paraphrasing a Ghanaian proverb: "We need all hands on deck."

Notes

1. Scholars and commentators usually employ some variant of this dichotomous model. Krauthammer, for example, in a recent op-ed piece in *Time* magazine, categorized African American political responses as "mainstream" versus "rejectionist" (1990, 80).

2. While many in this current refer to themselves as nationalists, "nationalism" is a contested term. Social theorists have distinguished between bourgeois nationalism, progressive nationalism, and revolutionary nationalism; or between cultural nationalism and political nationalism (Hutchinson 1992). West (1992, 256), for example, defining nationalism as based on the development of group solidarity and the assertion of identity rights, suggests that nationalist movements may include political movements seeking to exercise state power; social movements that develop in response to colonialism; affirmations of cultural identity not necessarily linked to territorial sovereignty; and minority movements for identity rights and political inclusion.

3. This caption of a poster publicizing the struggle of Memphis sanitation workers became a rallying cry for the civil rights movement.

4. The different streams from which this critique emerges, including some feminist scholarship and lesbian writing as well as the action-oriented Marxist movements, often differ on the weight and position they give to various relationships of oppression.

5. This has also been true for poor and working class Euro-American women. For example, the Eugenics movement at the turn of the century was concerned with limiting reproduction among immigrant women particularly those from southern and eastern Europe.

6. The Parks Department estimated 400,000; the march organizers claimed at least 1,000,000. Boston University's Center for Remote Sensing estimated the crowd to be 837,214 with a 20 percent margin of error.

7. *Final Call* 14, no. 22 (1995), p. 19.

8. *Final Call* 14, no. 21 (1995), p. 3.

9. *Final Call* 14, no. 21 (1995), p. 3.

10. Forum on the Million Man March, held at Columbia University Institute for Research in African American Studies, October 31, 1995.

11. *Final Call* 14, no. 22 (1995), pp. 17–19.

12. *New York Times*, November 17, 1991, p. A53.

13. *USA Today*, October 5, 1995, p. 1.

References

Afshar, Haleh. 1989. "Women and Reproduction in Iran." In Floya Anthias and Niral Yuval-Davis, eds., *Woman-Nation-State*. London: Macmillan.

Ali, Shahrazad. 1989. *The Black Man's Guide to Understanding the Black Woman*. Philadelphia: Civilized Publications.

Anthias, Floya, and Niral Yuval-Davis. 1989. "Introduction." In Floya Anthias and Niral Yuval-Davis, eds., *Woman-Nation-State*. London: Macmillan.

Asante, Molefi K. 1981. "The Black Male and Female Relationships: An Afrocentric Context." In Lawrence E. Gary, ed., *Black Men*. Beverly Hills: Sage Publications.

Baer, Hans A. 1993. "The Limited Empowerment of Women in Black Spiritual Churches: An Alternative Vehicle to Religious Leadership." *Sociology of Religion* 54(1): 65–82.

Black Panther Party. 1969. *Black Panther Sisters on Women's Liberation*. N.p.: Black Panther Party.

Bookman, Ann, and Sandra Morgen, eds. 1988. *Women and the Politics of Empowerment*. Philadelphia: Temple University Press.

Brown, Audrey Lawson. 1994. "Afro-Baptist Women's Church and Family Roles: Transmitting Afrocentric Cultural Values." *Anthropological Quarterly* 67(4): 173–86.

Busby, Margaret. 1992. *Daughters of Africa: An International Anthology of Words and Writings by Women of African Descent from Ancient Egypt to the Present*. New York: Pantheon Books.

Cole, Johnetta, ed. 1986. *All American Women: Lines That Divide, Ties That Bind*. New York: Free Press.

Collins, Patricia Hill. 1991. *Black Feminist Thought: Knowledge, Consciousness, and the Politics of Empowerment*. New York: Routledge.

Combahee River Collective. [1977] 1982. "A Black Feminist Statement." In Gloria Hull, Patricia Bell Scott, and Barbara Smith, eds., *All the Women Are White, All the Blacks Are Men, But Some of Us Are Brave*. Old Westbury, NY: Feminist Press.

Coyle, Marcia. 1992. "The Court Confounds Observers." *National Law Journal* 13: 1.

Davis, Angela. 1974. *An Autobiography*. New York: Random House.

———. 1981. *Women, Race, and Class*. New York: Random House.

Fairclough, Adam. 1987. *To Redeem the Soul of America: The Southern Christian Leadership Conference and Martin Luther King, Jr*. Athens: University of Georgia Press.

Gates, Henry Lewis. 1996. "A Reporter At Large: The Charmer." *The New Yorker*, April 29–May 6: 116–26.

Giddings, Paula. 1984. *When and Where I Enter: The Impact of Black Women on Race and Sex in America*. Toronto: Bantam.

Ginsburg, Faye, and Rayna Rapp. 1995. "Introduction: Conceiving the New World Order." In Faye Ginsburg and Rayna Rapp, eds., *Conceiving the New World Order: The Global Politics of Reproduction*. Los Angeles: University of California Press.

Gutman, Herbert G. 1976. *The Black Family in Slavery and Freedom, 1750–1925*. New York: Pantheon.

Hare, Nathan. 1989. "Solutions: A Complete Theory of the Black Family." In Nathan Hare and Julia Hare, eds., *Crisis in Black Sexual Politics*. San Francisco: Black Think Tank.

Harley, Sharon. 1978. "Northern Black Female Workers: 'Jacksonian Era.'" In Sharon Harley and Rosalyn Terborg-Penn, eds., *The Afro-American Woman: Struggles and Images*. Port Washington, NY: National Universities Publications.

Higginbotham, Evelyn. 1992. "African American Women's History and the Metalanguage of Race." *Signs: Journal of Women in Society and Culture* 17(2): 251–74.

Hill, Anita Faye, and Emma Coleman Jordan, eds. 1995. *Race, Gender, and Power in America: The Legacy of the Hill-Thomas Hearings.* New York: Oxford University Press.

Horne, Gerald. 1991–92. "The Thomas Hearings and the Nexus of Race, Gender and Nationalism." *The Black Scholar* 22(1–2): 45–47.

Hutchison, John. 1992. "Moral Innovators and the Politics of Regeneration: The Distinctive Role of Cultural Nationalists in Nation-Building." *International Journal of Comparative Sociology* 33(1–2): 101–17.

Jackson, Jacquelyne Johnson. 1991–92. "'Them Against Us': Anita Hill v. Clarence Thomas." *The Black Scholar* 22(1–2): 49–52.

Jacobs, John E. 1991–92. "Clarence Thomas: Affirmative Action and Merit." *The Black Scholar* 22(1–2): 153–54.

Jayawardena, Kumari. 1986. *Feminism and Nationalism in the Third World.* London: Zed Books.

Jones, Jacqueline. 1985. *Labor of Love, Labor of Sorrow: Black Women, Work, and the Family from Slavery to the Present.* New York: Basic Books.

Karenga, M. Ron. 1978. *Essays on Struggle: Position and Analysis.* San Diego, CA: Kawaida Publications.

———. 1991–92. "Under the Camouflage of Color and Gender: The Dread and Drama of Thomas-Hill." *The Black Scholar* 22(1–2): 59–65.

Krauthammer, Charles. 1993. "The Black Rejectionists." *Time,* 23 July: 80.

Laslett, Barbara, and Johanna Brenner. 1989. "Gender and Social Reproduction: Historical Perspectives." *Annual Reviews of Sociology* 15: 381–404.

Lowery, Joseph E. 1991–92. "The SCLC Position: Affirmative Action and Merit." *The Black Scholar* 22(1–2): 151–52.

Madhubuti, Haki R. 1978. *Enemies: The Clash of Races.* Chicago: Third World Press.

Marable, Manning. 1983. *How Capitalism Underdeveloped Black America: Problems in Race, Political Economy and Society.* Boston: South End Press.

———. "The Abortion Debate." [1991], In press. "The Abortion Debate." In *Black Liberation in Conservative America.* Boston: South End Press.

———. 1995. *Beyond Black and White: Transforming African American Politics.* London and New York: Verso.

Marable, Manning, and Leith Mullings. 1994. "The Divided Mind of Black America: Race, Ideology and Politics in the Post Civil Rights Era." *Race and Class* 36(1): 61–72.

Morrison, Toni, ed. 1992. *Race-ing Justice, En-gendering Power: Essays on Anita Hill, Clarence Thomas, and the Construction of Social Reality.* New York: Pantheon.

Morton, Patricia. 1991. *Disfigured Images: The Historical Assault on Afro-American Women.* New York: Greenwood Press.

Muhammad, Elijah. 1965. *Message to the Blackman in America.* Philadelphia: Hakim's Publications.

Mullings, Leith. 1976. "Women and Economic Change in Africa." In Nancy Hafkin and Edna Bay, eds., *Women in Africa*. Stanford: Stanford University Press.

Patterson, Orlando. 1991–92. "Race, Gender and Liberal Fallacies." *The Black Scholar* 22(1–2): 77–80.

Ransby, Barbara. 1991–92. "The Gang Rape of Anita Hill and the Assault Upon All Women of African Descent." *The Black Scholar* 22(1–2): 82–85.

Rapp, Rayna. 1987. "Urban Kinship in Contemporary America: Families, Classes, and Ideology." In Leith Mullings,ed., *Cities of the United States: Studies in Urban Anthropology*. New York: Columbia University Press.

Rosenthal, Jack. 1992. "The Youngest, Cruelest Justice." *New York Times,* 27 February: p. A24.

Samad, A. Asadullah. 1995. "One Million Reasons for Black Men to March (Without Our Women)." *Los Angeles Sentinel,* 31 August: p. A7.

Sudarkasa, Niara. 1991–92. "Don't Write Off Thomas." *The Black Scholar* 22(1–2): 99–102.

Thorne, Barrie. 1992. "Review of *Black Feminist Thought: Knowledge, Conciousness, and the Politics of Empowerment* by Patricia Hill Collins." *Gender and Society* 6(3): 515–17.

Walby, Sylvia. 1992. "Women and Nation." *International Journal of Comparative Sociology* 33(1–2): 80–99.

West, Lois A. 1992. "Feminist Nationalist Social Movements: Beyond Universalism and Towards a Gendered Cultural Relativism." *Women's Studies International Forum* 15(5–6): 563–79.

White, E. Frances. 1990. "Africa on My Mind: Gender, Counter Discourse and African-American Nationalism." *Journal of Women's History* 2(1): 73–97.

Wilson, William Julius. 1987. *The Truly Disadvantaged: The Inner City, the Underclass, and Public Policy*. Chicago: University of Chicago Press.

X, Malcolm. 1970. *By Any Means Necessary*. Edited by George Breitman. New York: Pathfinder Press.

8

Gender and the Application of Anthropological Knowledge to Public Policy in the United States

An introductory anthropology course may be enhanced by including a segment demonstrating the relevance of anthropology to real problems in the United States. Such concerns are often considered to be the realm of applied anthropology. If one aspect of applied anthropology is its interventionist direction, promoting advocacy and collaboration, the other is found in its contribution to understanding social issues, specifically the use of anthropological information to challenge, develop, or support public policy (Chambers 1987, 319). In focusing on the application of anthropological knowledge to public policy issues, this chapter will be primarily concerned with the latter aspect. After a brief discussion of some of the concerns of applied anthropologists, I will present examples of two social policy issues to which anthropology has the potential to make a contribution: ethnicity and inequality, and health and illness. I will discuss the way in which recent anthropological scholarship on gender contributes to, modifies, and in some cases restructures the basic understandings of these areas.

Applied anthropologists have been concerned with such topics as health and medicine, education, and development and inequality, and they have used intervention strategies such as action anthropology, community development, advocacy anthropology, and cultural brokerage (Van Willigen 1986). Though most scholars agree that anthropology—in particular the holistic approach, the

159

concept of culture, and ethnographic methodology—has the potential for a unique contribution to solving social problems, there are significant controversies about the nature and scope of the field. Among these are: the ability of anthropology to contribute to policy formation (Weaver 1985); the extent to which applied anthropology favors short-term, status quo solutions (see Chambers 1987, 310); the relationship of theoretical, applied, and advocacy anthropology (see Chambers 1987; Leacock 1987; Sanjek 1987); the issue of divided loyalties, that is, to whom is the anthropologist responsible (see Leacock 1987); and the limitations of anthropology as a policy science (see Gibbs 1982).

There have been several recent reviews and critiques of applied anthropology, and particularly the role of anthropology in public policy (Chambers 1977, 1987; Gibbs 1982; Hicks and Handler 1987; Hinshaw 1980). However, there is very little written about the consequences of gender bias in applied anthropology.[1] Yet the same gender biases that appear in academic anthropology and in conventional ethnography have palpable consequences when anthropology sets itself the explicit task of helping people make decisions. Thus conceptualizations of gender have enormous implications for public policy. Notions of appropriate gender roles, for example, have powerfully influenced policies on welfare, health care, child care, women's work, equal compensation, and the family.

Examining two examples—ethnicity and inequality, and health policy—I will argue that gender constructs have direct consequences for policy decisions and rationalizations. While suggesting that policy (in its broadest sense) often reinforces gender hierarchy, I will demonstrate how some of the new feminist scholarship raises important questions and suggests different directions. However, knowledge in and of itself does not produce structural change, which often requires social action. But scholars have at times worked with others, and I will cite examples of how feminist perspectives in health have been used to bring about change through advocacy. Though both these topics fall within the domain of applied anthropology, it is important to note that the use of anthropological research to support, develop, or discredit policy is not limited to the work of those consciously engaged in policy-relevant research, rendering the distinction between theoretical and applied anthropology somewhat questionable.

Ethnicity, Inequality, and Public Policy

Since the beginnings of American anthropology, concern with ethnicity—group identification, by self or others, on the basis of phenotype, language, religion, or national origin—has been central to the discipline.[2] Inequality has been a pervasive feature of American life, and racial and ethnic differences have often been associated with unequal positions in the stratification structure.

Specifically, African Americans, Chicanos, Puerto Ricans, and Native Americans, as compared to Euro-Americans, are disproportionately concentrated at the lower end of the socioeconomic scale. In our society there is a prevailing ideology of equal opportunity. The major question, then, is why does ethnic inequality exist? Differences in perspectives on such public policies as immigration, public schooling, housing, affirmative action, employment, and a range of other issues revolve around how the relationship between ethnicity and inequality is conceptualized. Public policy decisions are often rationalized by scholarly work, and recent social science explanations have attributed ethnic inequality to biological or genetic differences, cultural differences, or structured inequality that is societally produced and reproduced.

The Prevailing Views

The notion that inborn genetic differences are primarily responsible for ethnic and class inequality continues to be found in the work of such writers as Shockley (1970), Jensen (1969, 1970), Herrnstein (1973), and Rushton (1989). Much of this work concerns IQ studies, and the policy implications are evident in the pervasive practice of "tracking" in the public school system (see Kamin 1974, 1982; Lawler 1978; and Taylor 1980 for critiques of the genetic basis of IQ). However, it is the assessment of cultural differences as determinant of inequality that has been more apparent in recent public policy.

Oscar Lewis's (1966) formulation of the "culture of poverty"—a problematic subculture characteristic of certain poor people—was perhaps the anthropological thesis that received most attention from policymakers. His description of this culture and its setting includes many ambiguities and contradictory statements that allow for emphasis on different aspects of his argument. However, policymakers chose to emphasize his analysis of the cultural, rather than the structural, roots of the problem. The aspect of Lewis's work with the greatest influence on public policy was his depiction of the way of life of the poor and his characterization of their culture as self-perpetuating: that children absorb this "culture" by the age of six or seven and are subsequently unable to take advantage of any changing circumstances that might occur. The emphasis on culture as the major determinant of stratification is also put forward in Glazer and Moynihan's introduction to *Ethnicity: Theory and Experience.* Here they elaborate their theoretical position that differences in access to resources are the result of differences in culture content: "It is *property* that begins to seem derivative, and ethnicity that seems to become a more fundamental source of social stratification" (Moynihan and Glazer 1975, 17).

A variety of anthropologists and other social scientists questioned the validity of the culture of poverty concept and its applications. Critics cited theoretical and methodological problems with Lewis's framework as well as numerous studies contradicting these generalizations about poor people (see Leacock 1971). Research in various disciplines has demonstrated how discriminatory practices and recent transformations in the larger economy (the decline of the industrial sectors and the growth of service sectors of the economy; the movement of jobs from midwestern and northeastern central cities to the suburbs, Sunbelt cities, and finally the third world; and the decline in social services) have disproportionately affected the poorest segment of U.S. society and specifically people of color. Nonetheless, the culture of poverty perspective remained an entrenched assumption in public policy. Charles Valentine's (1968) analysis demonstrates how the view that the culture of the poor is responsible for their poverty served as a rationale for both directing programs toward changing the culture of the poor, rather than toward eliminating poverty, and for dismantling some of the programs of the War on Poverty.

The first wave of studies criticizing the culture of poverty concept (with the exception of those that were specifically directed toward reexamination of the African American family) tended to be primarily concerned with issues of race and class, without sufficient attention to gender. Yet it was women who bore much of the brunt of the negative characterizations of poor people's culture. Women are portrayed as inadequately fulfilling their gender-based roles. Oscar Lewis describes a trend toward "female- or mother-centered families" and the "high incidence of maternal deprivation" as part of a set of negative culture traits (Lewis 1966, 23). It is in the work of Glazer and Moynihan that this implied criticism of poor women becomes explicit. This is particularly true in Moynihan's (1965) *The Negro Family: The Case for National Action* (known as the Moynihan Report), in which the roles played by African American women are portrayed as a causative factor in poverty and social disorganization. While Lewis had taken pains to point out that the culture of poverty is not limited to any ethnic group but is rather associated with a particular type of social structure (industrial capitalism), Moynihan applies this formulation specifically to African Americans.

The focus of Moynihan's negative characterization of women has to do with their roles within the family. Although initially Moynihan is careful to document the negative impact of high unemployment on the African American family and community, he then proceeds to treat family structure essentially as an independent variable.

At the heart of the deterioration of the fabric of Negro society is the deterioration of the Negro family. It is the fundamental source of the weakness of the Negro community at the present time. (Moynihan 1965, 5)

At the center of the tangle of pathology is the weakness of the family structure, the principal source of most of the aberrant, inadequate or antisocial behavior that did not establish, but now serves to perpetuate the cycle of poverty. (Moynihan 1965, 30)

The major weakness of the family structure as he sees it is that "in essence, the Negro community has been forced into a matriarchal structure which . . . imposes a crushing burden on the Negro male" (Moynihan 1965, 29). Matriarchy, defined by the "often reversed roles of husband and wife" (Moynihan 1965, 76), is reinforced from generation to generation. These "reversed roles" seem to be primarily defined by the fact that a greater proportion of African American than Euro-American women work outside the home. Moynihan argues that this "matriarchal" family structure is deviant in regard to the rest of the society and results in low educational attainment, crime, and delinquency. Parenthetically, it also makes military service important for African American men, since the military "is an utterly masculine world . . . a world away from women, a world run by strong men of unquestioned authority" (Moynihan 1965, 42). As assistant secretary of labor and director of the Office of Policy Planning and Research in the Johnson Administration, Moynihan was in a position such that his report had a significant impact not only on national policy but also on scholarship and ideology. Its major effect—intended or not—was to shift attention from structural issues, such as unemployment and discrimination, to the African American family structure and the roles played by women as primarily responsible for the condition of the African American community.[3] (See Gilkes 1983 and Jones 1985, 312 for a discussion of the effects of the Moynihan Report on gender relations in African American communities and organizations.) An examination of more recent examples of this perspective in the popular press may be found in Collins 1989 and Baca Zinn 1989.

Unlike much anthropological research in which women were "invisible," this work was unusual in the emphasis placed on women. Indeed, one might surmise that researchers were negatively impressed by their high visibility. At issue, however, is the accuracy of the interpretation of women's roles. These women, who often work outside the home, are portrayed as "deviant," with deviancy having negative consequences for their communities. To whom were women being compared? Recent research suggests that these women were seen as deviant in terms of a class- and ethnicity-based notion of ideal gender roles that conformed neither to the experiences of Euro-American working-class women nor to those of women of color.

The New Scholarship

With the impetus of the civil rights movement in the 1960s and 1970s and the feminist movement of the 1970s, research on women and ethnicity in the United States challenged the prevailing views with studies that reexamined the roles of women in families, the workplace, and the community. Not surprisingly, much of it was done by women. Basic assumptions—that the role of a woman as worker was a "deviant" one and that the roles of poor and working-class women in families and in their communities were indeed pathological—were questioned. These studies laid the foundation for sophisticated theoretical explorations of the social and cultural construction of gender: the manner in which the experiences of women vary with race and class, and how these compare with the dominant cultural ideology of gender roles.

Early studies such as Lerner (1979) pointed to the class bias of the "cult of true womanhood": the set of ideas asserting a dichotomy between home and workplace, a contrast between male and female natures, and idealization of domesticity and motherhood (Welter 1966). Historians and anthropologists began to make working women more visible by documenting women's participation in the labor force throughout U.S. history and noting that only a limited proportion of the population had ever possessed the resources to be "ladies." Though much of the early work was done by historians, anthropologists have increasingly begun to study the experiences of working-class women (see Lamphere 1987, chapter 1, for a recent review of the literature on studies of working women; see also Sacks and Remy 1984). New research traced the ways in which the lives of women of color, particularly their participation in the work force, are shaped by institutionalized racism (chapter 2; Dill 1986; Glenn 1986; Higginbotham 1983; Jones 1985; Zambrana 1982).[4] This work reversed the causal order of Moynihan's analysis by emphasizing the social constraints within which people created viable lives, rather than blaming the victims for social conditions they did not create.

In particular, these studies demonstrated that racial and ethnic discrimination does condition the options of women. For example, because of the discrimination against both men and women, African American married women have historically worked outside the home in greater proportions than Euro-American women and have constituted a pool of low-wage workers. However, participation in the work force was not aberrant to the experiences of many other U.S. women. Euro-American working-class women worked outside the home in greater numbers than an idealized version of history would have us believe. Do these conditions produce "deviant" mothers, disorganized households, and alienated individuals, as claimed by Lewis, Moynihan, and others?

Along with the work discussed above was a set of studies reexamining women's roles in households and communities. Carol Stack's now classic (though somewhat romanticized) ethnographic study of poor African American families (1970) pointed to the special role women played in ensuring the survival of children in situations of high unemployment. Stack found that women were nodes in extensive networks of kin and friends that exchanged goods, resources, services, and child care in an effort to ensure the survival of children. She documented a variety of residential and domestic strategies, such as child swapping and gift exchange. By demonstrating that the household structure and the roles played by women, far from being pathological and disorganized, constitute a rational, highly organized response to poverty, her research speaks directly to the culture of poverty hypothesis. A number of studies in the 1970s and 1980s on the African American family made similar points (see chapter 4).

The relationship between gender roles and household structure in poor families is placed in perspective by Rapp's (1987a) comparative analysis. She summarizes much of the work to date and demonstrates that households of different classes vary in their ability to tap wages and wealth; family form and gender roles will, to some extent, reflect the household's access to material resources. Rapp notes that woman-centered networks, more critical in poor and working-class families, are in part a function of the gender arrangements of urban segregation but are also part of "community control" for women (Rapp 1987a, 229).

Women's work in creating networks also extends to the workplace and the community. Bookman and Morgen's (1988) edited volume provides, for the first time, a series of ethnographic case studies documenting the involvement of working class women and women of color in community, work place, and political struggles. Cheryl Gilkes's (1983, 1988) discussions of African American women's roles as mothers, caretakers, workers outside the home, and community workers deserves special mention in this regard. These studies challenge the portrayal of poor households as pathological and disorganized and the individuals in them as alienated and passive. It is important, however, that these households and women not be romanticized. As will be discussed later in the essay, the inadequacy of resources takes a serious toll on these households and the women in them.

One byproduct of the increased understanding of how the experience of gender differs with class and race was renewed attention to the cultural and social (although often rationalized as biological) construction of gender. It became clear that, to a great extent, the manner in which different women in the United States played out gender roles was very much a matter of their position in the racial and economic hierarchy rather than their physiological makeup. For example, these studies uncovered the evidence that despite the popular "mammy" stereotype, the majority of enslaved African American women worked in the fields alongside men as field hands. After emancipation, they worked outside the home, took leading roles in their communities, and had relatively egalitarian relationships within the household. Although these roles were portrayed negatively by leading social scientists, they (along with the cross-cultural data) provide evidence for suggesting that the confinement of women to a particular set of tasks and roles is based on social rather than biological constraints.

Despite the variety of gender experiences, it is the roles played by elite women that become the cultural model of what womanhood should be (see Rapp 1987a). Elite women, who alone can afford to indulge in a certain lifestyle, set the model for femininity against which women of other classes were judged. Hence African American women, largely by virtue of their assertiveness on behalf of their families and communities and because they are not sufficiently economically dependent on men, become "dangerous women and deviant mothers" (Gilkes 1983, 294).

These studies—by documenting the way in which the boundaries of class and race influence the meaning of gender and by highlighting the external constraints within which people operate—provided support for structural perspectives on ethnicity and inequality. By incorporating analysis of gender and challenging the cultural construction of normative notions of male and female roles, the structural position is advanced and made more compelling. But just as structural critiques often missed the significance of gender, feminist perspectives have often missed the significance of race and class. In the following curricular example, the need for taking all these variables into account will be evident.

Curricular Example: Women, Households, and Poverty

Objective

To stimulate thinking about how new conceptualizations of gender might transform the way we look at public policy issues in the United States, using the example of women, households, and poverty.

Discussion

The term "feminization of poverty" has been used by a variety of scholars, policymakers, and activists to refer to increasing levels of poverty among women.

Social scientists disagree on how to assess the high poverty rates, but much of the recent work influential in social policy and public opinion attributes it to the increased prevalence of households headed by women.

This dialogue has particular implications for people of color, among whom are found a proportionately greater number of households headed by women. A number of recent works assert or imply (see, for example, Lemann 1986; Murray 1984; Moyers 1989) that much of the contemporary poverty experienced by minority communities is attributable to the growth of households headed by women. Thus it is these women who are most frequently portrayed as "deviant" in regard to the mainstream community—the welfare mother burdening the society with her children remains a powerful image. Jones suggests that "the manifestations of racism—black mothers and children dependent upon the state—only reinforce racism, in much the same way that slavery was shaped by and then reinforced racial prejudice" (Jones 1985, 327).

Several interrelated assumptions discussed earlier in this essay also appear in much of this work. Implicit, or sometimes explicit, is the cultural explanation for poverty—that differences in beliefs, values, and so on are ultimately responsible for disproportionate poverty and the growth of what has been called the under-class. The argument goes something like this: The growth of households headed by women—the households themselves being a result of deviant values—perpet-uates poverty by providing inadequate income and socializing children into a maladaptive culture. The majority of these works assume that households headed by women are inherently problematic. Some explicitly state that they are to blame for the recent growth of poverty among some peoples of color. The role of welfare has received particular attention (e.g. Murray 1984; Moyers 1989). It is suggested that access to welfare, by decreasing the necessity for dependence on men, encourages female-headed families and thereby poverty.

Recent studies have addressed themselves to the question of the centrality of family structure in causing poverty. Several analyses have pointed to the lack of evidence that family structure causes poverty, noting in particular that the two-parent family is no guarantee against poverty for people of color (see Baca Zinn 1989 for a review of such studies); similarly, comparative analyses of Aid to Families with Dependent Children benefits in different states indicate that wel-fare does not have a major effect on family structure (Ellwood and Summers 1986).

Other work has pointed to economic (rather than cultural) reasons for the racial differences in the proportion of households headed by females. Wilson, for example, argues that while the rise in female headship among Euro-Americans may have to do with emerging values, increasing female headship among African Americans is directly linked to unemployment among men. Despite the picture painted by the popular press, the rate of childbearing among teenage African American women is not increasing; rather, it decreased by 40 percent between 1960 and 1983 (Wilson 1987, 194). There were, however, fewer employed men to marry, and the rate of marriage declined, resulting in higher rates for out-of-wedlock births for African American teenagers. In highlighting the economic reasons for the high number of households headed by women, this work turns around the causative relationship linking female headship to poverty and provides evidence for the view that public policies need to focus on transforming the economic situation rather than the culture of the poor.

While this work is important in pointing to the structural reasons for the racial disparities in the number of families headed by women, much of it uncritically accepts normative views of the roles of men and women and the premise that households headed by women are inherently problematic, without sufficient concern for class variables that bear on access to resources.[5] The feminist scholarship goes further in questioning the assumption that women can have decent standards of living only through access to the resources of men and questions the validity of solutions making women dependent on men, rather than on welfare, for subsistence (Baca Zinn 1989; Collins 1989). These critiques give more attention to the actual lives of women and suggest that women's reproductive and marital statuses are affected not only by the employment of the men in their communities but also by their own lack of employment possibilities in a sex-segregated labor force (Gordon 1989) where women of color are disproportionately found in the lowest-paid sectors.

Along these lines, scholars have examined the way in which state policies reinforce gender hierarchy. By failing to provide child care that would allow mothers to hold jobs and earn independent incomes, and by maintaining two-tiered social insurance programs that discriminate against women, public policies reinforce the traditional family structure of the male breadwinner and dependent, isolated female homemaker. Welfare and workfare programs, where benefits are even lower than prevailing wage rates, do not allow full independence for women and therefore maintain traditional gender relationships in which a woman's only option for raising her standard of living is marriage (see Gerstel and Gross 1987, 461–65, for a review of such studies). The welfare and workfare programs mesh with the employment system to produce a pool of low-wage labor (see Susser and Kreniske 1987 for a case study).

Finally, feminist approaches might challenge the assumption that families headed by women are inherently problematic. While being a single parent is no doubt difficult and the cost in health and realization of personal potential is often high, more attention needs to be given to the various roles played by men and how relative access to material and social resources condition the household's experience. We need to know more about the variety of ways in which people organize themselves to successfully ensure the survival of children. In this regard it may be interesting to have students discuss network formation for mutual assistance among poor and working-class women who head families (e.g. Stack 1970), as compared to that among Euro-American middle stratum women, for whom

> the cultural emphasis on nuclear family independence constrains middle-class divorced women to rely on their families of origin for help and makes it difficult for them to extend ties to individuals outside this narrow range. (Newman 1986, 242)

Here again, feminist writers will need to attend to race and class and the way in which they shape the experience of gender. For example, several writers have noted that the "feminization of poverty" is a problematic phrase. It obfuscates class and race differentiation among women and substitutes gender for class as the variable by which resources are divided. Further, it ignores the increasing poverty of African American men and other men of color. Indeed, not all female-headed households are poor: in 1984, though over 50 percent of households headed by African American and Hispanic women were poor, only 27 percent of households headed by Euro-American women were poor (Rodgers 1986, 10). As Maxine Baca Zinn (1987, 24) put it, "The formation of female-headed households is but one example of the closely intertwined fate of racial-ethnic women and men."

Policy implications that derive from this sort of analysis point to the need for societal transformations that address unemployment and race and gender wage discrimination, and strengthen commitment to the provision of social services such as child care.

Health Policy

In the first part of this chapter, I discussed alternative perspectives on the roles of biology, culture, and social structure in the production and reproduction of inequality. This debate takes on very concrete ramifications when we examine the topic of health and illness. As new infectious diseases ravage our cities, health indicators decline in some sectors of our population, health costs continue to spiral upward, and health services are less satisfactory for the majority of the population, social scientists are increasingly drawn into analyzing the crisis in our health care system. Medical anthropology, a growing subfield, has been concerned with the interrelationship of biological, social, and cultural factors in health and illness. Critical medical anthropology, a relatively new field, is particularly attentive to applying the critical tools of anthropology to biomedicine as well as to the medical systems of other societies, demonstrating that biomedicine is also a cultural system and not exempt from this sort of analysis. The new scholarship on health and gender has contributed to this body of work by expanding our knowledge of the social construction of illness and health, the cultural construction of medical knowledge, and the way in which the medical system contributes to the maintenance of hierarchy.

The Social Construction of Illness and Health

In light of the discussion in the first part of the chapter, it should not be surprising that among women, health status clearly differs by race. For example, in 1980 African American women had an average life expectancy of 72.3 years, as compared to 78.1 years for Euro-American women, and significantly higher rates of the diseases that are major causes of death: cardiovascular disease and cancer (Keith and Smith 1988). However, the reasons for these differentials are much debated in medicine, where, despite the body of literature in public health on the social causation of disease, there is a marked tendency to see differences in rates of illness and disease as a result of either genetic/biological differences, on the one hand, or individual lifestyle choices, on the other. The policy result of both of these perspectives can be seen in the increased emphasis on individual, rather than social, responsibility for health and illness (see chapter 3).

While clearly there are biological and genetic aspects of differential disease rates (see Polednak 1987), and it is often difficult to draw links between social conditions and specific disease states, the new research on gender has added to our knowledge of the way in which social conditions generate disease and influence its distribution. Some of the early studies sought to demonstrate that differences in male and female mortality could be largely attributed to behavioral rather than physiological factors (Waldrun 1986), and that as women's experiences change, so does their health status. Other studies have revealed the way in which apparent racial discrepancies (often attributed to biological differences) are mediated by class and racial discrimination (Basset and Krieger 1986; Mullings 1989; Polednak 1987). *Too Little, Too Late,* edited by Perales and Young (1988), brings together work on a range of issues affecting poor women. The effects of various societal forces on women's health are the subject of several chapters in Lewin and Oleson 1985.

For women of color in particular, recent work has examined the way in which the triple day—work outside the home, household responsibilities, and community work—may contribute to higher rates of disease (see chapter 3), and how ethnicity and socioeconomic status may condition options for reproduction, contraception, and sterilization abuse (Boone 1988; Clarke 1984; Fisher 1986; Lazarus 1988; Lopez 1987; Zambrana 1982). This research suggests that the multiplicity of roles women of color fill under adverse circumstances takes a serious toll on their health.

Society as a whole not only bears a portion of the financial costs of preventable illnesses but also—and more important—loses the potential contribution of productive human beings. Weiss and Mann (1978) propose a striking way to look at the biological toll exacted by racism. The six-year differential in life expectancy between African American and Euro-American women may not sound like much unless it comes off your own life expectancy. But in 1980 there were approximately 14 million African American women in the United States, each of whom, on average, will live six years less than if she were Euro-American. These women, "and American society, will lose [84 million] years of human life and productivity to discrimination based on an inaccurate view of human variability" (Weiss and Mann 1978, 502; see also U.S. Bureau of the Census 1987, 17).

With respect to health policy, this research suggests that while an understanding of cultural preferences and the role of biological and genetic differences is important, health strategists must also look at structural differences if we are to make inroads into health differentials. This is a formidable issue to confront in the United States, which, along with South Africa, is the only Western industrialized society without national health insurance. As long as the commitment is to a fee-for-service medical system and to genetic and lifestyle explanations for racial differences in health and illness, it will be difficult to give priority to equalizing access to resources—employment opportunities, adequate wages, decent housing, good nutrition, quality education, adequate recreational opportunities, and good medical care—that may make the real difference in health.

The Cultural Construction of Illness

The new scholarship on gender has raised questions about the cultural construction of medical knowledge. For many health professionals as well as consumers, biomedical definitions, concepts, explanations, and models are not historically and culturally constructed but rather are understood to be "natural" facts, applicable cross-culturally and historically. This is often rationalized with reference to "hard" sciences such as biology, physics, and physiology. Cross-cultural studies by anthropologists, however, have demonstrated that concepts of illness and health are socially and culturally constructed and distributed. Recent gender-based studies have assisted in extending this critique to biomedicine. These works suggest that knowledge is always socially constructed, that scientific knowledge is not entirely objective nor free from value judgments and cultural constructions, and that in many instances medical knowledge is construed around cultural views of the proper place of women. Diagnosis and treatment, then, often serve to reproduce the hierarchical system they reflect.

Emily Martin (1987), for example, raises important questions about biomedicine's conceptualizations of female physiology (see also Scully and Bart 1973). Martin notes that as medical discourse began to be characterized by metaphors stressing production, menstruation was conceptualized as "failed production"— with accompanying images of sloughing, hemorrhaging, and waste. Analyzing standard medical textbook terms applied to menstruation, she finds that "in rapid succession the reader is confronted with 'degenerate,' 'decline,' 'withdrawn,' 'spasms,' 'lack,' 'weakened,' 'leak,' 'deteriorated,' 'discharge,' and, after all that, 'repair'" (Martin 1987, 47).

Similarly, menopause is seen as "a kind of failure of the authority structure in the body" (Martin 1987, 45; see also McCrea 1986). Medical terminology, allegedly value-free, contributes to negative views of these processes that find expression in women's perceptions about how medicine views their bodies as well as in their own images of their bodies. This discourse has implications for treatment, evidenced, for example, by the high rate of Caesarean sections and the management of menopause. Similarly, one may question the "scientific" basis upon which signs and symptoms are organized into diseases. Laws, for example, argues that medical knowledge about premenstrual tension is not really constructed out of scientifically proven facts but is "at its roots a political construct" (Laws 1983, 20).

Reproductive systems and strategies have been the focus of much of the work on gender bias in the production and dissemination of seemingly neutral medical technologies. For example, both Lorber (1987) and Crowe (1985) argue (from different perspectives) that infertility, although seen as a biological failing, is a social rather than physiological problem in that it violates a culturally constructed notion of family and gender roles. Implicit in the use of in-vitro fertilization (IVF) are cultural values concerning the nature of femininity, masculinity, sexuality, and motherhood. Thus IVF is not a value-free technology; rather, it reinforces certain perspectives about gender roles and the family: a biological definition of motherhood, the idea that the nuclear family is a natural structure, and the ideology that motherhood is a natural state for women (Crowe 1985). In addition, since access to high-cost technology varies with race and class, one may raise questions about the extent to which differential availability of such technology allows some couples, but not others, to have their own children.

Other work on reproduction and reproductive rights (e.g., Arditti et al. 1984) picks up these themes. Abortion "technology . . . renders the fetus visible, and the woman by implication transparent" (Rothman 1987, 164). Rapp (1987b) concludes that the technology of amniocentesis gives science such authority in defining motherhood that "other voices" cannot be heard. "Other voices" are differentiated by class and race as well as by gender. Petchesky (1983) takes on issues of class and reproduction in the history of access to abortion. Fisher (1986) discusses the way in which the incidence and consequences of hysterectomies vary across race and class. This body of work has dramatic implications for public policy relating to contraception, abortion, surrogate motherhood, fetal diagnosis, and other uses of medical technology.

These works suggest that what is seen as neutral scientific knowledge is, to a great extent, socially and culturally determined. This is not to assert that objective facts do not exist, but that as we perceive, organize, and apply them, we are constrained by a discourse shaped by the power interests of a hierarchical society. These interests shape medical knowledge, which both reflects and reproduces notions about what women ought to be. Medical systems may do this in a particularly potent way—rendering as natural that which is actually social, and then deploying natural explanations in reproducing hierarchical social relations. These studies provide the foundation for questioning whether the influence of hierarchical relations upon the metaphorical structure of medical models may impede the pursuit of health, whereas other ways of thinking may get us further.

Hierarchy and the Health Care Encounter

Although feminist critiques began with specific concerns, such as the negative imagery of women in medical discourse, the devaluation of women's physical ills, the treatment of issues of reproduction, and the use of drug therapy on women (see Lewin and Oleson 1985), studies of women's health status and their experiences as recipients of health care have facilitated examination of the way in which the structure and organization of the health care system, conditioned by hierarchical gender relationships in the larger society, structure the health care experience. Sue Fisher (1986), for example, analyzes discourse in doctor-patient communication to demonstrate how medical authority (generally male) constructs and determines discussions about diagnoses, prognoses, and possible treatments.[6]

Feminist scholars have raised questions about the management of childbirth and pregnancy. In particular, they have argued that the medicalization of childbirth, in which the woman is placed in a passive role and the doctor in an active role, does not serve the interests of women (Danziger 1986; Michaelson 1988; Singer 1987).

> In little more than a century, birth was redefined from a natural process in which women helped each other give birth to a dangerous, high-risk activity in which birthing women needed the medical ministrations and the intervention-ist practices of the male physician who would "deliver" their babies. (Fisher 1986, 137)

However, Michaelson et al. (1988) suggest that the feminist critique of birth was largely pertinent to the interests of the middle class. These modes of analysis can be extended to the many other phenomena that have become "medicalized."

By elucidating the power, gender, and class relations implicit in the health care encounter, this body of work underscores the way in which health policy, like other public policies, reinforces hierarchical arrangements. It suggests that while providing access to health care is important, improving health conditions in the United States would also necessitate a restructuring of the entire health care system.

Knowledge and Action

Can the anthropological knowledge discussed in this essay be utilized to affect public policy? Perhaps one of the most striking examples of the use of the find-ings discussed above is the women's health movement. Using the strategies of political action organizations and self-help groups, the women's health move-ment sought to empower women through knowledge and to challenge the assumptions and practices of biomedicine (see Zimmerman 1987). The partici-pants were primarily middle-stratum women (but see Morgen 1988a) and, not surprisingly, the movement appears to have been more successful at challenging the cultural construction of medicine than at addressing the social construction of disease. However, effects of the use of such knowledge are still evident in self-help groups, the dissemination of publications (*Our Bodies, Ourselves* being a widely read example), well-woman clinics, midwifery, and other changes in the context of birthing.

As we mentioned at the beginning of the essay, anthropologists have played a variety of roles in attempting to affect public policy. Because the recent feminist scholarship emphasizes social, rather than biological or genetic, constraints to equal opportunity and consequently points to the need for fundamental struc-tural changes rather than the short-term solutions more popular with policymakers, these findings are initially more likely to have an effect through grassroots and community movements. Case studies of anthropologists who have done work in grassroots organizations may be useful in giving students some flavor of the range of issues. Sanjek's (1987) account of his participation in the struggle to save a Gray Panther clinic is not specifically concerned with gender issues, but his analysis of the academic, applied, and advocacy aspects of his work is very informative. Morgen's (1988b) description of her experience as a participant observer in Citizen Action for Health, a cross-class, multiracial women's organization, brings in issues of race, class, and gender; the coalition was successful in reopening a prenatal clinic and in establishing a neighborhood health center. Both accounts present challenging examples of the anthropologist as advocate, and demonstrate that when anthropologists can link their skills to an organized social movement or one on the verge of organizing, their work may attain a special significance and contribute to social change.

Notes

I would like to thank Lynn Bolles, Lawrence Hammer, Delmos Jones, Margo Matwychuk, Sandra Morgen, Rayna Rapp, and project reviewers for their comments. I would also like to acknowledge the fine research assistance of Lawrence Hammer and Margo Matwychuk.

1. It is possible, however, to find literature on specific topics of concern to applied anthropologists. In education, for example, see Pittman and Eisenhart 1988; Goetz and Grant 1988; Holland and Eisenhart 1988.

2. For example, Franz Boas's interest in these issues was evident in his work on European immigrants and his attempts to demonstrate that culture, not biology, accounts for differences in behavior (see Partridge and Eddy 1987). While most anthropologists would assert that anthropology, with its cultural rather than genetic explanation of ethnic differences, has much to contribute to the public debate, they do not agree about the extent of anthropology's effectiveness. For example, Hicks and Handler (1987) claim that anthropology has been influential in public policy, and Hinshaw states that "decision makers at all levels have internalized many of the lessons anthropology has been teaching . . . with respect to race, ethnicity and multiculturalism" (Hinshaw 1980, 516). Weaver (1985), however, concludes that anthropologists have generally been ineffective in influencing public policy and that racist, exclusionary ideas such as those of Jencks had more influence on immigration policy than those of Boas and Wissler.

3. See Wilson 1987 for a sympathetic treatment of the Moynihan Report.

4. Work that attempted to conceptualize the relationships among gender, race and class was particularly important. In this regard, Angela Davis's ground-breaking work *Women, Race, and Class* (1981), followed by studies stimulated by the working group on women, race, and class of the Center for Research on Women at Memphis State University (see "Preface"), were critical.

5. The fact that there is not much information on class variables, and relatively little ethnographic work on middle-stratum African Americans and poor Euro-Americans, tends to structure the discussion by ethnic categories and to obfuscate class with ethnicity.

6. See Leavitt 1984, part 3, for a series of articles on women in the health professions.

References

Arditti, Rita, et al., eds. 1984. *Test-Tube Women: What Future for Motherhood?* London: Pandora.

Baca Zinn, Maxine. 1987. "Minority Families in Crisis: The Public Discussion." Research Paper no. 6. Memphis: Center for Research on Women, Memphis State University.

———. 1989. "Family, Race, and Poverty in the Eighties." *Signs* 14(4): 856–74.

Basset, M., and N. Krieger. 1986. "Social Class and Black-White Differences in Breast Cancer Survival." *American Journal of Public Health* 76(12): 1400–03.

Bookman, Ann, and Sandra Morgen, eds. 1988. *Women and the Politics of Empowerment.* Philadelphia: Temple University Press.

Boone, Margaret S. 1988. "Social Support for Pregnancy and Childbearing Among Disadvantaged Blacks in an American Inner City." In Karen L. Michaelson et al., *Childbirth in America: Anthropological Perspectives.* South Hadley, MA: Bergin and Garvey.

Chambers, Erve. 1977. "Public Policy and Anthropology." *Reviews in Anthropology* 4(6): 543–54.

———. 1987. "Applied Anthropology in the Post-Vietnam Era: Anticipations and Ironies." *Annual Review of Anthropology* 16: 309–37.

Clarke, Adele. 1984. "Subtle Forms of Sterilization Abuse: A Reproductive Rights Analysis." In Rita Arditti et al., eds., *Test-Tube Women: What Future for Motherhood?* London: Pandora.

Collins, Patricia Hill. 1989. "A Comparison of Two Works on Black Family Life." *Signs* 14(4): 875–84.

Crowe, C. 1985. "'Women Want It': In Vitro Fertilization and Women's Motivations for Participation." *Women's Studies International Forum* 8(6): 547–52.

Danziger, Sandra Klein. 1986. "The Uses of Expertise in Doctor-Patient Encounters During Pregnancy." In Peter Conrad and Rochelle Kern, eds., *The Sociology of Health and Illness: Critical Perspectives.* 2nd ed. New York: St. Martin's Press.

Davis, Angela Y. 1981. *Women, Race, and Class.* New York: Random House.

Dill, Bonnie Thornton. 1986. "Our Mother's Grief: Racial-Ethnic Women and the Maintenance of Families." Research Paper no. 4. Memphis: Center for Research on Women, Memphis State University.

Ellwood, David, and Lawrence Summers. 1986. "Poverty in America: Is Welfare the Answer or the Problem?" In S.Danziger and Daniel Weinberg, eds., *Fighting Poverty.* Cambridge, MA: Harvard University Press.

Fisher, Sue. 1986. *In the Patient's Best Interest: Women and the Politics of Medical Decisions.* New Brunswick, NJ: Rutgers University Press.

Gerstel, Naomi, and Harriet Engel Gross. 1987. "Introduction to Part IV: State Policy and Employers' Policy." In Naomi Gerstel and Harriet Engel Gross, eds., *Families and Work.* Philadelphia: Temple University Press.

Gibbs, James L. Jr. 1982. "Anthropology as a Policy Science: Some Limitations." In E. Adamson Hoebel, R. Currier, and S. Kaiser, eds., *Crisis in Anthropology: View from Springhill, 1980.* New York: Garland Publishing.

Gilkes, Cheryl Townsend. 1983. "From Slavery to Social Welfare: Racism and the Control of Black Women." In Amy Swerdlow and Hanna Lessinger, eds., *Class, Race, and Sex: The Dynamics of Control.* Boston: G. K. Hall.

————. 1988. "Building in Many Places: Multiple Commitments and Ideologies in Black Women's Community Work." In Ann Bookman and Sandra Morgen, eds., *Women and the Politics of Empowerment.* Philadelphia: Temple University Press.

Glazer, Nathan, and Daniel P. Moynihan. 1975. "Introduction." In Nathan Glazer and Daniel P. Moynihan, eds., *Ethnicity: Theory and Experience.* Cambridge, MA: Harvard University Press.

Glenn, Evelyn N. 1986. *Issei, Nisei, Warbride: Three Generations of Japanese American Women in Domestic Service.* Philadelphia: Temple University Press.

Goetz, J. P., and L. Grant. 1988. "Conceptual Approaches to Studying Gender in Education." *Anthropology and Education Quarterly* 19(2): 182–96.

Gordon, Linda. 1989. "Feminism and the 'Underclass." *Against the Current* 3(6): 42–43.

Herrnstein, R. 1973. *I.Q. in the Meritocracy.* Boston: Little, Brown.

Hicks, George L., and Mark J. Handler. 1987. "Ethnicity, Public Policy, and Anthropologists." In Elizabeth M. Eddy and William L. Partridge, eds., *Applied Anthropology in America.* 2nd ed. New York: Columbia University Press.

Higginbotham, Elizabeth. 1983. "Laid Bare by the System: Work and Survival for Black and Hispanic Women." In Amy Swerdlow and Hanna Lessinger, eds., *Class, Race, and Sex: The Dynamics of Control.* Boston: G. K. Hall.

Hinshaw, Robert E. 1980. "Anthropology, Administration, and Public Policy." *Annual Reviews of Anthropology* 9: 497–522.

Holland, Dorothy C., and Margaret A. Eisenhart. 1988. "Women's Ways of Going to School: Cultural Reproduction of Women's Identities as Workers." In Lois Weis, ed., *Class, Race, and Gender in American Education.* Albany: State University of New York Press.

Jensen, A. R. 1969. "How Much Can We Boost IQ and Scholastic Achievement?" *Harvard Educational Review* 39: 1–123.

————. 1970. "Can We and Should We Study Race Differences?" In J. Hellmuth, ed., *Disadvantaged Child: Compensatory Education, a National Debate,* vol. 3. New York: Brunner-Mazel.

Jones, Jacqueline. 1985. *Labor of Love, Labor of Sorrow: Black Women, Work, and the Family from Slavery to Present.* New York: Basic Books.

Kamin, Leon J. 1974. *The Science and Politics of IQ.* Potomac, MD: Erlbaum.

————. 1982. "IQ and Heredity: Historical and Critical Remarks." *Journal of Academic Skills* 3(1): 30–50.

Keith, Verna M., and David P. Smith. 1988. "The Current Differential in Black and White Life Expectancy." *Demography* 25(4): 625–32.

Lamphere, Louise. 1987. *From Working Daughters to Working Mothers.* Ithaca, NY: Cornell University Press.

Lawler, James M. 1978. *IQ, Heritability, and Racism.* New York: International Publishers.

Laws, Sophie. 1983. "The Sexual Politics of Pre-Menstrual Tension." *Women's Studies International Forum* 6(1): 19–31.

Lazarus, Ellen S. 1988. "Poor Women, Poor Outcomes: Social Class and Reproductive Health". In Karen L.Michaelson et al., *Childbirth in America: Anthropological Perspectives.* South Hadley, MA: Bergin and Garvey.

Leacock, Eleanor Burke. 1971. "Introduction." In Eleanor Burke Leacock, ed., *The Culture of Poverty: A Critique.* New York: Simon and Schuster.

———. 1987. "Theory and Ethics in Applied Urban Anthropology." In Leith Mullings, ed., *Cities of the United States: Studies in Urban Anthropology.* New York: Columbia University Press.

Leavitt, Judith Walzer, ed. 1984. *Women and Health in America: Historical Readings.* Madison: University of Wisconsin Press.

Lemann, Nicolas. 1986. "The Origins of the Underclass," Parts 1 and 2. *Atlantic Monthly* (June): 31–35; (July): 54–68.

Lerner, Gerda. 1979. "The Lady and the Mill Girl: Changes in the Status of Women in the Age of Jackson, 1800–1840." In N. Cott and E. Pleck, eds., *A Heritage of Her Own.* New York: Simon and Schuster.

Lewin, Ellen, and Virginia Oleson, eds. 1985. *Women, Health, and Healing: Toward a New Perspective.* New York: Tavistock Publications.

Lewis, Oscar. 1966. "The Culture of Poverty." *Scientific American* 215(4): 19–25.

Lopez, Iris. 1987. "Sterilization Among Puerto Rican Women in New York City: Public Policy and Social Constraints." In Leith Mullings, ed., *Cities of the United States: Studies in Urban Anthropology.* New York: Columbia University Press.

Lorber, Judith. 1987. "In Vitro Fertilization and Gender Politics." *Women and Health* 13: 117–33.

Martin, Emily. 1987. *The Woman in the Body: A Cultural Analysis of Reproduction.* Boston: Beacon Press.

McCrea, Frances. 1986. "The Politics of Menopause: The 'Discovery' of a Deficiency Disease." In Peter Conrad and Rochelle Kern, eds., *The Sociology of Health and Illness: Critical Perspectives.* 2nd ed. New York: St. Martin's Press.

Michaelson, Karen L., et al. 1988. *Childbirth in America: Anthropological Perspectives.* South Hadley, MA: Bergin and Garvey.

Morgen, Sandra. 1988a. "The Dream of Diversity, the Dilemma of Difference: Race and Class Contradictions in a Feminist Health Clinic." In Johnnetta Cole, ed., *Anthropology for the Nineties.* New York: Free Press.

———. 1988b. "'It's the Whole Power of the City Against Us!': The Development of Political Consciousness in a Women's Health Care Coalition." In Ann Bookman and Sandra Morgen, eds., *Women and the Politics of Empowerment.* Philadelphia: Temple University Press.

Moyers, Bill. 1989. *The Vanishing Black Family: Crisis in Black America.* PBS documentary.

Moynihan, Daniel P. 1965. "The Negro Family: The Case for National Action." Reprinted in Lee Rainwater and William L. Yancey, *The Moynihan Report and the Politics of Controversy.* Cambridge, MA: MIT Press.

Mullings, Leith. 1989. "Inequality and African-American Health Status: Policies and Prospects." In Winston Van Horne, ed., *Race: Twentieth-Century Dilemmas—Twenty-first Century Prognoses.* Milwaukee: University of Wisconsin Institute on Race Relations.

Murray, Charles. 1984. *Losing Ground.* New York: Basic Books.

Newman, Katherine S. 1986. "Symbolic Dialectics and Generations of Women: Variation in the Meaning of Post-Divorce Downward Mobility." *American Ethnologist* 13(2): 230–53.

Partridge, William L., and Elizabeth M. Eddy. 1987. "The Develoment of Applied Anthropology in America." In Elizabeth M. Eddy and William L. Partridge, eds., *Applied Anthropology in America.* 2nd ed. New York: Columbia University Press.

Perales, Cesar A., and Lauren S. Young, eds. 1988. *Too Little, Too Late: Dealing with the Health Needs of Women in Poverty.* New York: Harrington Park Press.

Petchesky, Rosalind Pollack. 1983. "Reproduction and Class Divisions Among Women". In Amy Swerdlow and Hanna Lessinger, eds., *Class, Race, and Sex: The Dynamics of Control.* Boston: G. K. Hall.

Pitman, Mary Arme, and Margaret Eisernhart. 1988. "Experiences of Gender: Studies of Women and Gender in Schools and Society." *Anthropology and Education Quarterly* 19(2): 67–69.

Polednak, Anthony P. 1987. *Host Factors in Disease: Age, Sex, Racial, and Ethnic Group and Body Build.* Springfield, IL: Charles C. Thomas.

Rapp, Rayna. 1987a. "Urban Kinship in Contemporary America: Families, Classes, and Ideology." In Leith Mullings, ed., *Cities of the United States: Studies in Urban Anthropology.* New York: Columbia University Press.

———. 1987b. "Moral Pioneers: Women, Men, and Fetuses on a Frontier of Reproductive Technology." *Women and Health* 13: 101–16.

Rodgers, Harrell R. 1986. *Poor Women, Poor Families.* Armonk, NY: M. E. Sharpe.

Rothman, Barbara Katz. 1987. "Reproduction." In Beth B. Hess and Myra Marx Ferree, eds., *Analyzing Gender: A Handbook of Social Science Research.* Newberry Park, CA: Sage Publications.

Rushton, J. Philippe. 1989. "Evolutionary Biology and Heritable Traits with Reference to Oriental-White-Black Differences." Paper presented at the Symposium on Evolutionary Theory, Economics, and Political Science: An Emerging Theoretical Convergence, at the annual meeting of the American Association for the Advancement of Science, San Francisco, California, January 19.

Sacks, Karen Brodkin, and Dorothy Remy, eds. 1984. *My Troubles Are Going to Have Trouble with Me: Everyday Trials and Triumphs of Women Workers.* New Brunswick, NJ: Rutgers University Press.

Sanjek, Roger. 1987. "Anthropological Work at a Gray Panther Health Clinic: Academic, Applied, and Advocacy Goals." In Leith Mullings, ed., *Cities of the United States: Studies in Urban Anthropology.* New York: Columbia University Press.

Scully, Diana, and Pauline Bart. 1973. "A Funny Thing Happened on the Way to the Orifice: Women in Gynecology Textbooks." *American Journal of Sociology* 78(4): 1045–50.

Shockley, W. 1970. "New Methodology to Reduce the Environment-Heredity Uncertainty About Disgenics." Paper read before the National Academy of Sciences, Washington, DC.

Singer, Merril. 1987. "Cure, Care, and Control: An Ectopic Encounter with Biomedical Obstetrics." In Hans A. Baer, ed., *Encounters with Biomedicine: Case Studies in Medical Anthropology.* New York: Gordon and Breach.

Stack, Carol B. 1970. *All Our Kin: Strategies for Survival in a Black Community.* New York: Harper and Row.

Susser, Ida. 1986. "Political Activity Among Working-Class Women in a U.S. City." *American Ethnologist* 13(1): 108–17.

Susser, Ida, and John Kreniske. 1987. "The Welfare Trap: A Public Policy for Deprivation." In Leith Mullings, ed., *Cities of the United States: Studies in Urban Anthropology.* New York: Columbia University Press.

Taylor, H. F. 1980. *The IQ Game: A Methodological Inquiry into the Heredity-Environment Controversy.* New Brunswick, NJ: Rutgers University Press.

U.S. Bureau of the Census. 1987. *Statistical Abstract of the United States: 1988.* Washington, DC: U.S. Bureau of the Census.

Valentine, Charles A. 1968. *Culture and Poverty: Critique and Counterproposals.* Chicago: University of Chicago Press.

Van Willigen, John. 1986. *Applied Anthropology: An Introduction.* South Hadley, MA: Bergin and Garvey.

Waldrun, Ingrid. 1986. "Why Women Live Longer Than Men." In Peter Conrad and Rochelle Kern, eds., *The Sociology of Health and Illness: Critical Perspectives.* 2nd ed. New York: St. Martin's Press.

Weaver, Thomas. 1985. "Anthropology as a Policy Science: Part 1, a Critique." *Human Organization* 44(2): 97–105.

Weiss, Mark L., and Alan E. Mann. 1978. *Human Biology and Behavior: An Anthropological Perspective.* 2nd ed. Boston: Little, Brown.

Welter, B. 1966. "The Cult of True Womanhood: 1820–1860." *American Quarterly* (summer): 151–71.

Wilson, William Julius. 1987. *The Truly Disadvantaged: The Inner City, the Underclass, and Public Policy.* Chicago: University of Chicago Press.

Zambrana, Ruth E. 1982. *Work, Family, and Health: Latina Women in Transition.* Monograph no. 7. New York: Hispanic Research Center, Fordham University.

Zimmerman, Mary K. 1987. "The Women's Health Movement: A Critique of Medical Enterprise and the Position of Women." In Beth B. Hess and Myra Marx Ferree, eds., *Analyzing Gender: A Handbook of Social Science Research.* Newbury Park, CA: Sage Publications.

9

Race, Inequality, and Transformation

Building on the Work of Eleanor Leacock

With race once again on the agenda, it is important to challenge the erasure of history and to underscore that there has long been an alternative tradition to essentialist conceptualizations of race, ethnicity, and culture. This includes the work of Eleanor Leacock and some of her contemporaries, as well as people of color such as Oliver Cox, W.E.B. DuBois, St. Clair Drake, C.L.R. James, and Bernard Magubane, who have deconstructed notions of race and representation, often within the framework of political economy.[1] Their efforts to link the concept of race to political and economic relations of domination stand in dramatic contrast to contemporary analysts who retreat from confrontation with power by seeking refuge in the celebration of difference.

I will first briefly discuss the context of Eleanor Leacock's work on race and inequality and then describe some of the social transformations that condition the way new formulations of race and inequality play themselves out; finally I will sketch out some of the ways in which an emerging scholarship is helping us to develop and extend this alternative tradition upon which I believe a scholarship of race, culture, and power must be built.

Eleanor Leacock: Theory and Practice

First, I would like to say what a privilege it was to have known Eleanor Leacock. I knew Happy as a scholar and activist whose commitment was not merely acade-

181

mic but political and personal. Long before critiques of the canon become fashionable, Eleanor Leacock was one of the few established scholars to consistently cite and promote the work of women and people of color. She fought hard to democratize the academy, and a whole generation of us will remember how she encouraged us to publish, invited us to conferences, and wrote letters on our behalf.

It was most important to me that unlike some of the contemporary interpretations of engagement, Happy called for forms of practice that link the skills of scholars to social movements and that challenge the power relationships and institutions that give rise to negative representations of poor and working-class people. Her vision of anthropology and social change—one that encouraged me to remain in the field—is best summarized in her own words:

> When combined with a broad historical orientation and an advocacy stance, anthropological perspectives make it possible to examine ways in which the conflicts and ambivalence people experience in their daily lives express fundamental social-economic conflicts that are impelling change. They offer the possibility for defining the potentials for action and the ambiguities that hinder it, as individuals and groups in part accept and in part resist the existing power relations that oppress them. Advocacy anthropology enhances the possibilities for delineating practical short-range steps and meaningful long-range goals for solutions to the problems urban people confront. Commitment makes it possible to work toward an effective—a practical—theory of social change. (Leacock 1987, 334)

Leacock's work was central to the unfinished project of demystifying the ways in which different forms of inequality are produced and reproduced. Mainstream social science explanations of inequality have, for the most part, attributed the source of inequality to its victims, ascribing poverty to either the biogenetic makeup or the culture of those who are poor. At first glance, it would seem that after World War II the emphasis shifted from biological to cultural explanations for inequality throughout the world, as scholars, politicians, and the media adopted analyses of underdevelopment and poverty popularized by the modernization literature.

An examination of the relationship between scholarship and the politics of race is beyond the scope of this chapter, but clearly certain conditions provided a context for the initial decline of biological determinism. For example, while the labor and leftist struggles of the 1930s raised issues of class and race, the Great Depression demonstrated that poverty was not genetically determined. Not much later, the horrors of the Holocaust graphically illustrated the logical conclusion of Nazism's biological regulation. The anticolonial, national liberation, and civil rights struggles and the increasing participation of people of color in the debates about race further undermined scientific racism. In this context, the Boasian critique of the notion of race and the social science scholarship on structural and environmental relations all contributed to deconstructing biological discourse.

However, even as biological determinism declined, it was replaced by cultural determinism, expressed in explanations imputing inequality to the culture of those most vulnerable to poverty. In the United States, Oscar Lewis's work (1966) systematized these conjectures by formulating a concept of "the culture of poverty." Moynihan's *The Negro Family: The Case for National Action* (1965) was particularly instrumental in shifting attention from structural issues, such as discrimination and unemployment, to the culture of the poor as the source of African American poverty. These views gained ascendancy as a militant civil rights movement, which threatened to broaden into a poor people's movement, sought to confront structures of inequality.

In her introduction to *The Culture of Poverty: A Critique* (1971a), Eleanor Leacock took on the devastating political implications, as well as the intellectual weaknesses, of the culture of poverty perspective. She also produced a series of articles concerned with inequality and race in housing, education, and health. During the 1960s and 1970s, her work was particularly timely in challenging both the intellectual underpinnings and the policy implications of the culture of poverty.

Unfortunately, the culture of poverty notion Leacock critiqued was but one step in series of victim-blaming characterizations that were to set the parameters of the debate and justify neglect of poverty for the next decade. In the 1980s and 1990s the notion of the underclass performs these same functions, and Leacock's analysis of culture and inequality remains a critical challenge to the underclass theories. Ironically, in the 1990s the entire scope of her writings on gender, class, and race has become even more relevant as explanations for inequality attribute the rising rates of poverty experienced by minority communities to poor women, particularly those who head households. Leacock's observation that "each generation of social scientists makes and must correct the same mistakes when it comes to views of the poor" (1971a, 20) is unfortunately prescient.

Race, Gender, and the Urban Crisis

In the last few decades, global economic transformations, particularly the outmigration of jobs, which creates high levels of unemployment for working-class populations in the United States, have interacted with historically established patterns of discrimination. When linked with disinvestment in cities and cut-backs in federal funding for social services, these processes have brought about increased immiseration and segregation for poor and working-class populations. In this context, Leacock's work on education and housing has, unfortunately, demonstrated its predictive quality.

Access to education has become even more unequal by race and class. In New York City, where Leacock did her pioneering study of education and inequality (1969; 1971b), schoolchildren receive less funding per child than suburban children and schools in low-income African American communities may receive less funding then other urban districts (see chapter 5). Metropolitan cities are more segregated than ever before (Wilson 1987), and inner-city communities such as South Central Los Angeles and Harlem and Washington Heights in New York threaten to explode as they become more and more socially and geographically marginalized.

Contemporary discourse about race has continuities with old images and stereotypes, but it is also transformed by new conditions. For example, new immigrant populations which blur the boundaries between black and white; the rise of a small, but increasingly visible African-American middle class; as well as new work on race in molecular biology all continue to undermine the crude biological determinism more appropriate to rationalizing and supporting the caste structure of the pre-civil rights period.

At the same time, the perceived threat of growing numbers of immigrants, rising unemployment in certain sectors of the United States, the precipitous decline in real income for most people, and the challenge to cultural hegemony posed by the multicultural movement have contributed to the rise of an elite national chauvinism. As the cycle of unemployment, drugs, and crime ravages some minority communities against the backdrop of resurgent racism, white supremacy is increasingly defended in terms of cultural superiority. Culture—a set of values and behaviors by which the poor are measured—becomes the dominant model to explain poverty.

In this context, "traditional values" emerge as a dominant ideological theme. This was perhaps most dramatically illustrated in the 1992 Republican National Convention, which opened with a call to arms for "a cultural war for the soul of America." As "family values," expressed in the defense of the mythical traditional family, become "keywords," women increasingly carry the symbolic load for all sorts of notions concerned with family, race, and nation. Women of the dominant race are admonished to return to traditional gender roles, and low-income African American single mothers are demonized (see chapter 5).

But despite the dominance of culturalism, I would argue that in the United States, biological and cultural explanations for inequality are not necessarily competing explanations, but are rather parallel discourses that mutually support each other in complex ways. In explanations for inequality, biology is behavioralized and culture is biologized.[2] A wide range of behavioral and cultural traits are attributed to biological differences (such as skin color), which in themselves have no such behavioral consequences. Culture, on the other hand, is essentialized. In the culture of poverty theories, culture becomes immutable, inherited, passed down from generation to generation. As what is social becomes natural, cultural differences are rendered insurmountable.

In the United States, where inequality provides the foundation for racial meanings in all areas of society, biological and cultural explanations for inequality reinforce each other in minimizing the role of structured inequities of race and class. In education, for example, both IQ and family disorganization are dominant explanations for the failure of a school system in which the division of resources by class and race has been characterized as "savage inequality" (Kozol 1991). Similarly, in the area of health, despite obvious inequities in access to health care and other resources necessary for good health, racial disparities in morbidity and mortality are attributed to genetic variation, on the one hand, and cultural differences, on the other (see chapter 3 and Mullings 1989).

Contemporary Approaches

Those who currently continue the critique of essentialist meanings of race emphasize the ways in which racial meanings, identities, and ideologies are historically specific and therefore continually created, contested, and transformed. These analyses highlight the concrete links between race and other forms of oppositionality such as class and gender, and the manner in which all these are structured within a global context.

Thus contemporary approaches problematize the notion of race by seeing race and ethnicity as socially constructed, contextual representations that play themselves out at specific historical periods. Racial meanings are contested and transformed as people counterpose their own constructions of identity, community, and history. In this regard, it is essential to clarify the relationship between power and knowledge, between the struggle for power and the struggle for interpretation.

Central to this perspective is a view of identity as interactional, of race as inextricably linked to gender and class. A growing body of literature highlights the ways in which class, race, and gender configure relationships of both domination and resistance. This new work questions the notion of boundaries between struggles in the domestic and political arenas and demonstrates how transformative actions taken by African American and working-class women to sustain their family or neighborhood are frequently linked to measures to transform the larger society. This work builds on Leacock's studies of class and race, on the one hand, and gender, on the other.

Stephen Gregory, who was given the first Eleanor Leacock Award in 1993, is part of this developing alternative scholarship on race, culture, and inequality. Gregory (1993) has provided us with an important case study of women whose oppositional efforts include the contestation of representation. He demonstrates how the circulation of images becomes important in representing people and struggles. But in keeping with the work on reception theory, Gregory points out that people are involved in active struggle with images. He describes the way in which women appropriate patriarchal ideology to disrupt negative images of black masculinity.

His article raises important problems of national liberation and gender equality for people of color and subaltern peoples around the world. Here we must contend with the murky boundaries between accommodation, resistance, and transformation. We need to appraise how resisting one set of oppressions may produce or reproduce another set, as well as to examine the possibility that replacing a dominant ideology with alternative rather than oppositional ideologies impedes real transformation (see chapters 6 and 7). We must confront the dilemma women of color face in the actual practice of attempting to eliminate gender subordination, national oppression, and class exploitation.

As globalized capitalism simultaneously integrates and segments the workforce by gender, nationality, and race, it is important to situate local cases within the global context. We must continue to examine the strategic use of an essentialized notion of culture to draw boundaries, to advocate maintaining cultural differences, and to justify racist policies, on the one hand (Balibar and Wallerstein 1991), and the ways in which people imagine identities that transcend national boundaries and construct movements of opposition, on the other.

Similarly, local manifestations of gender relations in the United States are clarified in light of global restructuring. With the expansion of service jobs and other forms of "female" labor in many areas of the world, women enlarge their participation in the labor force and, as the number of households headed by women rises, they increasingly challenge the notion of men as breadwinners. For African American women, who are at the forefront of this process in the United States, it is the intersection of race, class, and gender, of social relations and cultural meanings, that critically shapes their experience.

Nevertheless, despite the rather dizzying flow of capital, people, and goods through mediascapes, ideoscapes, ethnoscapes, finanscapes, as Appadarai might put it (1990), Ajaz Ahmad (1992) reminds us that the vast majority of working-class people are still confined within the national boundaries of the land of their birth and that they continue to experience the structural inability of capitalism to provide for the majority of the world's people. Furthermore, the answering dialectic to globalization must be universalist and transnational, yet address the relations of power through class struggle within the national terrain.

It is in this context that I most miss Happy Leacock. Among U.S. anthropologists, she was unusual in systematically linking theory to practice. But the good news is that there are currently scholars who continue in this tradition, and that what we say, and particularly what we do, about "difference" can make a difference.

Notes

1. Some of the material about Eleanor Leacock in the first part of this presentation first appeared in Mullings 1993. I would like to thank Patricia Tovar for her assistance in researching the work of Eleanor Leacock and to acknowledge the contribution of Juan Flores, with whom I cotaught a seminar on race and ethnicity.

2. Sydel Silverman coined the phrase "culture is biologized" in the colloquium Does Anthropology have a Future? held at the Anthropology Department, City University of New York Graduate School, March 5, 1993.

References

Ahmad, Ajaz. 1992. *In Theory: Classes, Nations, Literatures.* London: Verso.

Appadurai, Arjun. 1990. "Disjuncture and Difference in the Global Cultural Economy." *Public Culture* 2(2): 1–24.

Balibar, Etienne, and Immanuel Wallerstein. 1991. *Race, Nation, Class: Ambiguous Identities.* London: Verso.

Gregory, Stephen. 1993. "Race, Rubbish and Resistance: Empowering Difference in Community Politics." *Cultural Anthropology* 8(1): 24–48.

Kozol, Jonathan. 1991. *Savage Inequalities: Children in America's Schools.* New York: Crown.

Leacock, Eleanor. 1969. *Teaching and Learning in City Schools; A Comparative Study.* New York: Basic Books.

———. 1971a. *The Culture of Poverty: A Critique.* New York: Simon and Schuster.

———. 1971b. "Theoretical and Methodological Problems in the Study of Schools." In Murray Wax, ed., *Anthropological Perspectives on Education.* New York: Basic Books.

———. 1987. "Theory and Ethics in Applied Urban Anthropology." In Leith Mullings, ed., *Cities of the United States: Studies in Urban Anthropology.* New York: Columbia University Press.

Lewis, Oscar. 1966. "The Culture of Poverty." *Scientific American* 215(4): 3–9.

Moynihan, Daniel. 1965. "The Negro Family: The Case for National Action." Reprinted in Lee Rainwater and William Yancey, *The Moynihan Report and the Politics of Controversy.* Cambridge, MA: MIT Press.

Mullings, Leith. 1989. "Inequality and African-American Health Status: Policies and Prospects." In Winston Van Horne, ed., *Race: Twentieth Century Dilemmas—Twenty-First Century Prognoses.* Madison: University of Wisconsin Press.

———. 1993. "Eleanor Leacock and Urban Anthropology in the United States." In Constance Sutton, ed., *From Labrador to Samoa: Eleanor Leacock.* Arlington, VA: American Ethnological Society.

Wilson, William J. 1987. *The Truly Disadvantaged: The Inner City, the Underclass, and Public Policy.* Chicago: University of Chicago Press.

10

Reclaiming Culture
The Dialectics of Identity

In the last decade, African Americans have once again become increasingly committed to reclaiming their culture and history. This has taken a variety of forms and is evident in phenomena as diverse as the iconization of Malcolm X, the struggle around the African burial ground in New York City, renewed interest in African hairstyles, jewelry, and clothing, mass participation in the movement for a free South Africa, and the rise of Afrocentric philosophy.

Among African Americans, the term *Afrocentrism* may be used rather broadly to refer to a range of loosely integrated beliefs, practices, values, orientations, and behaviors. For some, it merely signals a sense of continuity with Africa and loyalty to a community of African descent. For others, Afrocentricity may be manifested in modes of dress, ritual practices, or other cultural activities. For still others, Afrocentrism refers to recent attempts to systematize these orientations into a philosophical system of beliefs and practices. I would like to address one essential element in these various approaches—the notion of culture.

The resurgent turn toward culture is in part a reaction to the failures of liberal integration; in part a consequence of the state-sponsored destruction of the left; and in part a challenge to apologists for inequality who attribute the cause of increasing poverty to the culture of African Americans. But it also represents the continuation of a long tradition of activist social scientists such as W.E.B. DuBois, who marveled at the inherent duality of African American culture and the transformation of the African medicine owner from "a bard, physician, judge, and priest, within the narrow limits allowed by the slave system rose the Negro preacher and under him the first Afro-American institution, the Negro church" (DuBois 1961, 144). We walk in the footsteps of poets such as Countee Cullen, who pondered "What is Africa to me?" and countless ordinary people whose everyday practices of speech, style, music, art, and ritual recall a homeland three centuries removed.

The point of departure for these diverse perspectives—the importance of the struggle for history and culture—is not at issue. "Culture is . . . the product of . . . history just as the flower is the product of a plant," as Amilcar Cabral (1973, 42) poetically put it. A sense of culture history situates the individual in time and space, plotting the places occupied by ancestors gone before and descendants yet to come. Culture provides a framework through which communities interpret their past, understand their present, and imagine their future.

Therefore, as Amilcar Cabral and Franz Fanon have described, though from different vantage points, the dominant group's power to represent the history and culture of subaltern groups is an important tool in achieving and maintaining domination. Hegemonic cultural systems seek to impose preferences, to redefine standards of beauty, and to lay out appropriate categories of thought and action. But perhaps most important, by interpreting the past and defining the limits of action, these ideological systems seek to depict the potential for the future, framing the boundaries for struggle. Thus the recent struggle around the African burial ground in New York City was based on the knowledge that those who control the interpretation of the past also have a major role in charting the future.

In the 1960s and 1970s, attempts to confront the ideological underpinning of white supremacy within the academy were reinvigorated. Responding to the militant civil rights movement and antiwar struggles, African Americans and others fought for the establishment of black studies departments. Many ethnic, labor, and women's studies departments nurtured scholarship that produced the knowledge base for developing alternate approaches. This new body of scholarship laid the intellectual foundation for the contemporary challenge to the general curriculum; for contesting how knowledge is defined, created, and controlled; and for placing the experiences of workers, women, and people of color, rather than those of elites, at the center of the analysis. The challenge to the ideological hegemony of the dominant class—whether in the liberal form of a historian such as Arthur Schlesinger, the conservative form of an educator such as Diane Ravitch, or the many popular formulations denigrating African American history and culture from Myrdal to Moynihan—has been a critical aspect of our struggle.

But opposition to official interpretations of history and culture, particularly when linked to action, was generally met with derisive contempt or unrelenting hostility. Intolerance for rethinking history as experienced by people of color, coupled with institutional tolerance of racism, has shaped the conditions in which alternative frameworks have emerged.

Furthermore, alternative interpretations face the difficult task of disengaging from, even while critiquing, traditional categories, and of rejecting the hegemonic framework that structures its own form of dissent. Indeed, one attraction of Afrocentrism is the appearance of initiating a conversation from the vantage point of another place, of creating a new space for discussion rather than accepting the categories set out by the dominant culture.

Afrocentrism, then, is born of the unremitting Eurocentrism of the academy and other societal institutions. Considering the large-scale invention of history from the perspective of elite Europeans, Schlesinger's charge that Afrocentrism is the "invention of tradition" (1992, 86) is at best disingenuous and at worst blatantly dishonest.

I would argue, however, that though Afrocentrism represents an attempt to highlight the importance of culture, to reclaim history and to correct the distortions of Eurocentrism, there are ways in which it is the child of Eurocentrism. Caught in its mirrorlike negation of Eurocentrism, Afrocentrism often inadvertently reflects the reductionism of traditional thinking about race and culture. Because it is, in effect, trapped in a project of negation, Afrocentrism sometimes loses its cultural compass, straying from the land of our collective memories, contemporary struggles, and hopes for the future.

There are different varieties of Afrocentrism, which I am not able to treat here as fully as they deserve, but I would maintain that the more fundamentalist versions are based on a dangerously limited notion of the nature of culture, one that is remarkably similar to Oscar Lewis's static definition of culture in his formulation of the "culture of poverty" or to the underclass theorists' understanding of culture as a set of unchanging behavioral traits. Consequently, though Afrocentric philosophers seek to reinterpret history, their concept of culture tends to be fundamentally ahistoric. Further, despite disclaimers to the contrary, they often treat culture as independent of the social system, thereby precluding the development of a dynamic, revolutionary theory of culture necessary for achieving liberation.

Culture is not a fixed set of traits, values, or behaviors; nor is it transmitted unchanged from generation to generation; nor is it merely a set of principles. Cultures are dynamic, always developing, ever changing; as Amilcar Cabral (1973) put it, the manifestation on the ideological plane of the historical reality of a people. Despite the importance of deconstructing Eurocentric representations of African history, the foundation of African American culture is not to be found in the tombs of the pharaohs.

Cultures are historically created and therefore not hermetically sealed. The contemporary world in which information moves around the globe at nearly the speed of light brings new possibilities for domination, but also fresh potential for liberation. Diasporic cultures, for example, are continually formed and reformed through constant interaction and exchange: African Americans wear kente cloth, and South Africans sing "We Shall Overcome." Just as African Americans made an important contribution to the liberation of South Africa, it is to be hoped that the new South Africa will assist African Americans in their struggle for equality.

The essence of African American culture, and therefore its resilience, lies in our people's continuing struggle for survival, continuity, and liberation. Through this process, African Americans created their culture, transferring, transposing, rediscovering, and reworking elements from Africa and the Americas within the varied structural and cultural constraints of different locales. Under conditions of slavery, segregation, discrimination, and deindustrialization, our achievements have been enormous, and we need to reclaim them for ourselves and our children. Nevertheless, some aspects of culture, while perhaps initially responses to inequality, now facilitate the reproduction of domination and are an obstacle to progress. For example, many contemporary cultural expressions reflect an unfortunate valorization of the dominant society's hierarchical gender roles and accept stigmatization of African American women's lives and struggles. But the more progressive and enduring aspects of African American culture—which stand as a contribution to all of humankind—are best comprehended through the lens of our people's historical struggle.

Perhaps most problematic is the tendency of Afrocentrists to reify the ideological, to treat culture as independent of the social system and as reducible to geography, climate, or environment—in this sense not entirely dissimilar to the manner in which white supremacists reduce culture to a mythical concept of race. It is important to make the comparison between cultures in which the dominant theme is individual achievement and accumulation and those characterized by collectivism and egalitarianism. But with respect to the cultures cited by Afrocentrists, this is largely a distinction between the culture of capitalism, which had its earliest and most significant development in Europe, and the culture of the village community, which, until relatively recently, existed in much of Africa. African Americans have maintained some communally oriented cultural elements precisely because of their shared historical experience of struggle. But one has only to consider an Idi Amin, a Clarence Thomas, or a Thomas Sowell to understand that we cannot reduce contrasting cultural frameworks to geography, climate, race, or ethnic identification.

While ideas can act as a material force and the struggle for power involves the struggle for interpretation, white supremacy, as we all know, is not merely a cultural or literary project. As we are reminded every day—by the hundreds of thousands of homeless, unemployed African Americans, by the nearly six in ten African American children growing up in poverty, by every African American imprisoned and executed by the state, by the young men shot down in the flower of their youth, by all our assassinated heroes—at the foundation of racism is a system of savagely unequal economic and political relations. We must, along with others, address the social relations that give rise to the power to interpret. Despite the importance of the "black is beautiful" movement of the 1960s, which sought to turn dominant symbols on their head and to seize the interpretive initiative, cultural transformation could not be maintained without successfully challenging the institutions that produce these representations.

Culture is an important element of struggle. But it is by nature malleable and symbolic and can be deployed in different ways. For Amilcar Cabral, a revolutionary notion of culture was a tool in achieving liberation. For Mangosuthu Buthelezi, a reactionary notion of culture became a rationale for alliance with the white supremacists of South Africa. We cannot afford to cede the right to represent our culture and history. But those of us who are privileged to have the leisure to contemplate must place our skills at the service of social movements that critically reflect the lives, experiences, and history of our people. We must help to construct concepts that our people can use here and now to better their lives and ensure their continuity.

References

DuBois, W.E.B. 1961. *The Souls of Black Folks.* Greenwich, CT: Fawcett Publications.

Cabral, Amilcar. 1973. *Return to the Source.* New York: Africa Information Service.

Fanon, Frantz. 1963. *The Wretched of the Earth.* New York: Grove Press.

Schlesinger, Arthur M. Jr. 1992. *The Disuniting of America.* New York: W. W. Norton.

Index

abortion, 173
  use by slave women, 98
Abyssinian Baptist Church, xiii
Africa
  traditions of, 120
  women's roles in, xvi
African Americans
  in colonial period, 36–40
  education of, xiii, xiv, 91–92, 184
  gender roles in, 82–83, 119–122, 127(n9),
    131–158
  inequality of, xi–xii
  kinship in, 79–83
  low socioeconomic status of, 161
  political strategies of, 131–158
  racism against, 24
African-American liberation, women's roles
    in, 144–149
African-American men
  health of, 25–26, 52–53
  unemployment in, 89, 143
African-American women, xix–xx, xxi
  in colonial period, 33, 34, 36–37, 39–40
  Euro-American women compared to, 8
  feminist studies of, 1–5
  health of, 19, 52–68, 170–171
  images and ideology of, 109–130
  in labor force, 15–19, 23, 29(n4), 43–48,
    55–62, 84, 118–119

negative stereotypes of, xiii, 119, 126(n7)
  as nurses, xiv
  role in liberation, 144–149
  sexual exploitation of, 93, 113
  sexual images of, 94, 111, 112–113,
    115–116, 119, 121
  as slaves, 18, 43–47
  transformative work of, 18, 98–100, 121
"African American Women in Defense of
    Ourselves," 151
African National Congress, xvi, 147
*The Afro-American Woman: Struggles and
    Images* (Harley & Terborg-Penn), 3
Afro-Baptists, 137, 145
Afrocentrism, 108, 132, 134, 189, 191,
    192
Afshar, Haleh, 140
Ahmad, Ajaz, 186
AIDS, 93
Aid to Families with Dependent Children,
    91, 167
Ain't I a Woman (hooks), 5
Akron Convention for Women's Suffrage,
    24, 112
Ali, Shahrazad, 139, 146
*All the Women Are White, All the Blacks Are
    Men, But Some of Us Are Brave* (Hull,
    Scott, & Smith), 2
American Cyanide Company, 63

195